Instructors and their jobs

W. R. Miller
*Chairman, Practical Arts and Vocational-Technical Education
University of Missouri—Columbia*

Homer C. Rose
*Late Professor, Department of Industrial Education
Southern Illinois University*

AMERICAN TECHNICAL SOCIETY CHICAGO, ILL. 60637

Preface

This Third Edition is thoroughly revised and updated to set forth the most useful methods and techniques for today's instructional needs. The presentation is clear and concise and aimed at providing readily useable information.

The book is designed to give practical and substantial assistance to instructors, supervisors and others who are preparing to teach or, more appropriately, stimulate and direct learning. It contains the most practical and productive use of instructional methods and techniques used in modern schools, industry, business, government, the military services and other agencies. Every concept in the book has been applied and evaluated by the authors in a variety of educational programs.

Each person who has responsibility for instructing probably feels that his job is unique and requires a specialized approach. To a degree, this is true. Instructional programs vary and require different methods, as do the various parts of a single program. This book is devoted to the basic principles and techniques that are applicable to all educational programs and training situations. Many of the illustrations in the book are from technical education programs. One reason for this is that such programs involve tools, equipment and materials, and thus lend themselves to photographic presentation and to ease of understanding. The extensive use of pictures and other illustrations from common and basic technical education programs should not suggest that the concepts presented are limited to such programs. The fundamentals stressed here, when used with insight and judgment, will give positive results in any educational program.

Teacher educators, professional teachers, and those preparing for the profession should find *Instructors and Their Jobs* of real value in bridging the gap between the more detailed and theoretical aspects of psychology and education, and the practical everyday problems each instructor must solve with a given group of learners.

The authors thank the various organizations that provided photographs for the book.

The Publishers

Contents

The Instructor's Role

Skillful instructors are vital to every dynamic, successful educational program. Facilities, instructional materials, equipment and personnel with specialized technical knowledge are also needed but, without instructors fully competent in the art of teaching, no educational program can be completely successful.

This book deals with the vital processes of learning and teaching. Its objectives are to:

1. Summarize systematically the existing knowledge concerning modern instructional concepts and techniques.
2. State these ideas in a practical and straightforward manner. Whenever practicable each basic concept is immediately followed by specific illustrations and recommendations.
3. Add new concepts and balance. In thinking through the learning-teaching processes, in reviewing actual experience in a variety of types of educational programs and in evaluating ideas and procedures set forth by others, it is natural that some new insights and interpretations are possible.

Special emphasis has been given to adult level technical education.

At no time in history has the education of young and old alike been as complex and important as today. With each new scientific and engineering breakthrough, people must learn new skills and adjust to new situations. These changes are coming faster and faster. Corporate expenditures on employee training reached $4.5 billion in 1965. The nation's colleges and universities spend about $18 billion. If we add the cost of secondary level and technical schools (about $50 billion) and of military and other government training it is clearly evident that training and education is one of the nation's major activities. It is also evident that we cannot afford to use poor methods and techniques of instruction. Without practical and effective educational programs under expert instructors, much of the large investment will be lost.

The need for more and better educational programs for people of all ages is alarmingly evident. There is no standing still. Because so many of us must learn and keep learning as far into the future as anyone can see, it is imperative that the most practical and effective instructional procedures be used. Our progress and well being as individuals and as a nation depend greatly on how well we learn.

The Competent Instructor

The competent instructor in the classroom and on the job is the builder of bridges between expanding and changing subject matter on one side and a wide range of personalities on the other, personalities of people who must learn new concepts, new attitudes, and new skills.

Instructors are successful only to the extent that they enable their students to learn what they need to know at the right time, rapidly and well. The measure of their success is the learning which results from their instruction.

With this goal in mind, we may examine the qualities and techniques which contribute to effectiveness. We cannot do this scientifically, but the observation of skilled instructors in action and an analysis of the techniques they use provide a set of ideals toward which we may strive as well as a basis for self-criticism and self-help. These ideals can also serve as a guide for those who select, develop, and supervise instructors.

Identification of the desirable qualities in an instructor may be done in several ways. Many long lists have been prepared which include such hints as: stand on both feet, look at class, keep shoes shined, etc. Little is gained by listing such items. They vary from individual to individual and are accepted by the students as part of the instructor's total personality. Many of the personal qualities and mannerisms become important only in extreme cases. These six broad qualities stand out as absolutely essential:

1. Competence in the subject being taught.
2. Mastery of the techniques of instruction.
3. Resourcefulness and creativeness.
4. Knowledge and application of evaluation procedures.
5. The desire to teach.
6. Ability to develop good personal relationships.

Competence in the Subject Being Taught

The statement is sometimes made that a person who knows how to teach can teach anything. It would be more accurate to say that, in some instances, a skillful instructor can learn new subject matter in a shorter time than a subject matter specialist can learn to instruct. There is, however, no substitute for experience and detailed knowledge and skill in the subject being taught. The competent instructor will do a better job of staying one lesson ahead of the class and will be more at ease with students than an inexperienced instructor lacking in knowledge of the subject. However, the attempt to instruct without expert knowl-

A sound platform for effective instruction.

edge of the subject is evidence of bad judgment or unforseen emergency.

The instructor should be thoroughly competent in the skills to be taught as well as in the related information. This is particularly true where students are being prepared for positions involving specific and specialized tasks. Students are usually alert and capable and are quick to appraise their instructor. The competent instructor earns their respect. The class catches on in a hurry when the instructor bluffs or fakes and is likely to be suspected of inaccuracy and incompetence even in those aspects of the subject in which he is fully prepared.

The instructor must be competent in the subject he is teaching.

Mastery of the Techniques of Instruction

The competent instructor prepares each lesson to be sure that the best use is made of the student's time; that the planning of the lesson relates everything that happens in the learning situation to the objective of the lesson; that the planning is flexible enough to capitalize on special interests or special experiences of individuals in the class. The techniques of presentation include being able (1) to speak clearly without shouting, (2) to organize instruction according to student learning capacities, (3) to repeat and emphasize key material in such a way that it stands the best chance of being remembered, (4) to conduct a demonstration skillfully, and (5) to provide practice sessions and performance tests in such a way as to promote and develop desirable skills and attitudes.

Resourcefulness and Creativeness

Only the incompetent or lazy instructor uses the same method all the time. The methods that work well for one individual or for one class or for one lesson may not be satisfactory in another situation. The good instructor is alert to even the slightest evidence that confusion, misunderstanding, or lack of interest is present among the students, and is able to adjust his or her approach instantly to correct the difficulty.

One of the reasons for varying instructional procedures with different classes or individuals is that individuals differ to a marked degree in native capacity, in background of experience, and in learning pattern. By the time students begin to receive occupational instruction they have learned to walk, to speak the language, to count, to read, to write, and to get along more or less well with other people. Some of this learning has taken place in school, some in the home, some in sports, youth organizations, and in many other situations. In other words, the process of learning how to learn has begun; that is, the individual has developed a way of adapting to occurrences outside himself and is capable of profiting from vocational instruction.

This learning pattern or style differs for each person. The rapidity with which a particular individual learns a particular subject depends to a large extent on how well he adapts his learning pattern to the method by which the instructor presents the material. This instructor-student relationship should work both ways. The instructor must be quick to modify instructional procedures so that learning will be facilitated. An understanding of the principles of learning will help of course, but the really fine instructor learns to adjust general principle for the individual who happens not to fit the pattern.

Resourcefulness is demonstrated when the instructor designs a new instructional aid to help illustrate a principle, uses a current event to emphasize a concept, builds an advanced project to develop his own competence in the subject he teaches, or discovers a more effective way of measuring the progress of each student.

Knowledge and Application of Evaluation Procedures

The good instructor is like the good cook who keeps testing the food to see if the flavor is right, or like the craftsman who uses the senses of sight, smell, and touch to indicate when the power tool is cutting properly and safely. The instructor must be sensitive to the way the students are responding. There must be a constant desire to find out the extent to which students are learning. This can be done periodically by examinations if the questions are designed to find out whether or not the students have achieved the objectives specified for instruction.

In other words, can they demonstrate the level of skill, knowledge and attitudes for which the instructional program was designed to develop? However, the testing, like the tasting must be continuous. The good instructor makes every effort to tell by the expression on the faces of the students, by the questions asked, and by other indications the extent to which a particular idea, process, or skill is being assimilated by the learner.

It should be emphasized that the primary purpose of most course examination should not be to "rate" or grade the stu-

Facial expressions may indicate the effectiveness of the instruction.

dent, but rather to moniter the amount or quality of learning. The process of thinking through the material and assisting students to organize it in their minds, which results from the review preceding an examination and the discussion which should follow, is of tremendous value in fixing the important ideas and relations in the students' memory.

Desire to Teach

Possibly no single factor in the complex group of qualities and abilities that are considered to be absolutely essential for good instruction is, in the long run, so important as the attitude of the instructor toward the teaching role and the students. Few occupations make such demands on the emotional and mental composition of the individual as teaching. The instructor must always be projected into the thinking of others, and must do this not in the sense of command—of ordering students to do things—but as a sympathetic and understanding guide. The fumbling attempts of the beginner often "try" the patience of the expert. Nevertheless, the instructor must show, tell and guide patiently until the beginner has acquired the necessary competence.

It is natural for the instructor to feel

some resentment at being retained at the same level of instruction for a considerable length of time, as is necessary for the person teaching a single short course repeatedly. Yet, for effective instruction, material which has become commonplace to the instructor must be taught each time as though it were absorbing and interesting. Actually, this means that, except for those who teach in a field which is rapidly changing and expanding, the instructor must learn to transfer his interest from the subject to the students. He must make central in his thinking not what he is teaching, but "what are they learning?"

Ability to Develop Good Personal Relations

Students are people. Supervisors and administrators are people. The instructor must learn to get along with both groups. It has been proven that emotional factors influence learning. Favorable attitudes such as a feeling of confidence tend to increase the level of student achievement, while unfavorable attitudes or strong emotions such as the fear of failure may block learning entirely. A student who is angry or afraid or worried cannot learn effectively (a fact that parents should remember).

The instructor may be guilty of interfering with the development of good personal relationships. Many of the traits which aggravate students, such as aloofness and sarcasm, are protective devices which the instructor often uses to hide inadequate preparation or lack of confidence. The "ivory tower" notion of separation between instructor and student is a convenience for the person who does not want to make the effort to know the students even though it is a well established principle of learning that positive personal relations between instructor and students contribute to learning.

Students respond very quickly to genuine interest. If they believe that the instructor likes them and has confidence in them, they will generally have a greater desire to achieve. It must be remembered that the instructor who has good interpersonal relations with his students can require, and get, much more achievement from them in the long run than one who is disliked, resented, or not respected for his ability.

Students are encouraged by genuine interest.

It goes without saying that the instructor must work in harmony with his fellow instructors and with his supervisors. Demonstrating willingness to do more than is required is a great help in earning the respect of one's associates and superiors, unless this willingness is accompanied by qualities of aggressiveness or lack of consideration. The instruction in any educational program can be greatly improved by cooperative efforts toward improvement of method, instructional materials and devices, as well as evaluation procedures.

Here are a few specific suggestions:

Be friendly. The instructor who meets both students and associates with a smile and a word of greeting will find it easier to work and get along with them. A free and natural relationship should be maintained with fellow instructors as well as with students.

Be friendly with students and associates.

Cooperate. Since all instructors are working together for the benefit of the students, cooperation between instructors is essential. The instructor should discuss non-instructional responsibilities with the administration in order that there will be a clear understanding of the expected role. If this role is carried out in a friendly, cooperative manner, a positive reputation will result and a higher degree of cooperation from others can be expected.

Take part in social activities. The instructor should enter into the recreational and social activities of the group. Such participation outside the instructional setting promote rapport with the group that has positive implications for

program effectiveness. This does not mean an instructor must limit social and recreational contacts to fellow staff members but rather that an attempt be made to enter into and enjoy their conversations and recreational activities to an extent that will permit a congenial and informal relationship within the group.

Compliment achievement of others. From time to time instructors will have unusual success with a class or with a particular approach to some student's problem. When this happens, compliments should be given sincerely and in terms of benefit to the students. False flattery should be avoided. One of the most effective compliments is to merely show an active interest in the progress being made by a colleague as well as for the progress of a student.

Use tact and consideration. Consider the feelings of others. Since we cannot know how others feel about many things, we should be cautious in situations that may prove embarrassing. Dogmatic statements about such issues as politics, race problems, or the value of one school subject over another are best avoided. However, controversial matters can and should be discussed with tact and understanding by well-informed people, if we are to make progress. The important thing is to think first and talk second. We can seldom have meaningful discussions if we are judged to be unreasonably opinionated. We can be honest with our students and colleagues if we are perceived by them as willing to listen and consider other points of view which could alter our own beliefs.

Maintain good personal appearance. It has been said that a man gets no credit for shaving but much discredit for not shaving; and likewise, a woman may receive little credit for well groomed hair but much discredit for hair that looks uncombed or poorly styled. Cleanliness and neatness in appearance is an asset in any job, but an instructor is in a position to be observed closely, and poor grooming can have an adverse influence on students and colleagues alike. Your associates get their first impression of you from your general appearance, and this may last a long time.

Be a professional. In the best sense of the word a "pro" in the instructional arena takes pride in the role and demonstrates a high degree of ethical behavior in dealing with others. Further, the pro takes pride in being competent as an educated person. There is not always a direct relationship between education and the number of years of school attendance. According to the Carnegie Foundation for the Advancement of Teaching, the educated person is intellectually curious, thinks critically, weighs evidence dispassionately, is tolerant, temperate, balanced in judgment, possesses maturity, is not intellectually lazy or slovenly, and does not permit rational processes to be at the mercy of fears and prejudices.

Your Relationship With Your Students

As an instructor, you are always being observed and "sized up" by your students, and this impression has a major effect on the way they will respond to you as an instructor. If they respect you and like you, your job will not only be easier, but you will turn out a better product. The preceding section dealing with the development of *good personal relationships* are human relation techniques that apply to your students just as they do to your peers.

Let us consider some of the things an instructor might do and how these things affect learning:

Bluffing: The instructor who attempts to bluff when he does not know what to say or do is not respected by students. No instructor can know everything about the subject. It must be expected that students will ask questions that the instructor cannot answer. When this happens the instructor should not feel threatened and display, either through verbal tone or expression, disgust, frustration or irritation that might cause the timid student to withhold further questions. Instead the student should be complimented for raising the question; the instructor should admit he doesn't know and do one of four things shown on page 10.

Using sarcasm. There is never a place for sarcasm and ridicule in teaching. Be fair, firm and friendly. The use of sarcasm puts the student in a frame of mind where he is unable to learn because his attention is focused on the cause of the resentment and not on the lesson. Sarcasm is too frequently viewed as a "put down" and is a source of embarrassment that is avoided by effective instructors.

Acting as a comedian. There is a place for a good joke or a bit of humor while teaching because this helps to make the setting less formal and the instruction more interesting. It must be remembered, however, that the instructor's job is to teach, not to amuse the group. A good rule would be to mix a little humor in where it will help to reinforce the subject matter. But don't let your desire to be a comedian intefere with your job of teaching. Remember that jokes and stories that

SITUATION	PROPER TECHNIQUE
Something the instructor realized he should know and that should be taught in the lesson.	Offer to find out. Keep the promise and relate information back to the class.
Something of interest to an advanced student but beyond the scope of the course.	Tell the student where to get the information or help him find it at the proper time.
Something for which there is no exact information	Inform the student that the facts are not known. A brief comment about work that has been done so far toward finding the facts might be given.
Something that is too advanced or complicated for the students at this time.	Briefly describe the techniques or process and indicate its complexity. Suggest the question be asked again in a later lesson or course. If appropriate make a note to include it later.

do not contribute to the content being learned are better left untold.

Complaining. Few instructors have everything they need to work with, but many have more than are properly used. Regardless of your problems related to instructional setting it is always best to do the job to the best of your ability under the conditions without complaining to the students. They are not interested in excuses, but they will respect you for going ahead with the job of instruction in spite of obvious handicaps.

Being hard boiled. An instructor may seek to establish a reputation as being "tough" by using aggressive behavior, frowning, a commanding tone of voice and the display of a hard boiled attitude; by bragging or threatening that few A's are given or that extraordinary effort must be expended to pass the course; refusing to repeat anything that has been said or acting as though students must be driven rather than led; never considering the feelings of the students. The hard boiled instructor seems to believe that students can be bullied into learning. Such techniques discourage students from trying to cooperate with the instructor and fills them with fear or disgust. Very little learning can take place when the student feels fear, disgust or resentment. It is essential that an instructor develop a good measure of patience and tact. Sometimes it demands a great deal of self control and maturity, but the real pro does it because it facilitates learning.

The Rewards for being an Instructor

One of the most satisfying experiences a person can have is to know that through their efforts someone has become more competent, developed a better self image, become a better human being and more useful as a citizen. Through the applica-

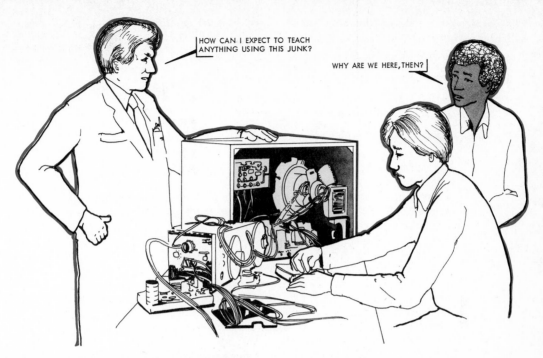

Students will not respect a complaining instructor.

tion of your skill as an instructor you can bring new opportunities to others.

One of the most exciting experiences an instructor can have, which is hard to imagine until it has happened to you, is to discover dormant talent in a student. To motivate, to develop interest, to discover latent abilities, to see the pleasure that results from new-found capacities, and to participate in the development of competence is a reward unique to the field of teaching.

Some of the contacts you make with your students will develop into strong life-long friendships because of the mutual respect and understanding gained through working and learning together. You will enjoy the exchange of ideas that takes place among instructors with whom you work, and you will develop interests

in ideas and engage in activities about which you have given very little thought previously. These new interests will broaden your horizon and make it easier for you to find something in common with others with whom you come in contact.

It has been said that the only way to really *know* something is to try to teach it. Since this is at least partly true, you may expect to find yourself studying the things your students must learn from a new and perhaps more analytical point of view. Such study and thought will add to your knowledge of the subject and make you better informed on all phases of your subject matter.

There will be many changes in your job and each day will be filled with problems for you to solve. These problems will be a challenge to you, but it is through such experience that you will become more skillful not only in your profession but also in working with other people. You, as an instructor, are in the "people" business.

QUESTIONS AND ASSIGNMENTS

1. State in one sentence by what standard an instructor must be judged.
2. Is it enough to say that the competent instructor enables students to learn the right things?
3. What are the major qualities of the good instructor? What are some things that may not make much difference?
4. Make up a short list of other good characteristics you have noted and indicate to which of the six major qualities each is related.
5. What factors make it possible for instructors to be very different in methods they use and still be equally effective?
6. In the subject you plan to teach which seems more important— knowledge of the subject or ability to instruct?
7. Why should a plan for teaching a lesson allow for flexibility?
8. Why does the experienced and skilled instructor use many methods in instructing?
9. If the good instructor continually evaluates the students' responses as he instructs, what does this suggest with regard to educational films, closed circuit TV, or other training aids?
10. If we recognize that the good instructor must want to teach, what can we do as instructors to develop this desire in ourselves?
11. What is apt to be the result of pretending to know something?
12. What purpose do examinations have other than determining a grade?
13. Why must an instructor like to teach if maximum effectiveness is to be achieved?
14. List some improper personal relationships you have seen between supervisor, instructor, and students.
15. How would you correct these poor relationships if you were the instructor? the supervisor? the student?
16. If another instructor develops a unique and successful way of presenting certain material, what would you do about it?
17. Of the six qualities a person needs to become an instructor, decide which you feel is your weakest and consider what you can do about it.

Gaining Insight Into the Learning Process

It is possible for a technician to wire a house or repair a radio without knowing much of the theory of electricity or electronics. Likewise the cook may use the correct ingredients and procedures to produce a culinary delight without knowing the chemical theories and principles that caused the successful product. In the same way, an instructor may use good techniques of instruction without knowing much of the theory of learning. However, the technician, the cook and the instructor will be more effective in the long run when confronted with new and changing situations if they have an understanding of the basic theory related to the specific techniques of the job. In this and the following chapter we will be dealing with some of the facts and principles involved in the learning/teaching process on which effective instruction is based.

We learn in many different ways—by reading, listening, watching, doing, thinking, and solving problems. The success of any of these learning processes depends on several elements of which attention and interest are the central overriding forces. No instructional approach can be very successful if it fails to hold the students' interest and attention. It is easy to learn when we are interested; it is most difficult if we are not. The person who has a strong desire to become an aircraft pilot finds that the required mathematics and science subjects can be learned even though he may have a poor record of achievement or avoided such courses in high school and college.

The learner's attention will vary with the nature of the subject, the level and quality of the instruction, and with the previous experiences of the students both in and out of the course. With advanced students, difficult problem-solving activities may hold attention over long periods of time; with beginning students, the instructor may need to involve students in a greater variety of participatory activities.

The skilled instructor uses techniques

The good instructor holds the attention and interest of all the class.

and learning activities that hold the attention and interest of the largest number of individuals possible. Other techniques may need to be used to reach individuals within the groups as the need arises.

Learning by Trial and Error

The baby's response to discomfort is kicking and crying. If the discomfort is the result of being hungry, the kicking and crying stops whenever he is fed. After a few weeks the child learns that a par-

ticular cry will bring food. Of course, the mother learns that cry, too. Later, the child and the mother learn that other activities, such as reaching for a cup, indicate the desire for food. The baby and the mother have learned to communicate by trial and error. The baby makes all kinds of movements and noises until the food comes. After a while the baby selects one kind of behavior to bring about the desired response from mother or father. In other words, the baby learns what to do to get results.

Adults learn many things by trial and

error. However, because of past experiences and their ability to reason or use knowledge gained previously, they don't have to make as many trials before acquiring the necessary behavior (learning). Many adult automobile drivers, however, have learned to drive more or less by trial and error and some still demonstrate the ineffectiveness of the method where exact standards or a high degree of skill is necessary. Considering modern cars and driving conditions, most people will agree that formal and organized driver training is necessary.

We all use trial and error to some extent, and the method is the only method that can be used at times. However, contrary to popular opinion, learning things "the hard way" is not necessarily the best way. In a humorous vein, it has been said that "good judgment comes from experience and that experience comes from using bad judgment." Later, we will discuss "learning by doing" which is related to, but different from trial and error.

Learning by Observation

We learn much by watching others do something we want to do. This helps to eliminate some of the trials we would have to make by our first method. However, there are many important things that cannot be learned by observation alone. No amount of watching a pilot would permit one to develop the competence or skill needed to become a pilot. We can't even learn to ride a bicycle by observation alone. We may get the general idea, but we can never get the "feel" of the skill by observation. When we learn motor skills, such as using hand tools, walking, throwing a ball or typing, a change must take place in our muscles and nervous system. This is often referred to as *psychomotor*

learning. This kind of learning comes only through doing and practicing over a period of time whatever it is we want to learn to do.

Such activities as operating a calculator, solving mathematical problems, running a metal working lathe, or even playing a card game is usually too complicated to be learned by this method alone. Observing things that go on around us is, however, a valuable habit. The scientist learns as he observes his experiments. He has learned to observe with great objectivity, see things in truth not as they might be or as the scientist might want them to be, but as they are.

Learning by Doing

Many instructors are too verbal as they use too many words in the process of telling. They have confused *telling* with *teaching*. Words are important, and no instructor can do without them, but words usually convey only part of the meaning. Some form of activity or participation is necessary for an individual to gain complete understanding. The city youngster's concept of a farm can never be very accurate until there is some direct involvement such as living or working on a farm. No amount of verbal education, TV or films can take the place of real experience. When physical skills must be acquired, there are obvious reasons for *learning by doing*. We learn physical skills, such as driving a nail or hitting a ball, by learning the correct movements. This is the reason for following the instructor's demonstration with a direct "hands on" experience by the learner.

Although it is more often neglected, the principle of learning by doing holds just as well for non-physical learning. Each major idea or concept in a lesson should

Learning by doing is an important part of instruction.

be followed by carefully prepared student assignments and problems that make use of or *apply* the idea or concept presented by the instructor. Students must summarize, review, discuss and apply new material. Frequently they should translate new ideas into their own words. Learning aids, including working models, performance tests and even achievement tests that require interpretation or application of facts are effective *learning by doing* processes.

Even while presenting material by lecture, it is possible to have the mental participation of learners as they relate new ideas to past experience or previously learned facts. The skilled instructor can apply the principle of learning by doing while lecturing by challenging the students through rhetorical questions and allowing time for them to:

1. Answer questions silently.
2. Criticize ideas.
3. Disagree and try to defend their ideas.
4. See relationships of principles to specific uses.

In other words, the skillful instructor gets students to learn by doing inside their heads.

Transfer of Training

Transfer of training in its simplest form refers to the learning of something in one setting or situation that permits one to gain insight or solve a problem in a quite different situation. Transfer is not necessarily automatic, although persons of high intelligence can generally transfer quicker and more effectively than persons of low intelligence. Many people still believe that one can train the mind like a muscle. Transfer can be facilitated by the teacher who continually causes students to think of alternatives, to look for new ways, to question and to apply knowledge. In other words, one must teach for transfer through generalized meanings and flexible habits.

A noted educator once said, "There is no single subject that has the key to rational thinking, any subject can make a contribution, but the way the subject is taught may make all the difference." Unfortunately some people think that by mastering certain difficult subjects the mind can be strengthened and will, therefore, have greater intellectual or rationale power and be more able to learn any subject. This concept of learning is not generally accepted by psychologists and careful experimentation has failed to support the theory. We do not learn to solve problems in human relations, for example, through the study of geometry, nor does a knowledge of human relations help in learning geometry. A respected historian whose work is of the highest level of scholarly endeavor may be unable to supervise others effectively, to lay out a good floor plan for a school building, or to understand a simple wiring diagram. This inadequacy is not because the historian does not have a good mind, but rather that he or she lacks certain competencies that are needed by a supervisor or architect or an electrician.

A factor that often contributes to confusion with regard to modern day problems is that well-known experts in their own fields of endeavor speak out on subjects or problems in which they are far from expert. Many complex occupations require personnel to have much specific education and experience before their judgment can be trusted. No amount of competence in a specific field of work makes one fully competent to render judgment in another field of work.

Value of specific knowledge. Learning one specific task or subject may, however, help us in learning some other specific task, if the two tasks or subjects are closely related or made up of the same elements and if the student recognizes these relationships. Knowledge of one language will help us learn another if the languages are related or similar. Because some English words come from Latin, a knowledge of Latin will help us to learn English. But it is just as true that a mastery of English helps us learn Latin. Mathematics will help us learn electronics because mathematics is a part of electronics. Simulators like electrical-mechanical trainers used for pilot training have great transfer value because they are designed to simulate the exact performance of the airplane. Great care is taken to keep such trainers in adjustment; however, since poorly designed or out-of-adjustment training devices may actually train the operator to do the wrong thing. The closer the learning environment resembles the actual occupational environment, the easier it will be for transfer to take place. Increasing use of these simulation techniques in instruction is being used at all levels of education.

Military drill is a good example of transfer of training. Probably no one would train raw recruits without some military close order drill. However, the value of a great deal of this type of training for today's military personnel cannot be justified unless it transfers to other required assignments. Many soldiers, sailors, and airmen are skilled technicians who act independently on their technical assignments. It is doubtful that intensive military drill will make the radarman, the electronic technician, the metalsmith more proficient in these duties. On the other hand, we would expect good transfer of training from military drill to such situations as handling lines while ships are refueling at sea or when the commander of a submarine gives the order to dive. These situations demand immediate response to command. In this situation team coordination of the efforts of many men under emergency-like conditions is typical. However, regardless of the amount of previous military drill, a great amount of specific training in the exact procedures is needed. One must not only be able to react instantly, but do the required task as well.

Other examples of transfer. If the student learns that $3 \times 8 = 24$, by transferring this knowledge he should know without further instruction that $8 \times 3 = 24$, and with minimum instruction that $30 \times 8 = 240$, and that $30 \times 80 = 2400$.

The geometry student knows that 5" is the length of the hypotenuse if the other sides of a triangle are 90° to each other and one side measures 3" and the other 4". If he understands the principle, and by using feet instead of inches, he should be able to lay out the 90° angles of a tennis court.

If such transfer does not take place, we can suspect that the instructor failed to illustrate the principle in such a way as to cause it to come to mind in new but related situations.

When many mathematical problems have been worked but the student fails in his effort to solve a slightly different problem in which the same mathematical principle should be used, we have reason to doubt that the instructor is teaching for transfer. Practice and drill are essential, but so is an understanding of the principles involved. A lot of unproductive student homework can be avoided where the principles are well taught and when examples are used to show how the principles can be applied.

Teaching the "principles of learning" to potential instructors is not apt to have much effect on their performance unless (1) the principles are applied in a variety of practice teaching situations, and (2) the relationship of these principles to specific teaching situations is evaluated and emphasized.

Some may feel that in technical or vocational education there is little need for transfer, as specific techniques are taught and used on the job as soon as the student completes the course.

It should be remembered, however, that technical subject matter changes rapidly. It is not enough to know the specific steps of procedure. The principles and the "why" must be understood if we are to adjust to changing situations.

The habit of seeing the relationship of basic principles to a variety of practical

An airline crew and instructor at work in a DC-8 flight simulator. Simulators such as this duplicate the real situation which greatly aids in transfer of learning. (United Airlines)

uses should be developed in any course of instruction. This is the reason in this book for giving examples and for the end-of-chapter questions and assignments which require application of the text material to the subject.

Aiding transfer of learning. As instructors we can aid the positive transfer of learning if we:

1. Emphasize the underlying principles and ideas of the content being learned, and make sure they are fully understood. Then the student will be more likely to apply them to a new or different task or subject.
2. Help students to see the relationship of parts of the subject being taught to other parts of the course or to other subjects or courses.
3. Let students know when to expect transfer, the benefits to them, and how to facilitate the transfer.
4. Use projects, problems, discussion, and leading questions to give practice in transfer.
5. Give attention to the differing ways in which individual students learn and their approach to problems as well as to results.

Under some circumstances, skill in one activity or one way of doing something may actually interfere with learning a new skill. This is called negative transfer. There is research evidence to show that one should not attempt to learn two very similar physical skills at the same time. Learning two similar languages at the same time may also result in negative transfer. Parents who speak a language different from the one their children are learning in school are frequently asked by the school not to try to teach the second language at the same time. Riding a motorcycle with a sidecar will have a negative transfer effect compared to riding without a sidecar because the feel and balance are different. Can you think of other related skills that may cause negative transfer?

Plateaus in Learning

Plateaus in the process of learning are like the landings in a long flight of stairs. They are particularly evident in the development of psychomotor skills which are complex combinations of physical coordination and mental processes. After we have mastered the steps of procedure in performing a skill, we may become discouraged because we do not seem to be making any further progress toward a higher level of skill. One cause may be that, although we know how to perform the skill or task, we have not practiced it enough to make it a thoroughly established habit. We still have to think about each step of procedure as it is performed. At this point, we may feel as though we have bogged down——that further progress is impossible. We might feel like giving up. Golfers and other athletes experience plateaus in developing their game. Students should be informed of this characteristic of learning so that they will recognize it as natural and something experienced by everyone who strives for perfection.

One typically overcomes a learning plateau by continued practice assuming that

LANDING

Plateaus in learning are like the landings in a flight of stairs.

the physical movements are correct; however, specialized instruction may be required to overcome the plateau if there is a flaw in the techniques of performance. As practice is continued and coupled with a strong effort to learn, and a thorough knowledge of the procedures involved in the task, the process will gradually become automatic, just as walking or talking is automatic to most human beings over three years of age. From this point on, progress is again possible in the same way that running is possible after walking has become automatic. However, other delays in progress are likely to occur along the line of developing additional skill. The solution of the problem is usually the same: *continue practice after the procedure is thoroughly understood until the movements become so automatic that it can be done without thinking.* The mind is then free to concentrate on new problems.

Several plateaus may be encountered along the road toward a high degree of skill. The instructor should:

1. Recognize the existence of plateaus.
2. Inform students of the nature of the plateaus in learning
3. Analyze student performance to detect any performance flaws that require remedial instruction.
4. Help to increase the learner's understanding of the task.
5. Emphasize the need for additional practice.
6. Provide encouragement and continued practice until the steps of procedure become so automatic that the student can concentrate on the next phase or level of achievement.

If plateaus are of long duration it may mean that (a) improper habits have been formed, (b) that the student is attempting to learn something beyond his potential ability, or (c) that the instructor has failed to give needed assistance and motivation.

Emotions such as fear, hate, and boredom may create plateaus in learning because the student's mind is not free to concentrate on the task being learned.

Individual Differences

To understand people we must recognize two truths: (1) all people are different, and (2) we are often unaware in what way, to what degree, and why people are different. We are all acting and reacting in an environment that is seen from our own personal point of view.

Hence, each individual can be understood only through careful observation, thought, and insight. The professional instructor consistently observes, listens to, and tries to understand each student. In our casual thinking about learning and teaching, we tend to visualize an instructor and a group of students, the one teaching, the other learning. However, the instructor must understand and teach *each* individual in his group. The *group* does not learn anything, only individuals within the group learn. The instructor must decide which individuals need guidance, encouragement, extra instruction, more practice, or more challenging assignments. Decisions must be made regarding each individual's level of achievement and ways must be found to assist learners achieve their maximum potential. Individuals differ in their emotional maturity, in their ability to understand complex concepts, in their physical

Mental and emotional differences are more important in learning than physical differences.

coordination, in their learning rate or speed and many other ways that may influence their performance in a learning situation.

In short, the instructor must know each member of the group as a unique person and this knowledge must help to determine the approach to use. This is one reason why large classes in our schools are not very successful and why mass media such as radio and TV can only supplement, or be a part of the educational process rather than take over the instructional process.

If we look at the differences in people, the picture is striking. Of course they differ in the physical characteristics we can see: height, weight, length of legs, color of skin, eyes and hair, and size of head. More importantly the instructor must be sensitive to the many other less obvious differences which have a tremendous impact on their learning such as

their mental ability, their interests, the keenness of their senses, their emotional stability, experience, background, knowledge level. As a result of basic aptitudes, training, and experiences, they differ widely in what they have learned and the level of competence they can reach in a given period of time.

Human characteristics. With regard to human characteristics, we should remember, however, that while there is a great range (some people very tall, some very short), a very high percentage of us are close to being average. A few of us may be blond, a few brunette, but most of us are somewhere in between the two extremes. We should also remember that certain characteristics are possessed by every person although these characteristics might have extreme variations from one individual to another. For the average person a little daydreaming is normal; excessive daydreaming or no daydreaming is not. To say that a person is *bright* has little meaning unless we know to what degree or in what ways the individual is bright. One bright student may be able to learn twice as fast as another bright student. Brightness is a misleading term since abilities are specialized. For example, one person may be able to read literature rapidly and comprehend it well while another person may be much more effective in the calculation of mathematical problems.

In some situations, small differences are very important. A tenth of a second difference in reaction time can be very important in the training of pilots, athletes, and some technicians; however for most vocations people with great differences can be successful. What they lack in one way can be compensated for by other characteristics. Many gifted persons are not as successful as they might be because they lack adequate drive and ambition. A less gifted person may have more success because of desire and the willingness to work harder.

Research studies regarding the characteristics of great military leaders have shown that great leaders did not have many characteristics in common nor do they lead in the same way. Note the great differences between Grant and Lee. It is said that Lee was the greatest strategist in the field; Grant led more by common sense and great will or drive to win.

An understanding of the following terms is necessary for further discussion of individual differences.

Aptitude, Ability and Achievement

Aptitude refers to the individual's potential to achieve in a given area. A student may have great aptitude for music, but not be able to play any instrument because of lack of training. Aptitude, then, is the potential or "built-in" characteristics that can be developed through training and experience.

We might think of aptitude as clay in the ground. It can take the form of mud in the street, be made into bricks for a building or, in the hands of the artist, into a great piece of sculpture. The clay is the same. The result is dependent on the way it is used.

When we use aptitude tests, of which there are many types, we are attempting to measure or predict what the student can do after appropriate educational experiences. Aptitude refers to latent or potential ability.

Ability refers to the individual's actual level of performance as contrasted to aptitude or potential. It refers to what a student can do after education or experience.

Ability means demonstrated performance over a period of time. The skilled carpenter with a sore hand may not perform well today, but we can still say he has the ability to perform. He may do very well a few days later. We say he has the ability to do well even though he does not perform well at all times. The sick student may fail an examination, but he may still have the ability to pass the examination because he knows the content.

Achievement refers to the present. When a young student gets a high mark on his tenth grade mathematics test, this is evidence of achievement as measured by his teacher's standards. A good aptitude test given, perhaps, years before the course, would have predicted that the student could do this. When an aptitude test predicts success but achievement does not result during the educational process, we must consider the student's interest in the subject, the instructor's methods, and perhaps other factors that affect learning.

If the student gets good grades in mathematics but not in English, this may mean a difference in his aptitude for the two subjects. However, it may mean that one teacher is doing a better job than the other. It may mean simply that one teacher has different standards than the other. Or it may mean that the student, for some reason, works harder on mathematics than on English. These factors and many more must be considered in understanding the progress of a given student. It is sad that so much emphasis is placed on school grades by some parents who have little understanding of the basis for grades.

Differences in Intelligence

Intelligence is hard to define, but basically it refers to a general aptitude based on many specific aptitudes. It is measured by aptitude for such factors as solving problems, speed in learning, understanding of relationships, and dealing with abstract ideas.

Intelligence always refers to aptitude rather than achievement. An individual can be very intelligent yet accomplish very little in an educational setting. The term I.Q. (Intelligence Quotient) refers to a means of relating general aptitude to age. It is determined by standard intelligence tests given under controlled conditions. If we want to know how one person compares with others of the same age, as measured by intelligence tests, we can compare his score on a test with the average of hundreds of others of the same age. A person may have a score on a test that is equal to the average of others who are the same age or it may be higher or lower. If the individual is twelve years old and his score on the test is the same as the average of thousands of other twelve year olds from a given population for which the test was constructed, we say he has an I.Q. of 100.

Traditionly, the I.Q. was a ratio of mental age (MA) and chronological age (CA). For instance, if a 10 year old had a mental age of the average 12 year old, the mental age (12) was divided by the age in years (10) and multiplied by 100, giving an I.Q. of 120. A mental age of 8 and a chronological age of 10 would result in an I.Q. of 80.

However, the 1972 Stanford-Binet standardization testing program revealed that the average mental age in the U. S. has shifted upward and as a result a child five years of age must have a mental age of 5 years and 6 months to be classified as average. As a result, I.Q. is now *derived* at each age level rather than calculated as a direct ratio of chronological age and mental age.

The growth of mental ability, like physical growth, is more rapid during the early years of life, and then gradually levels off. For practical purposes, we can assume that full mental maturity is reached by most people by age 20 to 25. The mental growth rate of the very intelligent person is faster and continues to a higher level than that of the person of average or below average intelligence.

If the intelligence test was well constructed, and if the person being tested is from the same cultural background assumed by the test development team, and if the test is taken under ideal conditions when the individual is free from emotional or physical discomfort, a true measure of intelligence can be expected. Under the above conditions, the same test or similar forms of the test could be administered to an individual at different times during life, and the I.Q. would remain relatively stable although the M.A. and C.A. would both increase. Even though the Intelligence Quotient is fairly stable and constant for individuals, the mental growth rate may fluctuate in individuals. For example, after four years in which the schools were closed, junior high students in Virginia's Prince Edward County returned to class in September, 1963. As measured by standard I.Q. tests the average I.Q. of these students rose 18 points during the next 18 months.

Factors such as intensity of interest, attitudes resulting from home conditions, as well as physical and emotional health may affect the individual's score on a specific intelligence test. These same factors, of course, affect his success in learning.

Shown below is the distribution of Intelligence Quotients as found by intelligence tests known as the Stanford-Binet Scale.[1]

It is estimated that General Grant had an I.Q. of about 110. Lincoln, 125, and Jefferson, 145. Of course, they didn't take an I.Q. test, so the estimate is based on what they said or wrote at various times during their lives.

As instructors, we must bear in mind that achievement is based on much more than I.Q. What a person does with the gift of intelligence depends on opportunity, personality, general health, ambition and other factors. Many people have done very well in difficult tasks in spite of handicaps of all kinds. The individual with a measured intelligence of average or below, under the right conditions of education, environment and with appropriate personal characteristics, can

DISTRIBUTION OF INTELLIGENCE QUOTIENTS

CLASSIFICATION	I.Q.	PERCENTAGES OF ALL PERSONS
Gifted	149 or above	.14
Very Superior	133 - 148	2.14
Superior	117 - 132	13.59
High Average	109 - 116	17.065
Normal or Average	92 - 108	34.13
Low Average	84 - 91	17.065
Dull or Borderline	83 - 68	13.59
Mild Retardation	67 - 52	2.14
Retarded	51 or below	.14

[1]Terman, L. M., and Maud A. Merrill, *Stanford-Binet Intelligence Scale Manual For Third Revision.* Boston: Houghton Mifflin Publishing Co., 1973.

make contributions that are clearly above average and frequently superior to those who may be more intelligent. As an instructor, you must not limit an individual's performance level by low expectation any more than you should frustrate a learner by demanding a higher level of performance than ability will permit. This is a fine level of distinction that the superior experienced instructor can make much more easily than the novice. It is an instructional skill worth cultivating as it permits individuals to maximize their potential as human beings.

Physical Characteristics and Learning

The physical characteristics, such as shape of head, distance between eyes, angle of chin, give little or no indication of intelligence, ability, or personality. Our feelings and attitudes toward physical characteristics, however, may cause us to distort what we see or think we see. We too frequently over generalize from one or two examples which cause us to misjudge. We may think we see differences that are not really there. If you think that women don't make good drivers, you are more apt to notice when a woman driver gets into trouble. If the instructor thinks a high forehead indicates high intelligence he is apt to think he sees better achievement with students who have high foreheads.

A good instructor does not put all people of the same physical characteristics, sex, age, or race into one classification. He knows, for example, that some older persons are "set in their ways" but that other older people are liberal-minded and flexible. He knows that members of a given racial group may be either good or bad, but the pro must not pre-judge others of the same group. The instructor must real-

ize that very little, if anything, can be really known about a person's ability, personality, honesty, etc., by their appearance and even less from a photograph.

As instructors we must evaluate constantly our own attitudes in order to be as fair and objective as possible with each student.

While physical characteristics, such shape of head and brow, size and shape of nose and color of skin, in themselves do not determine the individual's aptitude for learning, they may have an influence on how he learns in some situations. Any characteristic from freckles and red hair to small stature may cause feelings of insecurity and embarrassment which may prevent students, especially young or timid students, from feeling that they are accepted by their fellow students or by you, their instructor. This in turn may result in emotional reactions that have a significant effect on learning. Unfortunate social experiences caused by the reactions of others to the student's physical characteristics or home background often lead to learning behavior difficulties.

The good instructor is alert to these possibilities and should promptly take whatever action he can to help the individual fit into the group in a normal way. Sensitivity to the feelings of your students is part of your role as an instructor, but even more important is the strategy you use in helping individuals overcome their "hang ups" so that they can achieve their full potential.

Sex and Learning

In addition to the obvious physical differences between men and women, for which most of us are grateful, there are other differences. Men usually test higher on mechanical aptitude, but it is recognized that most of this test difference is due to early experience with mechanical things. Little girls traditionally have not been encouraged to play with mechanical toys but rather with dolls. Probably, most differences in the averages between men and women, except in physical strength and related characteristics, are due to environment and educational experiences. The evidence is overwhelming that many women perform well in jobs tradi-

tionally reserved for men when they are given an equal opportunity for educational experiences whereby they may gain the necessary competencies.

Age and Learning

It is easy to exaggerate the importance of age. The fact that we can estimate a person's age makes it easy to think we see a difference in performance, hence individuals don't always get the same chance to show their abilities. Compulsory retirement at sixty-five, regardless

Age does not necessarily affect a person's ability to learn.

of the individual's level of competence, is being challenged by many competent psychologists and administrators.

In the ability to learn new mental skills, most individuals reach a peak by age 20 to 25. From then on, during the person's working life, there is usually no significant decrease in the capacity to learn. Of course, some older people do not wish to learn anything new or are out of the habit of learning because they have been coasting on past achievements. These factors do influence the rate or speed of learning. It must be recognized that some physiological factors related to aging such as visual or hearing impairment can adversely affect learning.

Scientists, business leaders and writers often reach their peak performance around age fifty. We should recognize, however, that younger persons might do as well if they were in the same favorable position to demonstrate what they can do.

In skills of a physical nature age is more significant. The average age of maximum performance in sports varies with the sport. For football it is between 20 and 30, but for less physically demanding sports like golf the maximum is between 20 and 45.

Differences in Performance

If we give the same instruction to everyone in the group, we must expect differences in performance, and the larger the group the greater the range of differences to be expected. Even in simple types of work one person may produce several times the amount of another. As instructors, we must contend with built-in differences. Educational programs will not erase these differences in individuals. In fact, if we provide individuals who are of different aptitude and different achievement the same instruction, the differences among them with regard to achievement is likely to become greater. The person with the greatest aptitude for a given task is likely to perform the task better at any stage of training, and typically can gain more from the training received. Instruction will improve the performance of each student, but it usually has the greatest effect on students who have consistently demonstrated good achievement. For many reasons, success tends to beget success.

What should you do about individual differences in a class? Here are three important suggestions:

Encourage individual abilities. Don't try to force everyone into the same mold. Make use of the best abilities of each student so that he or she can develop at his own rate of speed. The instructor will find that it is not possible or desirable to keep all students on exactly the same problem or assignment. Students should develop to the full extent of their abilities, and it would be foolish to hold the fast learner back to the pace of the slow learner.

Get the facts. In order to make the most of the student's educational opportunities, you may wish to gather a few facts about each student. A simple form such as shown on page 29 will help to compile these facts in an orderly manner. In designing your form avoid asking for unnecessary information. An interview should be held with each student after the form has been completed to help you get better acquainted and to assist you in interpreting the facts.

Give both group and individual instruction. The characteristics of typical classroom instruction are well known to anyone who has attended the public schools.

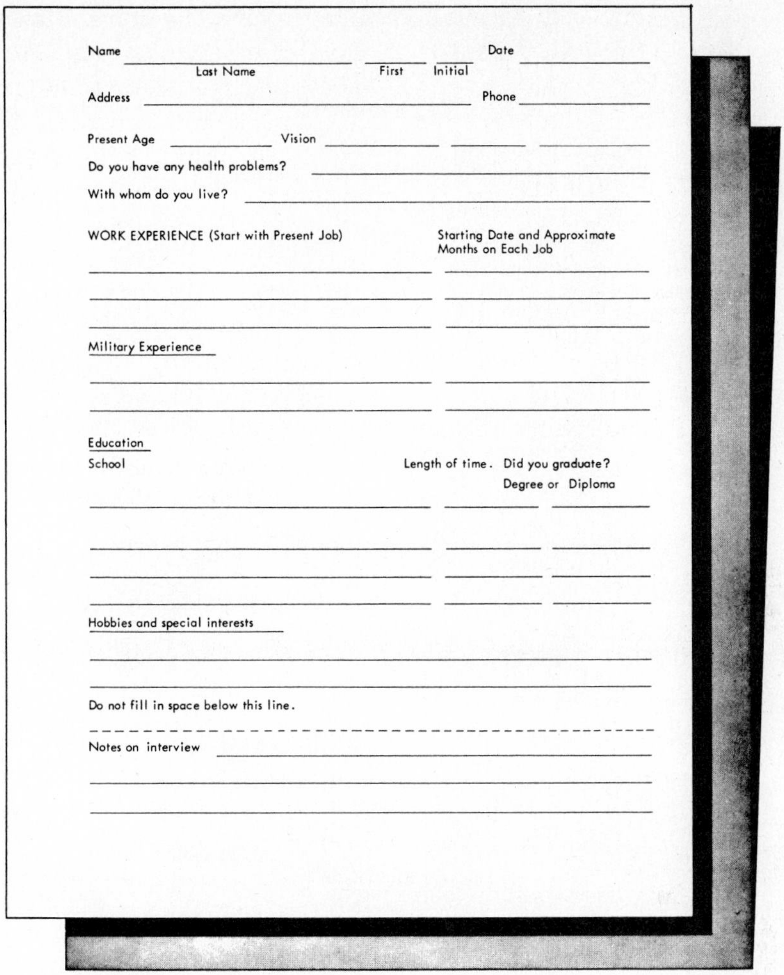

Name _____ Date _____
             Last Name   First   Initial

Address _____ Phone _____

Present Age _____ Vision _____ _____ _____

Do you have any health problems? _____

With whom do you live? _____

WORK EXPERIENCE (Start with Present Job)   Starting Date and Approximate
                                      Months on Each Job

Military Experience _____

Education
School   Length of time. Did you graduate?
                                             Degree or Diploma

Hobbies and special interests _____

Do not fill in space below this line.
- -
Notes on interview _____

A typical form for determining a student's past education and experience.

The chief advantage of group instruction over individual instruction is the saving of time which can result when the students are at the same level of accomplishment and need the same instruction. There is also a tendency for instructors to make more thorough preparation and to put on a better demonstration for a class than for an individual. This is one of the advantages claimed for instruction by mass media such as television or films.

The chief disadvantage of group instruction is that individuals who make up a group rarely need exactly the same instruction at the same time. The more advanced students are held back to the rate of progress made by the group as a whole. When demonstrations are given to a group, considerable time may lapse before some of the students have an opportunity to apply the information or procedures and much of it may be forgotten.

Group instruction is the primary method for presenting basic material.

The best plan in most instructional situations is found in a compromise. Instruction to the group should be given when the material is basic and needed by the entire group. Individual instruction should follow and be employed all through the program by means of written instruction sheets, short on-the-spot demonstrations, and continual coaching of individuals.

There are some real advantages in group instruction which result from the interaction of individuals to the group as a whole and to other individuals within the group. Because of the interplay of ideas and the resulting motivation, group instruction is most effective in some situations. For example, in supervisory training a major objective is the development of attitudes. The skilled instructor can draw on the experiences and ideas of the group as a whole to influence the attitudes of individuals in the group.

QUESTIONS AND ASSIGNMENTS

1. Why does a small child frequently use the trial and error method of learning?
2. What are some of the things adults are likely to learn by the trial and error method?
3. What other methods of learning would be applicable for each of these.
4. Do you believe that skills learned by trial and error are remembered longer? Do they lead to the highest level of skill development?
5. What handicap would the student have in learning to play chess or other games by observation only?
6. Why does the principle of "learning by doing" tend to be neglected when teaching some subjects?
7. How can "learning by doing" be brought into a lecture?
8. Under what conditions does the learning of information or skill help us learn other subjects or skills?
9. Give an example of positive transfer of training between subjects you have mastered.
10. Would it matter if you had learned the second subject first?
11. What is negative transfer?
12. Select a specific part of the course you plan to teach and explain the actions you might take to motivate students.
13. If we "learn by doing," why are other forms of instruction necessary?
14. When is copying a mechanical drawing or an illustration from a book a form of "learning by doing?" What is being learned?
15. Give a specific example of ability, of aptitude, and of achievement.
16. If a boy's actual (chronological) age is twelve but his mental age as measured by standard tests is fourteen, what is his I.Q.?
17. Design a form for gathering important facts you need about each student in the class you plan to teach.
18. Do you think you should know the I.Q. of your students? Why?
19. If you were a student would you want the instructor to know your I.Q.? Why?
20. How would you make sure the older person in your class is given an equal opportunity to achieve in the class?
21. In your subject or class, how would you adjust for individual differences among the students?

Influences on Learning

3

In all effective learning, the need or desire to know comes first. When our level of knowledge or skill is not adequate to satisfy a conscious or felt need, we have a desire to learn.

Children who listen to interesting stories read to them may not try to read until they want a story at a time when no one is available to read to them. The child often looks at the pictures at first and makes noises or calls words in an attempt to imitate the story teller. As the child gets more mature and independent, he realizes that if he could read he would have the story. At this point, he has a conscious need. With help and guidance, he will begin to learn to read.

As adults we acquire many highly complex competencies, such as getting along with other people in various kinds of situations, because we feel a need for these abilities. We cannot satisfy our desire for achievement in most fields of endeavor without first developing a degree of competence in working with others. Sometimes we forget that adults, as well as children, must have a conscious need if training is to be effective.

Motivation

One seldom does anything except as a result of motivation. Sometimes the motivation is obvious. There was the story of a 130 pound woman who lifted one end of a 3,000 pound automobile that had slipped off its jack so that her teen-age son could be pulled out from under the auto with only minor bruises. That's motivation!

It is not always easy however to discover the type of motivation to which a person will respond. The youngster who says, "I don't know why I did it," may be telling the truth. The motivation to "do it" was there; he simply doesn't know where it came from. Sometimes the motivation is known to an individual, but purposely concealed from others. The story is told of a fellow who insisted on having his dog's tail cut off all the way.

After some persistent questioning by the veterinarian, he finally admitted that his mother-in-law was coming for a visit and he didn't want anything around to suggest that she was welcome.

Of course, the thoughtful instructor attempts to provide the student with reasons why the content is important and should be learned. All too frequently, however, the instructor has a hard time relating the subject to immediate needs of students. This is not always the instructor's fault. Some courses, or parts of courses, just don't have any discoverable value, but continue to be taught because someone thinks they are good for the student. Much of the alienation of youth in today's schools comes from the conflict between what the student wants to learn and what the teacher wants to teach, or perhaps what the school system or the board of education or the college entrance examinations require. Some people still think in terms of *train the mind* rather than working at the task of making education relevant for the learner.

Dr. Glenn Frank when he was President of the University of Wisconsin said: "Since both college life and human life are short, and it is impossible to learn everything, we should study the things that will most directly minister to our efficiency and happiness."

Some instructors think of motivation as a sort of pep talk at the start of a lesson, but real motivation cannot be a separate and distinct step in teaching. Everything that happens in teaching has an effect on the student's motivation. In a sense, all of the techniques described in this book are good only if they have a positive effect on the student's desire to learn (motivation).

For instruction to be effective or meaningful to the learner, we must start at the learner's level. If the learner does not know or understand the material just preceding or basic to the new learning task, it is the instructor's responsibility to see that the prerequisite level is reached before going on to the new material.

Proper Orientation

One common difficulty with the technical specialist who becomes an instructor is that he doesn't appreciate or understand the student's viewpoint. The specialist, with a high level of competence, has long passed the beginner's level and often has forgotten how he felt and the difficulties he had as a beginner. He is unable to put himself in the students' places and to appreciate their feelings. The technical specialist who takes on the instructor's role frequently talks as though the class is comprised of other specialists like himself. Too often the subject is the specialist's only concern. The classroom may become a stage from which to impress the audience.

The effective instructor knows the students entering capabilities, knows the language they understand best, and knows how fast new material can be learned. To the professional instructor, the student and the subject matter are both important.

We can assume that most adults who have voluntarily entered an educational or training program want to learn. Yet many come with only the vaguest notion of the nature of the instructional program or what will be expected of them. Some come because they are sent by their employers; others think going to school will result in a better career, changed life style, resulting in increased prestige and status.

It has been said that an education is the

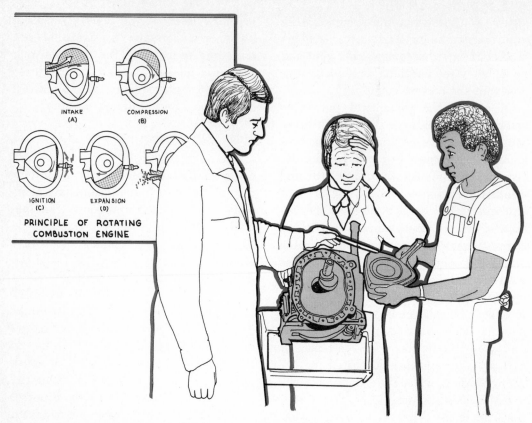

Something that is simple to the instructor may be bewildering to the student.

only thing a college student will gladly pay for and not get. In other words the student may want the degree but will care little for the learning experiences that are part of the educational process.

No instructor can be successful in the long run who is unable to set the stage or stimulate students to want to learn. Most courses of instruction can, at best, provide only a start toward the goal of mastery of the subject. Students should be motivated in such a way that they continue to learn and develop their abilities long after they complete the course. Students who are driven to get high grades by the constant threat of failure or punishment are not

being motivated in a way that will carry over once they are out of the course. Many of us have learned much about a subject, but in the process we also learned to dislike it. What was gained? Would it not have been better to have had another type of instruction through which we learned to like the subject and wanted to continue with it at every opportunity?

Needs and Desires of the Student

Here are some desires or needs characteristic of many students and a few practical ways of responding to them for motivation.

Desire for recognition and approval by

others. Call students name. Let students work in groups occasionally. Find ways to provide recognition for good achievement by known standards and in terms of progress. Use exhibits and displays of outstanding work. For example, a drafting instructor might post drawings that illustrate different types of good work—the lettering on one drawing, the dimensioning on another, original design, etc. By this method, most students in a class can receive some degree of recognition. A word of caution must be provided to instructors who flaunt the work of good students to the point where other students begin to resent the "star" pupil's achievement. The high achiever should not be singled out for frequent praise. Be discrete and provide the words of praise through private conversation, or a note on the student's paper. When posting examples of good work or test results protect the student's identity. This saves much grief for both high and low achievers.

Desire for security. Give a word of approval for a job well done. Provide reasonable opportunities for the students to talk over their special problems with you. See that classroom shop and laboratory conditions are as positive as you can make them. A good environment that makes people feel secure aids learning.

The good instructor shows a personal interest in the achievements of each student.

Desire for new experiences. Let students assist in the development of a process or special projects, allowing them to work at their own rate of speed. Make equipment and material available for advanced work. Keep the content of your course as up to date as possible.

Desire for acceptance and social relationships. Treat students as individuals worth knowing. Encourage friendships in the group. Get to know each student. Occasionally have after-class informal discussions on topics of mutual interest. The good instructor is rewarded by the achievements of his students and their respect and friendship through the years. When the situation permits, allow students to work in groups and help each other. Occasionally an advanced student may be assigned to help the beginner. On the rifle range, for example, expert riflemen are expected to help coach others. Both the helper, and the person being helped, must be instructed in the proper relationships.

Need for self respect. The attitudes and feelings of the student determine to a large degree the extent and effectiveness of learning. Every student wants to be respected as a person. Human beings yearn for recognition. Society provides many examples of persons who have sought recognition in both positive and negative ways in a desire to "be somebody." The surest method of teaching, and for that matter, of getting along with others, is to help them satisfy some of their basic desires. All skilled manager are aware that good wages, steady employment, and physical comfort are not enough to develop high morale and productivity among employees. One of the most important needs is for a feeling of self-respect and of being respected.

Need for physical comfort. More will be achieved when students and instructor are comfortable; the students are ready to learn, the instructor to teach. If feasible, students should be seated for chalk talks, lectures, and demonstrations. Clean, well-lighted classrooms and laboratories as well as safe, well-organized tools and equipment facilitate learning.

Need for success. Satisfying this need is very important. Good progress records should be kept and students should know their level of achievement in comparison with recognized standards. Projects, problems and other activities should be consistent with the objectives of the course, provide the proper emphasis, and be as practical and worthwhile as possible. All assignments should be carefully prepared so that success is possible with reasonable effort. Assigned problems and tasks should increase in difficulty from day to day and continue to challenge students to do their best. In some types of instruction, provision can be made for assigning tasks of varying complexity so that each student can achieve to a maximum level, irrespective of the achievement level of others. However, where occupational competence is required, all persons who are to be certified by the instructor as "occupationally competent" must reach some established minimum standard even though individuals may vary in the length of time that it takes to become competent.

Attitude of Instructor

The unconscious influence of the attitude of the instructor upon the students is difficult to estimate, but it is tremendously important. The genuine enthusiasm displayed by the instructor is always a major factor in motivation because it is contagious. It engenders a pleasant atmosphere in the classroom and contributes to high motivation. Enthusiasm cannot be forced, but it can be developed. If you discover a better way of explaining something, or if you discard dull useless material and add new, interesting and useful material, you should feel a surge of enthusiasm. The basis for creating enthusiasm is this: you must believe that your role as an instructor is worthwhile. Hence the development of enthusiasm depends on thorough preparation for each lesson to be taught.

If you believe in your job, are well prepared and physically energetic, you will show enthusiasm and your students will tend to respond in the same way. Just as you prepare students to learn through proper motivational techniques, you must maintain or develop your own interest. Enthusiasm and pride in your own work not only helps you do a better job, but these characteristics are transmitted to your students and reflected in their attitudes.

The continuous search for effective ways to motivate the learner is so important that the following are suggested: After a given course of series of lessons are completed, prepare a few questions and ask the students for their reactions and opinions regarding ways by which instructional procedures could have been improved. Since some students will take the easy way out and say they like everything, it may be desirable to include such questions as: What do you find least interesting? If you were able to shorten the course by four hours, what would you take out? Where can class time be saved? List some things you would like emphasized or added to the course. Insist that students are not to identify themselves. To insure honest answers, you might designate two members of the class to collect the suggestions and summarize them so that all students will be assured that you will not see their papers and thus identify them through their handwriting. If you want honest answers, students must be able to remain anonymous.

A friendly and objective group discussion following an analysis of the class answers to the questions may prove valuable. Care must be taken not to develop a defensive attitude. Only an instructor who has developed rapport with the group and is judged by students to be open-minded will gain from this kind of discussion.

The instructor must keep his "ear to the ground." Take note of but do not necessarily comment or react to "off the cuff" remarks made by students which may be an indication of their *true* feelings. Individual comments should be encouraged by careful listening and a friendly attitude.

The opinions of qualified outside observers may prove valuable, especially if they know the objectives of the course and observe long enough to get a true sample of student attitude.

Frustrations and Their Effect on Learning

When we want to do something we cannot do for one reason or another, we feel annoyance and perhaps tension. The psychologist would say we are frustrated. Frustration in modern life is frequent and unavoidable for all of us. It may come from simple things like rain when we want to go on a picnic, a telephone busy signal or, at the other extreme, from unsatisfactory progress in our chosen occupation.

Frustration occurs whenever there is conflict between an individual's desires and the complicated world of which he is a part. When we are frustrated, strong emotions are apt to affect our behavior in ways that, to the casual observer, make very little sense. The person who seems hard to understand may be frustrated. Regardless of the cause, frustration may interfere with an individual's attention to the learning task. While it should be acknowledged that some degree of tension may cause an individual to pay attention and work harder at the learning task, too much tension leads to frustration and interferes with the learning process.

As instructors, it is important that we have a working knowledge of the causes and reactions to frustration in order to understand better our own behavior and that of supervisors, students, and others with whom we work. Let us consider some of the common sources of frustration.

Impersonal things. A busy intersection, a stalled engine, a flat tire are all good examples of impersonal things that cause frustration. A common tendency when we are faced with such situations is to feel tension and perhaps to become angry.

People. Although people may help us obtain our goals in life they may also stand in our way. Every person is a complex combination of needs, characteristics, values, abilities, desires, opinions

Frustration may hinder learning.

and attitudes; it is inevitable that we get in each other's way. Good human relationships satisfy many of our desires. However, even the most perfect relationships are apt to be frustrating at times. The parent loves the child but sometimes the one frustrates the other because each wants something different as a result of the relationship at any one time. The boy wants to build a tree-house; his mother wants a neat yard.

Most adults learn to let-someone else have his way at least temporarily and to at least partially hide their feelings. Frustration in adults, therefore, may be less obvious than in children. There are fewer fist fights among adults, but frustration shows up in other ways.

Rules and regulations. Whenever there is an organization of people, there must be rules and regulations. We recognize that most of these are necessary and good for everyone in the long run. At the same time, these regulations seriously interfere with our freedom as individuals as they restrict our actions from time to time. The people enforcing the regulation, whether they be instructors, policemen, supervisors, members of organizations, become the target of frustrations even though the source may be a rule or regulation.

Our own limitations. We are frustrated when we can't remember something as quickly as we want to, when we can't get someone to see our point of view, when we can't drive a nail without bending it, or when we can't back into a parking place that we *know* is big enough.

Sometimes we must choose between two equally appealing goals. The skilled technician may have to choose between staying at his bench, where he gets satisfaction from doing high quality work, or

moving to a supervisory position, which means more money and responsibility. Regardless of which he chooses he is likely to feel frustration at first and from time to time thereafter. How many times have you heard a supervisor express a wish to be back in the production area where life is remembered as being simpler with fewer frustrations? Instructors who become school administrators frequently long for the "good old days" when they were classroom teachers.

Another type of frustration occurs when a highly desired achievement is in conflict with a code of conduct or personal conscience. A common example is the ruthless go-getter, highly motivated toward financial, social, or similar goals; whose desires in those areas are in conflict with his desire to be well liked by his associates. Could this be a possible reason for a rich person giving money to charity in advanced years?

Our reactions to frustration. Frustrations resulting from contact with individuals are far more disturbing and significant than those which come from the traffic light or the stalled engine because people are more difficult to understand. Also, the individuals can fight back if we show our frustration in certain ways. We can kick the door that won't open and get away with it. It is more difficult to take comparable action with individuals without feeling afraid, guilty, or ashamed. These feelings in turn tend to increase our frustrations.

Let us think of a person who is confronted with a barrier of some kind. Perhaps it is some impersonal thing like a stalled car on the way to the hospital, or perhaps something of a built-in personal nature like the conflict between conscience and desire for financial success.

Unreasonable aggression is a common reaction to frustration.

For a time, the individual may look for some way of getting around the barrier. Different ways to start the car, or try to make money without hurting anyone else may be attempted. Failing in this, there is a tendency to become somewhat emotional which may give him some temporary relief, but the resulting behavior may seem very strange to others who do not realize the source of the frustration.

When major frustrations occur over a period of time, individuals may resort to one or more unproductive forms of behavior, including aggression, regression, fix-

ation, apathy, and escape. Since even the well adjusted person may resort to mild forms of such behavior, they deserve attention.

Aggression. The most common form of aggression is anger and attack in a childish fashion, such as a grown man kicking and swearing at his car. A more complicated form of aggression is seen in the father who returns home from a hard day at the office and takes out his frustration on his family. It should be kept in mind that the man may not understand or admit, even to himself, that he is frustrated or the cause of the frustration. He simply feels a need to kick the dog or argue with his wife. Perhaps this is because he does not dare to do so to his boss, but won't admit this even to himself.

Another form of aggression is seen when individuals blame their problems on the supervisor, the president of the company, their relatives, or anyone else who might make a convenient scapegoat.

Regression. When an adult behaves like a child as a result of frustration, we refer to this behavior as regressive behavior. Child-like and unquestioning dependence on some powerful person or group to solve our problems, a strong and continuous desire to return to the good old days, striking out at someone or something, or crying are examples of regression. The latter examples may not always be undesirable, as they may serve to relieve frustration and permit resumption of normal activity. Obviously, repeated behavior of this type is not helpful or healthy.

Fixation. Fixation is characterized by repetition of certain behavior long after it should be apparent that it is getting one nowhere. In simple form we see this is continued stepping on the car starter after it should be clear that something else is necessary. The person who dwells on questions of world affairs, economics, the meaning of life, and other complex problems to which there are no simple answers, but who continues to insist on simple answers may in time develop his own pattern of beliefs and attitudes which are very fixed. Such an individual does not meet new problems with an open mind. Any information contrary to preconceived beliefs is rejected. New ideas and points of view that are in conflict with his pat answers are painful to him.

Such a person may blindly follow and fight for some group or "movement" that happens to fit his pattern of thinking. Milder forms of fixation are observed in persons who have very narrow conversation patterns such as their children, their work, football.

Apathy and negativism. Some individuals, when faced with many frustrations and perhaps poor health, simply give up and quit trying. They may take on a negative and sour attitude toward almost everything. They expect nothing good to happen and make no effort to cause the right thing to happen.

Escape. An individual facing too many frustrations may try to escape either physically or emotionally. Some may keep moving to another state, another job, another girl friend or boy friend. The soldier may go AWOL.

Others may escape emotionally by daydreaming, by going to the movies or to the nearest bar, by taking up a hobby, or by just going fishing. A certain amount of escape of this type is normal. It may bring about some enjoyment and provide helpful relaxation. Such psychological escape is harmful only when carried to extremes. For example, when we begin to really believe that we are something other than what we are. If you think you are Napoleon, you need help now!

Learning to live with frustrations. We differ in our ability to adjust to frustrations. Some of us seem to have more ability than others in resisting frustrating situations. You may have learned to deny yourself some pleasures today in order to enjoy more important things later. If you had not learned this, you would not be preparing yourself as an instructor. Probably our ability to withstand frustration comes partly from early training and experience with frustrations that were not too severe. Parents, by necessity, will frustrate their children in some things, because the child's demands cannot and should not always be met. They need this experience as a normal part of living as a human being. On the other hand, the child who is greatly and consistently frustrated in all or most of his desires may develop habits of mental escape that will be harmful when reality must be faced and dealt with in a positive and constructive way.

It follows that we, as individuals, can learn to tolerate frustration if we understand its nature and attempt to make reasonable adjustments. As instructors, we must keep in mind that individuals learn and act as they do because of their own drives, frustrations, and attitudes.

The existence of frustration in instructional situations might sometimes be recognized by the symptoms of poor achievement, many discipline problems, damaged school equipment, the spreading of gossip and rumor, exaggerated complaints, absence from class, and accidents in the shops and laboratories.

What the instructor can do. Remember that behavior is always a result of something. People are not born lazy, mean, aggressive, stubborn, or fearful. We can look for the causes rather than just the symptoms of behavior. Does the student know exactly what is expected? The professional instructor knows what he wants and clearly communicates this to the students. Does he have the instructional materials and supplies necessary for achievement? Can we modify our own

Too many words is a common cause of boredom and frustration.

point of view with new and more objective information? If a student is resorting to daydreaming, why?

Remember that most of us at certain times become frustrated, if only to a relatively mild degree. No one is completely free of frustration. Remember that a degree of tension is necessary if one is to try to achieve to a higher level. Recognize, but don't try to treat extreme cases of reaction to frustration. If you think you recognize a case of extreme frustration, obtain advice or assistance from the medical staff or other professional sources with regard to action that should be taken.

To some extent an instructor can reduce frustration by helping to reduce or eliminate the feelings shown in the table below which are commonly found in the learning-instructing situation.

An instructor may be able to help some of his students face reality and live with situations that are beyond their power to change. They should be helped to see that there are times when the attitude of "if you can't lick 'em, join 'em" is the best approach. There is no sense in beating one's head against a stone wall forever. We can work hard and take pride in our achievements and still accept the fact that many things we would like to change cannot be changed. We must not advocate or encourage cheap compromise or "copping out" when the going gets rough, but at the same time reason and reality may dictate acceptance of a new course of action if long range and more important goals are to be achieved.

Reward, Punishment, and Reprimand

Rewarding and punishing. Both reward and punishment are useful tools for the instructor. Reward is the more useful, and the psychologists refer to it as *positive reinforcement.* When we give reward

FEELINGS THAT MAKE LEARNING DIFFICULT

Fear and worry	Fear of failure Fear of ridicule from class or instructor Family and home problems—sickness—worry over money
Discomfort	Standing too long Eyestrain Dirty working conditions Dangerous tools and equipment Poor ventilation Poor shop-laboratory organization
Boredom	Instructor talking too long at a time Little chance to use equipment Instructor not prepared Teaching aids not used Instructional methods not varied

for doing the right thing and ignore little mistakes, we are using positive reinforcement. When we focus on things that are wrong and on the mistakes, we are using negative reinforcement. Negative teaching, in most instances, is not very effective. It tends to make a learner, whether the child learning to use a spoon or an adult learning to speak in public, concentrate more on errors, rather than on the right procedure. Even dog trainers know that it is better to pet the dog for holding up the right foot for the hand shake than to punish the dog for holding up the left foot. Of course we must correct errors, but this should be done in a friendly, helpful and positive manner which is mixed with recognition of good performance. An encouraging smile or comment from a respected person is a real reward for most students.

While reward or approval from the instructor is a common form of positive reinforcement, the intrinsic reward that comes from the individual's competence, demonstrated through performance, is needed in the long run. The instructor should encourage and help the student to develop the ability to judge and take pride in a job well done. In this way, greater skill becomes its own reward.

Some instructors find it easy to criticize but hard to praise. This is a matter of orientation. Students seldom do perfect work, but the instructor should see the good elements of even a mediocre performance, just as errors must be identified and corrected.

There is no need to use praise when it is not deserved, but some honest praise can be given in almost every situation. Others should be praised for only outstanding achievement. Often a friendly remark over the student's shoulder is all that is

needed. It is safer to praise when the student and the instructor can talk privately, since peers may resent the "teacher's pet." However, praise may be given publicly if the achievement is truly outstanding, if it can be recognized as such by everyone and if it is not given too frequently to the same person.

Grades properly used can provide useful motivation. However, there is too much emphasis on grades in some programs since a letter or numerical grade, at best, is only a partial indicator of competence. To be effective, grades must not become the major source of drive for learning. Also grades, if they are to motivate and not discourage, must be determined by careful judgment of several factors or criteria. The instructor has a responsibility to grade in such a manner as to stimulate and not discourage his students.

Reprimanding. Attempts to coerce or compel students into right habits of thought and action nearly always fail. The instructor who applies more "heat" than "light" is more likely to arouse resistance than compliance. However, when the student is compelled from within, when the instructor is able to kindle a flame of desire and interest in the student through stimulation and a fair, firm, and friendly relationship, the results in terms of student achievement are often outstanding.

We have all seen examples of reprimands which are done in such a way as to develop resentment and a strong desire on the part of the student to retaliate or "even the score" with the instructor. Obviously such experiences do not pay dividends for anyone. When we reprimand, only those methods should be used which will help the student to progress to a

The instructor should reprimand like this   **. . . not this.**

higher level of achievement, and if possible, stimulate a feeling of respect for the instructor and an increased desire to participate in the teaching/learning process. When a reprimand is necessary the good instructor:

1. Remains calm.
2. Knows and uses facts.
3. Considers the feelings of the student.
4. Talks to the student alone.
5. Includes some encouragement and praise for work well done.
6. Suggests a constructive course of action.
7. Criticizes the mistake—not the individual.
8. Ends the conversation on a positive note by acknowledging past achievement and the student's positive attributes.

The weak instructor may:

1. Become angry.
2. Fail to know or use the facts.
3. Fail to consider long term results.
4. Fail to consider the effect of others present at the time.
5. Deflate the individual's ego which often results in resentment and retaliation.

Knowledge of Progress

In target practice, we expect to be told when we hit the bull's eye. If we miss it, we want to know by how far and in which direction we missed. Knowing how well we are doing helps us to improve our performance. This is true whether the subject is target practice, roof framing, or English composition. Knowledge of progress toward a goal or level of skill helps us to correct our errors and motivates us to do our best. For example, the class in clerical practice should visit the offices at a large business firm so students can compare their work with the standards of the occupation. The instructor should evaluate each student's work at frequent intervals and let each individual know how well he is doing by some known standard. The instructor plays an important role in helping students establish standards and in evaluating their achievement in terms of the standard.

Competition among individuals and groups may motivate them to greater effort, but intense rivalry and the "win at all costs" attitude is not beneficial. The medical profession has expressed concern over some forms of organized and highly competitive sports for children. Ruthless competition between students in an instructional program can be disastrous when emphasis is shifted from *learning* to *winning*.

Repetition, Drill and Skill Development

Repetition and guided practice are essential in skill development. We practice a selection on the piano, we drill on multiplication combinations, we swing at many golf balls before we really have these neuro-muscular or mental and muscle connections correct so that they can be repeated without constant thought. This is skill: a thoroughly established habit of doing something in the most efficient and effective manner.

Since drill takes instructional time, it should be used for the most important and fundamental skills, such as learning the multiplication combinations in arithmetic. Drill or practice to be effective must be taught with understanding of the process rather than by blind imitation.

There is much evidence, experimental and otherwise, to support the assumption that distributed practice in learning is more effective than long periods of con-

tinuous practice. For example, in learning freehand lettering as a part of a mechanical drawing course, it is more effective to schedule five 15-minute periods per week than to have one concentrated period of 75 minutes. Factors such as boredom and fatigue are critical to decisions regarding length of practice sessions. The periods of practice should not, however, be too brief, nor need they be of equal length.

The principle of distributed practice is most important in the development of physical skills; however, the principle is still valid in a general way for all types of learning. However, there are times when one reasonably long period of concentrated study is more effective than several shorter periods. A two hour period of concentrated effort in the drafting room where a sequence of design elements is being applied to a practical drafting assignment or problem may be better than several shorter periods. Adults can generally profit from longer periods of study than can children because of their typically longer span of interest.

The experienced instructor learns to judge the effectiveness of various lengths of concentrated study and practice periods for each level of student and each type of subject matter.

When the number of errors in the student's performance begins to increase, it may be time to stop the practice until the student is more rested or until more time can be given to thinking through the task to get the steps or procedure and the principles more clearly in mind.

Continued practice after something to be learned is understood and can be remembered readily or performed with a high degree of accuracy results in a high level of competence. Some refer to this as *over-*

learning. Subject matter than can be remembered without hesitation after a considerable period of time may be said to be overlearned. Many facts and principles that are used for further learning need to be learned beyond the point of mere understanding; they need to be "grooved in." Skills such as writing, spelling, speaking, or hand tool processes need to be mastered to the point where we can use them easily without much thought.

As instructors, we must decide frequently whether to teach a subject by breaking it into small parts and teaching each part well before going to the next, or to teach the whole subject to some extent before drilling on the parts. (This is often referred to as the "whole vs the part" method). In learning a five minute speech, the whole speech should probably be learned at one sitting. A longer speech might be learned in segments over a period of practice sessions before eventually "putting it altogether." In coaching basketball, we would probably allow some team play almost from the start but continue to drill on such elements of the game as the free throw, passing and dribbling during each practice period.

Long tasks involving many separately identified skills and much information obviously cannot be practiced as a whole from the start. In these situations, logical divisions must be made and learned separately. A method of analyzing an occupation or subject into logical learning units is discussed in Chapter 4.

Forgetting

The more meaningful and the more opportunities we have to use subject matter, the longer we will remember it. It is much easier to remember a poem if we understand the meaning of the words and their "message." In fact, if we were to take the same words and mix them up so that they made no sense at all, we would have great difficulty in learning to repeat them in a given order; we would tend to forget them quickly. As soon as a subject has been learned, however, forgetting starts, unless we continue to use the subject and keep it fresh in our minds. As forgetting will always occur to some degree, it is foolish to try to remember everything. It is important that the student know those elements of content that must be ready for recall and application, as well as the content that can be derived or located easily when needed at infrequent intervals. The instructor who places the same emphasis on relatively minor details (details which are used only to illustrate a point) as that placed on basic principles of the subject, is not helping the student to retain the important elements from the course.

Forgetting is most rapid soon after the subject has been learned. Normally one will forget a lot of the content during the months just following the learning of new subject matter and forget less and less of the residual knowledge as time goes by. Concepts or ideas are frequently forgotten to a greater degree than manipulative or manual skills. Adults can usually skate, swim, ride a bicycle, or find the chords on a banjo after years of disuse of these skills. Probably this is the result of the combination of mental-physical learning in valued skill development gained through a great amount of practice.

Things learned as a result of an individual's special interest or under special circumstances tend to be remembered. The telephone number of a girl friend is easy to remember. An automobile accident may never be forgotten. On the other hand, some of us can't remember the food we had for lunch yesterday because little attention was given to it at the time.

Using Emphasis

We cannot instruct effectively without emphasizing the important elements in the lesson so that they stand out. Several techniques may be used when speaking. These are listed in the relative order from most to least effective:

1. Repeating the statement several times during the lesson.
2. Writing the word, term or phrase on the chalk board or using a chart or poster.
3. Preceding the material with such words as "Remember that," "Make a note of this," "Now this is an important part," etc.
4. Pausing before and after a statement.
5. Reinforce the information or idea with a visual device (diagram, photo or illustration).
6. Variance in speech pattern (speaking more slowly or loudly or softly).
7. Using physical gestures.

It should be kept in mind that the overuse of a technique for emphasizing decreases its effectiveness. Then, too, the nature of the subject may dictate which form of emphasis is most appropriate.

The story of a true experience illustrates how the individual aspects of learning and teaching we have considered are combined in real life situations.

In 1957, an Instructor Training Program for Air Traffic Controllers was or-

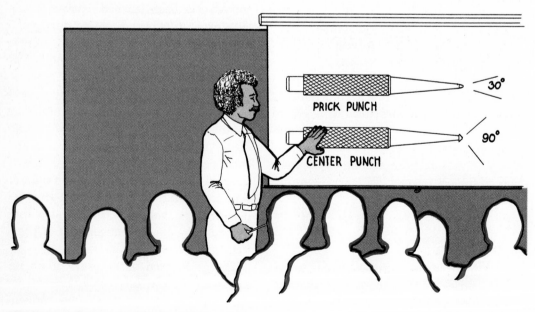

Visual aids help in emphasizing key points in the lesson.

ganized. The class was made up of mature, successful men with great skill in a critical and difficult occupation. As is usually done during the first day or so of the course, each member was asked to give a short talk on a subject of his choice.

Immediately after the class in which the assignment was made one of the men said to me: "I can't make a talk. I've tried and each time I have frozen. Everything has gone blank and I have walked out of the room. I will quit my job before I'll go through that experience again." I believed him because he gave every evidence of sincerity and anxiety. Without

delay I had to make a decision which might result in the loss of a valuable employee. After a moment's thought I said, "Joe, I won't require it of you if you will promise to go to someone who knows more about these things than I do and get some help. It's foolish to go on with this bothering you." He answered with a promise to do just that. His relief from worry was obvious.

The next day after about half of the class had made their short talks and a friendly atmosphere had been established, Joe walked to my desk and said, "I think I can do it." I put him on at once. He

A sympathetic and experienced instructor can instill confidence in a student speaker.

gave a simple but effective little demonstration on how to tie a fish line and hook. Members of the class asked questions and made several favorable comments. Joe went on to finish the course, which included several short talks and demonstrations and a full length practice lesson, without difficulty. Fear had been overcome by the feeling of success and security.

Try to illustrate each one of the following statements about learning with an example of what you as an instructor may do to make use of them.

1. The mind is not a muscle and cannot be trained like a muscle.
2. Interest is essential to effective learning.
3. Learning must start where the learner is. He must see a need for and be ready for the next step.
4. All new learning is influenced by learning environment and past learning.
5. We learn best when we have exact information on our progress toward a known objective.
6. Learning is more effective and is retained longer when it is based on first hand experience. We learn more by action rather than by absorption.
7. We tend to continue doing things that are pleasant and to avoid those things that are unpleasant.
8. Our behavior is controlled by our emotions as well as by what we know.
9. Learning is aided by feelings of success and security.
10. Emotional tension and frustration as well as physical handicaps are detrimental to learning.
11. Learning is aided through the use of several senses.
12. Individuals learn at differing rates.
13. We learn more effectively through stimulation and guidance than through threats or coercion.

QUESTIONS AND ASSIGNMENTS

1. What is motivation and why is it so important in learning?
2. Name some things you might do to motivate a learner.
3. How would you give each student in your class the proper recognition and approval?
4. Do you think everyone has a need for security? How can you contribute to this in a teaching situation?
5. What specific things could you do in teaching your subject to give your students new experiences?
6. What purpose may after-class informal discussions serve?
7. If you feel that a student is not cooperating and you ask him to give you a hand with some specific task, what results might you expect?
8. Did you feel any frustration on your way to your job or to class today? What did you do about it? Was your action aggressive in nature?
9. Have you ever kicked a dog? Why?
10. What are common causes of frustration to students in a school? To a person learning on the job?
11. Can you think of someone whose behavior suggests frustration? What could you do to help?
12. What feelings have you had that made learning difficult?
13. Why must you be concerned with the feelings of your students?
14. How can you tell when students are bored?
15. Why is reward more useful than punishment? When would you use some form of punishment with a student, such as making it difficult for him to get to see you?
16. In the subject you teach what standards can be used as goals for the student?
17. How can students be kept informed of their progress throughout the course?
18. Describe a situation requiring a reprimand. How would you handle the situation?
19. Give an example of a humorous story that would help to put across an idea in your course.
20. Discuss the statement "Practice makes perfect." When can practice be harmful?
21. Why is it important to give the student a bird's eye view of the whole task before focusing on its parts?
22. List some skills you may teach. Estimate the length of time that should be spent each time a practice period is scheduled.
23. If a theory is important and you wish to make sure it will be remembered, what steps would you take?

Identifying Content and Specifying Behaviors

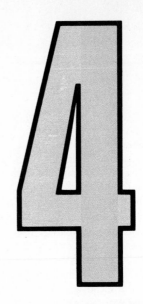

As instructors, our goal is to increase student competence in a predetermined area or subject. The professional instructor knows precisely the objectives to be achieved by the students at the end of the course. Certain behaviors are to be exhibited if the instructional program is to be judged a success. In other words, the student should *know* more, be able to *do* more, and/or exhibit different *attitudes* as a result of the instructional experience.

We think in terms of the student being able to do something better after instruction. The goal may be broad or it may be very specialized. It may involve developing general abilities in a wide field or a high degree of skill in a specialized field. Regardless of whether the goals are broad or specialized, they must be defined and understood before an instructional program can be designed and conducted effectively.

Performance and Knowledge

Some readers may question the emphasis on *doing* when we say that a student should be able to do something better after instruction. They may feel that *knowing* rather than doing is most important; however, all knowledge, education, and training influence behavior in the long run.

In recent years, educators have done a more systematic job of classifying behaviors. In fact, a series of books edited by Dr. Benjamin Bloom, which is referred to as the *Taxonomy of Educational Objectives* classifies all human behaviors into three domains: (1) the *cognitive* (knowledge and information related behavior), (2) the *psychomotor* (hand-eye, mental-muscle or doing related behavior) and (3) the *affective* (attitudes, feelings and value related behavior). Most of this chapter will deal with knowing and doing or the cognitive and psychomotor domains, as they are the easiest to identify and describe. The affective domain will be dealt with separately near the end of this chapter.

In an agricultural mechanics course, for example, the student may be required to measure, cut metal, drill holes, weld, etc. These must be done with some predetermined degree of speed and accuracy and in a step-by-step manner. Each step follows another in a certain sequence. Later the student must learn to solve certain types of problems in a step-by-step manner, using some of the skills previously developed.

While these are examples of behaviors that focus on *doing,* it is essential that the student understand certain underlying theory and possess certain knowledge if the doing behavior is to be performed at a high level.

By definition, learning is the modification of behavior. The electrician learns a great deal of theory, but this is justified only if it helps him to *do* something—find the short circuit, figure out a new circuit, design an effective and safe wiring plan, etc. Even the most general of subjects in a broad curriculum are intended to exert a positive influence on performance. It follows that we can identify and select the content to be taught only after consideration of the precise behaviors that should be exhibited after the instructional program.

Relationship Between Objectives and Instructional Content

When preparing a course or instructional program through which individuals are to develop or increase their occupational competence, the long range objective is that the individual will become *occupationally competent.* There will be many short range objectives or behaviors that the individual must be able to exhibit in some way, in order to be judged occupationally competent. These specific behaviors which educators typically call instructional or behavioral ob-

jectives are the same as the *knowing, doing* and *being* content that professionals in the practical arts, vocational and technical education fields have been talking about for years.

Much time and effort is wasted in educational programs because of overlapping of course content, unintentional omissions of important content, and improper emphasis. As all knowledge has some relationship to performance, our major problem in planning instruction is to identify, select, and teach those elements of content that are most appropriate in terms of our objectives. If the objectives change, we may then add or remove certain content and change our methods of instruction.

Selection of Content

The need for some instruction can be accepted on the basis of observation and common sense. The prospective or new employee needs to be told and shown certain things which experience indicates are needed by one who is to function in a given occupation. The selection of content for other more general types of educational programs, including both formal and on the job types, is more difficult.

Several methods which may be used to identify this content are: (1) interviewing individuals or groups to identify the tasks they perform and get their suggestions of content needed for those being trained for positions of a similar kind, (2) submitting questionnaires to a large number of people to obtain their opinions, (3) using formal tests, either the paper-and-pencil type or the performance type, to ascertain the strengths and weaknesses of individuals or of groups with regard to specific occupational requirements and (4) making a detailed analysis of each task performed to identify skills and knowledge required at all levels of performance. In this chapter, we will describe a method which produces consistently good results with a reasonable expenditure of effort. This process is called the *Analysis Method.*

The Analysis Method[1]

Any occupation is based on information (facts, concepts, ideas, etc.) which individuals must know as well as the skills (operations, procedures, techniques) they must be able to perform with an acceptable degree of proficiency. In preparing to instruct individuals in any subject, the first step is to identify and organize these skill and knowledge elements (psychomotor and cognitive behavior, if you prefer).

In the body of this chapter the principles and procedures involved in the analysis process are described with the aid of illustrations from common subjects. At the end of the chapter are examples from

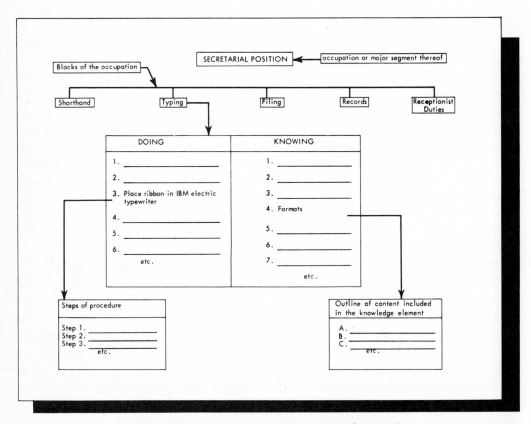

This chart shows the terms used in the analysis method.

[1]Credit is given to Verne C. Fryklund for certain basic principles of the analysis method discussed here. These concepts are presented in greater detail in his book *Occupational Analysis: Techniques and Procedures* (Milwaukee: Bruce Publishing Co., 1970).

the fields of air traffic control, machine metal working, photography, electronics, and secretarial work. Any subject that is to be learned can and must be analyzed for effective instruction.

The following brief summary of the analysis method is given to define certain terms and to reveal the relationship of the parts of any analysis before we examine each part in detail. Wage-earning jobs, occupations, and major work segments of these, may be divided into major parts which may be referred to as *blocks* or large units of content. For example, three of several blocks of the secretarial occupation are filing, typing, and shorthand. Each block is made up of at least two kinds of content: (1) *Doing* content which refers to specific skills, operations or procedures which occur over and over in the individual daily work routine, and (2) *Knowing* content which consists of concepts and useful information directly related to performance. "How to place the ribbon in an I.B.M. electric typewriter" is an example of doing content within the typing block or large unit. "Subject matter divisions" is an example of knowing content in the block on filing.

Doing elements of content are further analyzed or broken down into steps of procedure, listed in the order in which each step is taken. Knowing elements of content are further analyzed into specific items of information, and normally recorded in standard outline form. In reading and understanding this chapter, it will be necessary to keep the meaning of these words and the relationship of the parts of an analysis in mind.

Step I. *Determining the blocks or major units.* The first step in making an analysis is to identify and name the major segments, areas, or types of work found in the subject you plan to teach. These are the *blocks* or *major units*.

The purpose of blocking is to identify categories of content or required behaviors under which we can later list closely related elements of performance and elements of information. Determining the blocks may be done in several ways and will depend to some extent on the occupation or subject being analyzed, the amount of content in the subject, and the type of instructional situation. In machine shop practice for instance, we might list the blocks according to major work processes or major pieces of equipment as follows:

```
BLOCK 1 BLUEPRINT READING.
BLOCK 2 BENCH WORK AND MEASURING.
BLOCK 3 DRILL PRESS WORK.
BLOCK 4 LATHE WORK.
BLOCK 5 MILLING MACHINE WORK.
BLOCK 6 SHAPER WORK, ETC.
```

Some instructors may prefer to list *measuring* as a special block or to combine it with blueprint reading. There are many such choices that the instructor must make. The important thing is to list the blocks in such a way that all related content on the subject can be grouped in a given block. It would be ideal if each block contained about the same amount of content and be of about the same importance; however, this seldom happens in practice. In Basic Photography the blocks could be:

```
BLOCK 1 BASE BLOCK (A BLOCK CONTAINING UNITS OF SKILL
        AND KNOWLEDGE THAT ARE BASIC IN RELATION TO
        ALL OTHER BLOCKS).
BLOCK 2 EXPOSING FILM. (TAKING THE PICTURE).
BLOCK 3 DEVELOPING BLACK AND WHITE FILM.
BLOCK 4 MAKING BLACK AND WHITE PRINTS, ETC.
```

Before you read on, we suggest you identify and list the blocks in a subject, preferably the subject you plan to teach. Remember, this is the first step of the analysis.

Step II. *Determining and listing the doing content.* The second step is to list the specific skills, processes, and procedures found in each block. These are called the *doing* elements of content.

Doing content involves those operations or skills that, regardless of the specific task to be done, remain basically the same and are used repeatedly by the worker. The skills of adding, subtracting, dividing, and multiplying in arithmetic are good examples. We may perform these doing units in the same way regardless of the problem being solved.

In the identification process, certain doing content will be easy to classify because it is clearly *manipulative* or *psychomotor* in nature. However, some performance elements have such a close tie to knowledge that they are harder to classify. One key that will help in your classification is whether or not the content statement indicates action or performance requiring a degree of skill. You should remember, however, that the *identification* of all necessary content is more important than the classification.

Examples of doing units from Basic Photography, Block 3, *Developing black and white film,* are:

```
1  MIX DEVELOPER
2  MIX AND TEST HYPO.
3  MIX  SHORT STOP.
4  PLACE CUT FILM IN FILM TANK.
5  PLACE ROLL FILM IN FILM TANK.
6  DEVELOP NEGATIVES.
7  FIX NEGATIVES.
8  WASH NEGATIVES.
9  DRY NEGATIVES, ETC.
```

In listing *doing* elements, always state them in terms of action or doing something (mix developer, fix negatives, test chemicals). One could say "mixing developer"; however, in this text we will consistently use the infinitive form "to mix developer" which is really a shortened version of the behavioral objective "the student should be able to mix developer." Consistency in wording is strongly recommended.

In evaluating the doing elements, ask yourself the following questions. Does the element contain several steps to be taken in a given order? Is the element of the appropriate length for a good demonstration or lesson? If not, elements of content may be combined or divided. Is there only one recommended way to perform the doing element? If there is more than one recommended procedure, each should be listed separately. In arithmetic, each way of finding the square root would be listed separately if the learner is to be expected to master each of the different ways. Note the three ways of turning a taper in the machine metal working analysis example at the end of the chapter.

Is the wording specific enough to convey the behavior to be developed? "Take measurements with micrometer" or "read micrometer" is superior to "use micrometer" because "use" does not specify the precise behavior. In an engine repair analysis, the title "take measurements of cylinder" would be more specific because there is a definite procedure to follow and a definite behavior that can be observed.

The word *use* is not recommended in listing doing content since it is seldom specific enough to indicate the precise behavior required.

Now list some of the doing elements found in one or more blocks of your subject. In the following chart, note that some doing elements of an analysis become *steps of procedures* in doing elements more advanced in the analysis.

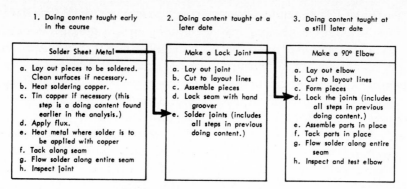

Doing units are cumulative in nature.

Step III. *Determining and listing the knowing content.* Having carefully listed the doing elements of content, the next logical step is to identify the concepts and information necessary for occupational competence. Many of the *knowing* elements of content will be essential if one is to perform with understanding and confidence. A tool may be sharpened exactly to specifications without knowledge of such things as cutting angle, clearance, and tool steel characteristics. However, a knowledge of these facts and concepts makes the work more meaningful and allows the worker to use his judgment in situations which vary from routine procedures. This is related to transfer of training discussed in Chapter Two. Our major problem in the identification of the knowledge elements is the extent to which we should include information and concepts that may not have a direct bearing on performance.

Although identification of doing elements of content is basic to good analysis and should be done first, it is no less difficult than identifying the knowledge-related content required for effective performance with understanding and judgment. Several things interfere with the logical identification of information.

1. The analyzer tends to feel that whatever he has previously learned (perhaps the hard way) is useful and necessary. Of course, all knowledge is useful in certain situations, but some is more useful than others. Our problem is to identify the knowledge that is necessary or most useful and, therefore, must have priority in the establishment of an instructional program. The goals or long range objectives for the instructional program may be helpful in deciding the extent to which "nice to know" content, that is not absolutely essential to performance, should be included.

2. The highly skilled person may have forgotten a great deal of the content initially learned and may minimize the importance of basic concepts and principles because he has applied them by habit and without much thought for a long time.

3. The basic preparation of students for whom the course content is being identified by the analysis process is likely to vary considerably. Some members of the class will have more information which can be applied to the learning of

specific skills. For example, a person with training in physics will have an advantage over those not trained in physics when learning such exact skills as electrical armature winding. This great difference in the general educational background of students (entering student capabilities) makes the analyzer's job more difficult. It is best to include too much rather than too little through the analysis process; it is relatively easy at a later date to omit portions of the content when experience suggests that this should be done.

4. There is still much misunderstanding regarding the learning process. Content to be used in a course of study is occasionally justified solely on the basis that it will strengthen the student's ability to think. We are on much safer ground if we justify each element of content because we know that the student will need this information in order to perform with judgment. Good attitudes and study habits have been considered to be natural by-products of well organized and effective training programs. This is true to a degree. However, educators are coming more and more to realize that the identification and development of behavior in the *affective* domain (feelings, values, attitudes) must be given greater attention. In other words, they must be identified more precisely and developed through carefully planned learning strategies just as we have done for other forms of behavior (doing and knowing).

Here is a suggested procedure for listing knowing contents. Think through the first doing element for the purpose of remembering the concepts and other knowledge elements that are required in order to perform in a satisfactory manner. Statements of knowledge related elements should be kept short. If it would take longer than one or two instructional periods to teach the content element, it should be divided into two or more parts, listing these parts in precise language.

In basic photography, for example, we find such knowing elements as:

1. Theory of development.
2. Types and characteristics of film developers.
3. Time and temperature controls in the dark room.
4. Types of developing tanks.
5. Contrast and development time.
6. Rates of fixation.
7. Defect identification in negatives.
8. Care of chemicals.

In the machine tool trade, we would find such knowing elements as:

1. Machining characteristics of cast iron.
2. Machining characteristics of brass and bronze.
3. Types of lathe cutting tools.
4. Causes of chatter.
5. Gages and their uses.
6. Standard machine fastenings.
7. Safety precautions.

Since the knowledge related content element does tell how to do something, they are not listed in the infinitive or "to do" form.

Re-examine each knowing element with the following question in mind: Can the individual perform in a satisfactory manner and with judgment without knowing the concepts or information specified in the knowing element? If the answer is yes, then you must decide to retain it or exclude it because it contributes to some type of behavior that the course is designed to develop other than performance. This is a decision that *you* must make. In a quite specific or narrowly designed training program, a considerable amount of valuable time can be saved through the relatively simple process of teaching only the information and concepts that are clearly related and necessary to the effective performance of required skills and procedures. More broadly designed educational programs will be justified including concepts and information which is valuable for its long range value, use in problem solving, and generalized transfer.

The content should be arranged in such a way that closely related *doing* or *knowing* elements follow each other or are grouped logically. When this step in the analysis process is completed, some *knowing* elements will be seen to be related to only one *doing* element. Other *knowing* elements will be related to several doing elements. This information will help in planning the order in which the content should be taught.

It is customary to list the doing and knowing content elements in chart form as shown below. This is called an *analysis chart* or *content inventory*. This particular chart shows a block of learning derived from an analysis of the plastics industry. The doing elements are identified with the knowing elements through the use of codes. D stands for doing, K for knowing and B for block. Thus K 4 corresponds with B5 D 6–7.

BLOCK 5: ACRYLIC PLASTIC SHEET STOCK

Doing (Skills to be developed)	Knowing (Information to be learned)
D 1. Handle and store acrylics	K 1. Chemical characteristics of acrylic plastic (basic to all doing contents)
D 2. Saw acrylic plastic	
D 3. Drill acrylic	K 2. Working characteristics and use of acrylics (Block 5 D 1–8)
D 4. Tap and thread acrylic plastic	
D 5. Heat and form acrylic plastic	K 3. Tests used to identify all types of clear plastics (basic to all doing contents)
D 6. Join acrylic plastic by soak method	
D 7. Join acrylic plastic by glue method	K 4. Types of cement (B5 D 6–7)
D 8. Sand and buff acrylics	K 5. Types of metal fastenings for acrylics (B5 D 3–4)

In the Air Traffic Controls outline, page 69, we have added the numbers of the knowledge elements after the doing elements. Either procedure is satisfactory.

Step IV. *Listing the steps in a doing element of content.* When we have identified carefully all of the doing and knowing elements of content, we are ready to analyze them further. As a matter of practical consideration, however, further analysis may be delayed until after the general outline of the course has been developed and we are ready to plan each lesson in detail. However, if time permits, it is better to complete the analysis process prior to the planning of lessons.

The content (both doing and knowing elements) in a thorough application of the analysis process are always sub-divided to show in detail the precise behavior to be learned and later observed. The knowledge related elements contain an *outline of concepts and information,* while the doing elements contain *steps of procedure.* In listing the concepts, information and procedural steps, the instructor is getting down to the specific behavior which the learner must be able to exhibit and, therefore, the content to be taught. Let us take the doing content first.

When an attempt is made to teach without first listing the exact steps of the doing content, the instructor, even though the subject may be well known, will generally leave out some of the essential steps, double back, or over-emphasize unimportant facts. One reason for this is that since the skilled person performs many steps by habit, each movement does not result from conscious thought. As a result, the "specialists turned teacher" may not emphasize or explain these "habit steps", and the student is left with an incomplete and inac-

curate set of procedures to follow. To get results the steps must be listed carefully so that the instructor knows the exact procedure to be taught. The procedure for listing the steps in a doing element is:

1. In their normal order, list the specific steps taken in the performance of a given task. Be sure to include every significant and essential step, but it is not necessary to specify every little step.
2. If possible, perform the task and check each step against your list.
3. Under each step list the key points and information essential to the performance of the step; these points must be emphasized to help the student remember. It is good practice to underline with a red pencil those points that refer to a potential hazard to students or to equipment, since these points are vital to instruction.
4. Have the steps read and corrected by another specialist in the field.

Step V. *Outlining the knowledge related content.* The knowledge related content is listed in the usual outline form. The outline should be sufficiently complete for the instructor, or anyone else using the outline, to be able to determine the exact content to be covered.

Certain technical information was included in the *doing* content. This type of information is so closely related to the process of doing that it must be taught with demonstrations, and by on-the-job coaching. Knowledge related content includes basic concepts, characteristics of tools equipment, and materials, and safety precautions. These elements of content are typically presented through the lecture with the help of visual aids, such as wall charts, samples of materials, as well as through reading assignments. The procedure for outlining a knowing element of content is as follows:

1. List the major headings under the title of the knowledge element. If the information is to be presented by lectures or discussion, keep the sub-headings to a reasonable number, say around 8 to 12 main points to the lesson. If there are more, perhaps the content element should be subdivided further.
2. Under each heading, list points which are specific and sufficiently detailed to leave no doubt regarding the content to be learned.
3. Have the outline checked by another instructor or specialist in the subject. An exchange of ideas on all units of instruction will help to prevent errors and omissions. Note example outlines at end of chapter.

Further Suggestions on making an Analysis

So far we have discussed the process of analysis as though you alone would be involved, depending primarily on first-hand knowledge of the subject. There are a number of things which can be done to help you with the analysis and to assure you that when it is finished it will be as accurate as possible. One practical way is to use a team approach.

A team can be made up of two or more skilled persons in the subject or occupation being analyzed, and another person or two to guide and control the analysis process. This approach has the advantage of bringing different points of view to bear on the subject. As each team member will have had different experiences, the team approach helps to avoid over-emphasis on certain elements of content by one person.

Another useful technique is to make use of books, curricula, articles, operating instructions, etc., as reminders of content that should be included; they may also prove helpful to identify detailed content to be included. It is wrong, however, to assume such publications can be used as a basis for the entire analysis. Published materials are designed for a specific purpose and frequently omit important material and overemphasize other material. Books should be written as a result of an analysis, not vice versa.

On unfamiliar and complex content elements, it may be necessary to observe a skilled person at work and confer directly about each step of procedure and each concept or informational item required.

After the results of the analysis have been completed, either by the individual or the team, it should be read and evaluated by others who have recent and first-hand knowledge of the field including, if possible, someone who has taught the subject.

In most occupations, the analysis chart or content inventory is never complete because of new developments and changes in procedures, but it is relatively easy to keep a well-developed content inventory up to date. The important thing is to start with a good analysis chart or content inventory as early as possible in the instructional planning process.

The direct relationship of the analysis to courses of study, written instructional materials, and on-the-job training programs will be discussed in later chapters.

Examples of practical analyses follow: the results of an analysis of the occupation of the Air Traffic Controllers are included on page 69 because of its non-mechanical nature and because it has been used as the basis for training decisions in a program directly affecting over 18,000 employees who carry the life and death responsibility for the control of air traffic.

PHOTOGRAPHY ANALYSIS

BLOCKS

I Basic block
II Exposing film
III Developing black and white film
IV Developing color film
V Making black and white film

I BASIC BLOCK

Doing–The learner should be able to:

1 Set up the camera
2 Focus the camera with:
   Range finder
   Ground glass
3 Place film in camera
4 Adjust shutter speed
5 Adjust lens opening
6 Test camera
7 Set up and adjust tripod
8 Read light meter

Knowing–The learner should know the:

1 History of photography
2 Principle of the camera
3 Camera parts and accessories
4 Elementary photographic optics
5 The theory of development
6 The nature of photographic emulsions, development, and fixation
7 Depth of focus and field
8 Types of cameras
9 Types of black and white film
10 Properties of light
11 Filters and their use

II EXPOSING FILM

Doing–The learner should be able to:

1 Use artificial light
2 Use natural light
3 Calculate lens opening and shutter speed with exposure meter
4 Mount filters and determine filter factor
5 Use tripod
6 Set up lights and camera for still objects
7 Set up lights and camera for moving objects
8 Set up lights and camera for portrait
9 Set up lights and camera for copying

Knowing–The learner should know the:

1 Film sensitivity and exposure of specific films
2 Factors of exposure
3 Composition of pic
4 Factors of good composition
5 Effects of lighting

V MAKING BLACK AND WHITE FILM

Doing—The learner
should be able to:

1 Mix chemicals for printing
2 Determine exposure
3 Make contact prints
4 Make enlarged prints
5 Determine desired contrast
6 Mask pictures
7 Develop prints
8 Fix prints
9 Wash prints
10 Dry prints on ferrotype tin
11 Dry matt papers
12 Straighten prints
13 Mount prints with rubber
cement or dry mounting

Knowing—The learner
should know the:

1 Types and characteristics of
paper developers
2 Available papers
3 Characteristics of contact
and projection printing
4 Types of enlargers
5 Safelights
6 Print defects
7 Characteristics of materials
used in mounting prints (photo
parts, rubber cement, gum
arabic, dry mounting tissue

MACHINE METAL WORKING ANALYSIS

BLOCKS

I Blueprint reading
II Bench work and measuring
III Milling machine operations
IV Drill press operations
V Lathe operations
VI Shaper operations
VII Heat treatment

V LATHE OPERATIONS

Doing—The learner
should be able to:

1 Center drill stock
2 Turn stock between centers
3 Turn shoulder on stock
4 Cut threads
5 Mount round stock in universal
chuck
6 Mount round stock in independent
chuck
7 Knurl on the metal lathe
8 Turn taper with compound rest
9 Turn taper by offset method
10 Turn taper with taper attach-
ment, etc.

Knowing—The learner
should know the:

1 Characteristics of carbon tool
steel
2 Machining characteristics of
cast iron
3 Basic requirements of a cutting
tool
4 Shapes and sizes of cutting tools
5 Screw threads systems
6 Lubricants for cutting operations,
etc.

NOTE: Each doing element is stated
in the infinite form, to **do**. The knowing elements are broad general topics
and may be related to one or more
doing elements.

CONTENT ELEMENT 7 OF BLOCK V ANALYZED INTO STEPS OF PROCEDURE

To Knurl on the Metal Lathe

1 Mount work between centers in lathe
NOTE: Size of center drilling in stock must be large enough to stand maximum pressure
2 Set knurling tool
NOTE: Set knurls square to work. Center of revolving head should be level with center of work. Knurling tool should be as near tool as possible
3 Set speed of lathe
NOTE: Speed of lathe should be about that used for rough turning
4 Set feed of lathe
NOTE: A medium feed should be used
5 Check knurls to make sure they are clean
CAUTION: Knurls should not be cleaned while in motion
6 Apply oil
CAUTION: Knurls will be ruined and the knurl produced will be rough if no lubricant is used
7 Start lathe and force knurl into the work
CAUTION: Stop lathe if tool is not tracking properly and start knurl at new place on the stock
8 Engage power feed
NOTE: Do not stop feed until tool has traveled the full length of section to be knurled
CAUTION: Do not wipe off knurls while in motion
9 Release pressure on tool before stopping lathe
10 Inspect knurl
NOTE: If knurl is not deep enough, the tool may be reset and the knurls run over the work a second time

KNOWLEDGE ELEMENT 1 OF BLOCK V

Knowing elements 1. Characteristics of Carbon Tool Steel

A Classifications
  1 Low carbon tool steel
    (a) Carbon content below .50%
    (b) Uses
      (1) Machine parts
      (2) Screws and bolts
    (c) Effects of heat and chemical treating
      (1) Chemicals—case hardening
      (2) Heating and quenching
      (3) Results
    (d) Common terms applied to low carbon steel
      (1) Cold rolled
      (2) Mild steel
      (3) Machine steel
  2 High carbon tool steel
    (a) Carbon content .65% to 1.50%
    (b) Characteristics
      (1) Harder than mild steel
      (2) Stronger than mild steel
      (3) More brittle than mild steel
    (c) Uses—tools
      (1) Tools requiring hard surfaces

              (2) Tools requiring sharp edges
              (3) Tools requiring durability
          (d) Effects of heat treatment
              (1) Heating
              (2) Quenching
              (3) Tempering
    B Machinability
        1. etc.

SECRETARY ANALYSIS (CIVIL SERVICE)

BLOCKS

       I Personal and telephone contacts
      II Correspondence review and composition,
    III Obtaining and presenting information
    IV Conference and committee work
     V Files and records
    VI Dictation
   VII Travel arrangements
  VIII Instruction to other secretaries
    IX Inducting the new secretary

VII TRAVEL ARRANGEMENTS

Doing–The learner should be able to:

1 Make reservations
2 Prepare travel authorization
3 Prepare transportation request
4 Get ticket
5 Arrange travel advance
6 Prepare travel voucher

Knowing–The learner should know the:

1 What type of accommodation supervisor prefers
2 Determining length, time, and place of trip
3 Location and number of airline ticket offices
4 Regulations for travel authorization
5 Regulations for advance
6 Regulations for Transporation Request
7 Regulations for voucher
8 Which forms to use, number of copies
9 Procedure within office for distribution of copies
10 Procedure for securing approval and authority

DOING ELEMENT 2 OF BLOCK VII ANALYZED INTO STEPS OF PROCEDURE

Prepare Travel Authorization

1 Gather pertinent information about the travel (essentially answers to: who, where, when, how and why?)
NOTE: Boss may supply this information voluntarily; if not, secretary must seek out answers.
2 Read Standard Practice Manual Part 2119.1, to familiarize yourself with Agency regulations concerning authority to travel

3 Assemble original and three copies of Form CD-29, "Travel Order"
NOTE: Four copies of Form CD-29 are to be forwarded to travel branch. If secretary wants to keep a record, she should make an additional copy

4 Type in the designated spaces the date, purpose of travel, name and title, itinerary, organizational unit, present official station, estimated cost, appropriation, period of travel, mode of transportation, per diem rate
NOTE: Although per diem rate is always $12.00 in the United States, it varies outside the United States. Please check Standard Practice for exact rate for foreign travel

5 Check form for accuracy, neatness and completeness

6 Have the designated authorizing officer approve the travel order
NOTE: The authorizing officer is usually the traveler's supervisor

7 Send original and three copies to the travel branch (MS-22) for final approval, and numbering

8 When approval copy is returned to you, record the travel order number which is assigned
NOTE: It is essential to remember the order number, since it will be referred to in later processing

KNOWLEDGE ELEMENT 4 OF BLOCK VII

Regulations for Travel Authorization

A Travel authorization terms
1 Authorize versus approve
2 Per diem
3 Itinerary
4 Common carrier

B Authority
1 Temporary travel
2 Change of official station
3 Actual expense bases

C Types of travel orders
1 Trip travel orders
2 Change of official station
3 Annual travel
4 Travel by privately owned vehicle

ELECTRONIC SPECIALIST ANALYSIS

BLOCKS

I Teletype maintenance
II Receiver maintenance
III Transmitter maintenance
IV Speech and audio equipment maintenance
V Voice recorder maintenance
VI VHF omnirange system maintenance
VII Instrument landing system maintenance
VIII Distance measuring equipment system maintenance
IX TACAN system maintenance
X Driving passenger and special purpose vehicles
XI Establish and maintenance stock of spares

II RECEIVER MAINTENANCE

Doing-The learner
should be able to:

1 Make receiver performance measurements
2 Analyze receiver operation utilizing results of receiver performance measurements
3 Read and interpret schematic diagram
4 Perform preventative maintenance and locate potentially defective components
5 Replace defective components and restore faulty receiver to normal operation
6 Align receiver
7 Analyze antenna and transmission line system.
8 Coordinate with operating personnel when installing or removing receiver from the system

NOTE: Example knowing elements, except 1 and 5, are not sufficiently specific to indicate the level, kind or amount of knowledge to be learned, unless one is to assume that everything about the item is to be learned.

Knowing-The learner
should know the:

1 Theory of L, C, & R circuits
2 Tuned circuits
3 Coupled circuits
4 Lumped and distributed constants
5 Vacuum tube operation
6 RF, IF, and audio amplifiers
7 Oscillators and mixers
8 Superheterodyne receivers, both single and double conversion
9 Fixed tuned and variable tuned receivers
10 Servo tuning systems
11 Transmission lines
12 Antennas
13 Sound reproducers
14 Special receiver circuits; i.e. squelch, noise limiters, AVC, AGC, crystal and mechanical filter, etc.
15 Diode crystals
16 Transisters
17 Transister circuit
18 Signal generators
19 Output measuring instruments
20 Oscilloscopes
21 Sweep generators

DOING ELEMENT 6 OF BLOCK II ANALYZED INTO STEPS OF PROCEDURE

How to Align Receivers

1 Read any special alignment instructions on schematic diagram or in instruction book
2 Remove receiver from rack and disconnect from external circuits if necessary
3 Connect an accurately calibrated signal generator to the grid of the 1st detector stage and the chassis ground
   NOTE: Many receivers require a blocking condenser or special coupling circuit
4 Set the signal generator to deliver a modulated signal at the IF frequency of the receiver
   NOTE: The output of the signal generator, throughout the alignment procedure, should be just high enough for accurate measurement on the output meter
   CAUTION: Insure that the output is never great enough to cause blocking in any of the receiver circuits
5 Disable the AVC circuit
6 Set the audio gain well advanced
7 Connect the calibrated output meter to the speaker terminals
   NOTE: The output meter must match the output impedance of the receiver

8 Turn on the receiver and set the IF gain high enough so that a usable indication is obtained on the output meter

9 Carefully adjust the IF trimmers for maximum output. Begin with the IF coil following the mixer state and proceed to the second detector
NOTE: On many receivers special alignment tools must be used and when an IF strip is broad band the coils are not adjusted to all peaks at the same frequency

10 Disconnect the signal generator and connect it to the antenna terminals through the proper matching network

11 With the signal generator delivering a signal at the operating frequency of the receiver, adjust the oscillator trimmer for maximum receiver output
NOTE: A crystal controlled or secondary standard type generator must be used for this step. This step considers fixed tuned receivers only. Variable tuned receivers would follow a different procedure

12 Adjust the rf amplifier and 1st detector trimmers for maximum receiver output

13 Check the overall receiver sensitivity.

KNOWING ELEMENT 1 OF BLOCK II

Theory of L, C, and R Circuits

A Electrical characteristics of inductance
   1 Self inductance: Henry's Law (one henry is the self-inductance of a coil in which, by changing the current 1 ampere per second, 1 volt is induced)
   2 Inductive reactance in coils (many turns of wire, soft iron core, high frequency alternating current)
   3 Charging an object by induction
   4 Magnetic induction

B Electrical characteristics of capacitance
   1 Charging and discharging action taking place in a circuit is dependent upon the capacity of a condenser
   2 The capacity of a condenser depends upon the area of the plates, the distance between the plates, and the quality of the dielectric between the plates
   3 Unit of capacity is the farad—one millionth of a farad is a micro-farad (mf), one millionth of a micro-farad is a micro-micro-farad (mmf)

C Electric characteristics of resistance
   1 Resistance is the opposition to electron flow
   2 Resistance in a conductor depends upon four factors
   (a) Length
   (b) Cross-sectional area
   (c) Temperature
   (d) Material
   3 The ohm is the unit of resistance (one ohm is the resistance caused by a column of mercury 106.3 centimeters long and 1 square millimeter in cross section, at 0°C
   4 The resistance of material may be expressed by using the mil (one thousandth of an inch) as a unit of length and the circular mil (the area of a circle which is one mil in diameter) as a unit of area

D Impedance
   1 etc.

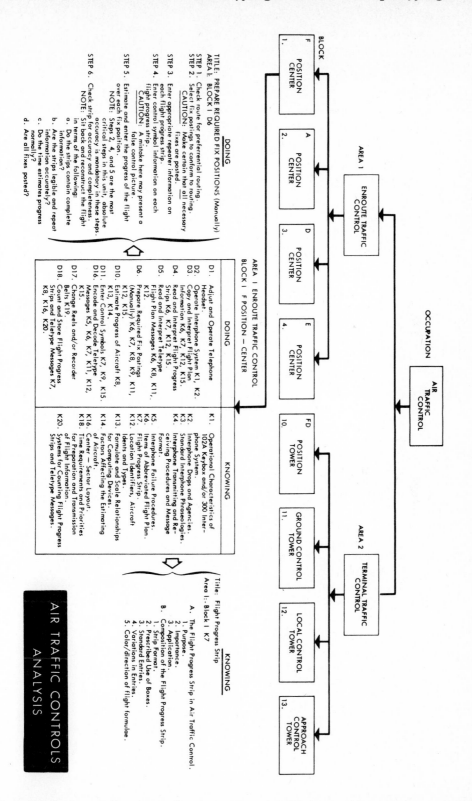

QUESTIONS AND ASSIGNMENTS

1. Define the following terms:
   Occupational analysis
   Block
   Doing content
   Knowing content
   Steps of procedure
2. Draw a chart from memory to show the relationship of the terms of Question 1.
3. List the blocks in your occupational or subject matter area.
4. What are the characteristics of a doing element of content? How long should it be? What should it contain?
5. Identify and list several doing elements of content.
6. Identify and list several knowing elements of content.
7. What is the relationship between content elements and behavioral objectives?
8. Code the knowledge elements of content to show their relationship to the doing elements.
9. List the steps in a doing element of content and add the points of information and the cautions related to each step.
10. Outline a knowing element of content.
11. What advantages do you see in making an analysis before starting to plan a course of instruction?
12. Pick out the parts of this chapter that are based on knowing and doing elements of content of the instructor's job.
13. What is meant by cumulative nature of doing elements of content?
14. To what uses, other than instructional planning, may a good analysis be put?

Preparing Courses of Study and Lesson Plans

When the architect designs a house, consideration must be given to the client, the trends in design, the characteristics and costs of materials suitable for the locality, the location selected for the house, and many other factors. When the plans are complete, the builder may proceed with confidence because he knows that all of the elements with which he will be concerned have been developed into a unified pattern.

Planning a course of study is a similar process. The course of study is a written document that provides a planned and logical organization for the content and the instructional processes designed to meet a given educational goal(s).

By the process of analysis as described in Chapter 4, we determined the knowing and doing elements. When combined with the attitudinal dimension, they will comprise the instructional program to be carried out. The analysis is similar to an inventory of the kinds of building materials on the market. It lists the materials

and supplies available, but it does not plan a building or indicate which materials are to be used in any specific design. An occupational analysis provides an inventory of potential content that may be taught; it may contain enough material for several courses of study. However, it does not indicate how or the order in which elements of content should be taught. For this, a course of study and plans for one or more class sessions during a given time period are needed (unit and lesson plans).

Components of a Course of Study

Assuming that the rectangle in the illustration on page 72 represents all the content that is in a given occupation or subject area (the theoretical body of knowledge), the analysis process would identify a portion of the whole. In the diagram, the irregular figure within the diagram symbolically encompasses the content identified through the analysis procedures. The content thus identified

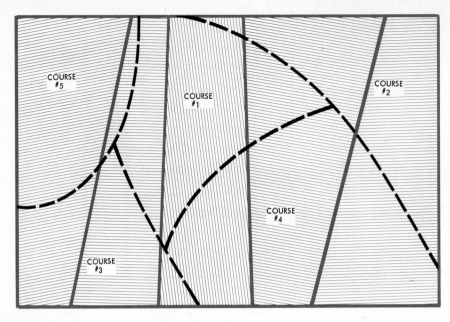

Interrelationship within the body of knowledge to be taught; content identified by analysis, blocking and content selection.

is categorized into Blocks or Major Divisions represented by diagonal cross-hatched areas. The next step in the process involves dividing the total content into manageable components which we typically call courses. In our diagram these are illustrated by the dashed lines cutting across several major divisions of content.

In the construction of a course of study, the instructor takes into consideration the relationship of this course to the entire educational program of the organization, the objectives of the course, the needs of the student, the content to be taught, the equipment and facilities available, the most appropriate methods of instruction for each part of the course, student learning activities, resource materials (including instructional aids), as well as procedures and instruments for evaluation.

In building a course of study, we deal not only with the content to be taught, but the instructional processes as well. The process involves a number of steps. Each of the steps involved in building a course of study results in a component or section of the instructional document.

This chapter, by necessity, provides

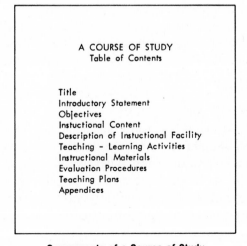

A COURSE OF STUDY
Table of Contents

Title
Introductory Statement
Objectives
Instuctional Content
Description of Instuctional Facility
Teaching – Learning Activities
Instructional Materials
Evaluation Procedures
Teaching Plans
Appendices

Components of a Course of Study

only an overview of each of the components of a course of study since entire chapters are provided to deal with the components in depth such as Chapter 10, Instructional Aids and Devices. The primary focus of this chapter, therefore, is upon the process of planning the course and lesson within the course. The organizational framework suggested by the course of study and lesson plans have been found to be helpful by the authors and many other successful instructors.

Naming the Course

Some thought should be given to the selection of an appropriate and descriptive title. Be as specific as possible and avoid naming the course in such a way as to suggest that it includes more than it does. The title should, if possible, indicate the content to be covered, as well as the type and level of instruction. Some examples are:

Machine shop mathematics,
Radar electronics,
Under water welding and cutting,
The steel square in roof framing,
Sheet metal layout for ventilating systems,
Basic nutrition for homemakers,
Clerical practice,
Computer programming-Fortran,
Residential landscape design,
Retail salesmanship.

Introductory Statement

After an appropriate name has been chosen, it is important that an introductory statement be prepared which clearly defines the grade, age or experience level at which the course is considered appropriate. In addition, any pre-requisites or conditions for the course should be specified and a paragraph prepared which

indicates the length and nature of the course. This will tell, in general terms, the purpose and content of the course.

Stating the Course Objectives

Here we describe briefly those behaviors we expect graduates of the course to know and be able to do. The objectives should specify the information and concepts to be learned, the skills to be developed as well as the attitudes, appreciations, or points of view that are desired of one who completes the instructional program. For a course in beginning photography, the following objectives might be listed:

1. To know the characteristics of roll, film pack, and cut film cameras, the relationship of lens size and speed of exposure, the measurement and control of light and the elementary chemistry of development.
2. To take pictures with common hand cameras, to mix photographic chemicals, to develop black and white film and to make contact prints and enlargements.
3. To recognize good composition and technical quality in photography.

The objectives should be realistic. There is always a temptation to give objectives that are far out of reach in the time allowed or with the facilities available. The examples above could be made even more precise by indicating the conditions under which the behaviors should be observed and the level of competency required.

Objectives should be more than grand claims. The instructor must expect the learner to reach the objectives. They should be realistic and consistent with

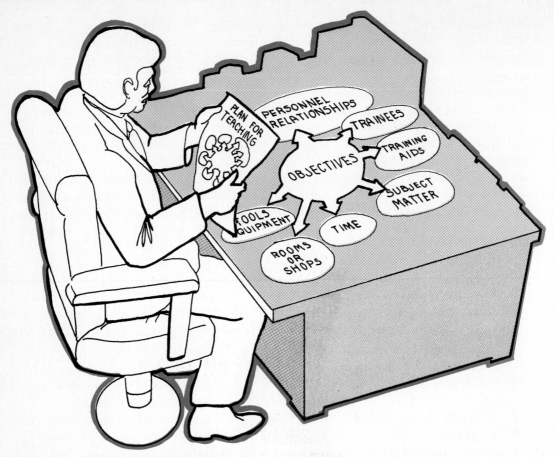

All elements of the lesson plan must be consistent with the objectives.

entering student capabilities and with the time and facilities available. Careful consideration should always be given to the educational level of the students, as well as their interests and aptitudes. The objectives should be such that, with effective instruction, almost every student of a typical group will be able to exhibit the desired or specified behavior.

In some cases an instructor may find that a course which has a reputation of being a snap or easy course may be made more meaningful and challenging by clear specification of the objectives to be achieved. Even in school programs where certain worthwhile courses have become the dumping ground for low ability and poorly motivated students, the really competent instructor can raise the standards to an acceptable level and build a better reputation for the course.

Determining the Specific Content and Listing Major Instructional Units

With the objectives in mind, select from the analysis those knowing and doing elements of content that you wish to teach. If the course must be taught in a

Discuss your lesson content with other instructors.

limited time, care should be taken to select those units that can be included within the time limits and which will contribute the most toward the objectives.

This is not as easy as it sounds. All content in the analysis has value in the occupation. As an instructor, you may have had more experience in certain parts of the occupation or subject and tend to favor what you know the most about. After you have made a tentative selection of knowing and doing units which are consistent with your objectives and time limitation, you may want to get opinions from other instructors and perhaps adult students who are familiar with your subject. Good decisions at this point will save a lot of time and effort later.

The interrelationship between *content* identified through occupational analysis procedures and *behavioral objectives* is striking. In reality, they are both statements of behavior and they become different only in the way they are expressed. Through analysis, the behaviors of an individual in an occupation are identified, while in an instructional program behaviors are specified as the desired end results of instruction. The behavior itself may be identical.

Arranging Units in Proper Order

When possible, the least difficult unit should be taught first. Also, some of the knowledge related content must be taught prior to the doing or performance content to which it is related. It is generally not wise, however, to teach too much theory before the students have had a chance to apply the theory, use tools and materials, or solve problems. Some courses have been designed so that all of the related mathematics and theory is taught at the beginning of the course. However, from the standpoint of motivation and ease of learning, it is usually better to teach each unit of related knowledge and theory just prior to the time it is needed by the student to solve practical problems. Where possible, information and theory should be taught in small segments throughout the course.

Selecting and Preparing Instructional Materials

The selection or preparation of visual aids, textbooks and all other instructional materials should, of course, follow decisions on course content to be taught and the methods of presentation. Instructional materials must be consistent with student ability, must emphasize the key elements of the course, and must be effective in presenting information and concepts.

A good textbook is essential for effective instruction in most courses. Many textbooks, however, are written with general objectives in mind. They are designed to be used in a variety of situations. As a result, supplemental materials are usually required for each specific course. If an appropriate text is available, it should normally be used for much of the assigned individual study.

Short units of programmed instruction may be valuable in assuring the development of the desired level of competence in the basic or most critical areas of the course.

The selection of films is important; however, their use may depend on availability from a film library. Therefore, films should be requested for a specific date as early as possible. Films from business, industry and trade associations should be used if they can clearly contribute to the instructional objectives. If not, they may waste valuable class time. In some instances only a portion of a film may be used. If especially valuable, the total film or a portion of it may be shown more than once.

Other instructional aids, including charts, illustrations for the opaque projector and overhead projection transparencies, should be selected or prepared as the course and each lesson are developed. If special equipment and supplies are needed, they should be placed on order well in advance of the time they will be used.

Tests and assignment sheets should be prepared and reproduced as early as possible after the objectives, course content and schedule have been determined. Some instructors have found the preparation of examinations along with the development of the course of study helps to sharpen the objectives and improve the course of study.

To avoid confusion and to reduce the use of inadequate materials, assignment sheets, written examinations and performance tests should be prepared well in advance of their use. These materials should be designed so that the most essential elements presented in the course are covered adequately. The content and coverage of an assignment or test should not come as a surprise to the student. They should be a logical step in the instructional pattern.

Learning Activities

The real purpose behind the process of planning for instruction is to facilitate *learning*. Therefore, the selection of appropriate and effective learning activities becomes a critical factor in the planning process and a most significant component in the course of study. Learning activities may be as varied as the instructor's creativity and imagination will permit. They range from the commonplace reading assignment through student prepared notebooks, field trips, repetitive drill, projects and other application experiences, to name only a few examples.

Projects. The term project is used to identify a wide variety of student learning experiences which emphasize the application of skills and knowledge that result in some type of product. A project may be a notebook in a class in distributive education, a set of house plans in architectural drawing, a garment in home economics, raising a garden in agriculture or a coffee table in wood working.

When projects are used as a means of instruction, the order of instruction is influenced by the practical nature of the project. For example, in the photography course the taking of pictures would normally precede the development of the film and the making of prints.

The fundamental purpose in using projects during a course is to provide an opportunity for practical application in a context that is meaningful for students as they learn specific skills. When students are required to make practice pieces which are then thrown away, there is usually less motivation or desire to succeed than when the same skills are developed through construction of useful and desirable projects. Projects must, however, be designed so that the right skills are emphasized to the right extent. A common failure is to use projects without a careful analysis of the skills and knowledge inherent in the activity or to use projects in which there is a disproportionate amount of time spent in the development of relatively unimportant knowledge.

In selecting or designing projects for instructional purposes, a number of objectives should be considered and used if appropriate:

1. The projects should require the development of the skills selected for the course and specified through the course objectives.
2. The finished projects should be something that the student sees as having either intrinsic or extrinsic value, or both—something which the student can be proud of.
3. Readily available materials and supplies should be used where practicable.
4. The finished project should be consistent with known principles, and

standard practices in the occupation.

As a simple example, suppose we wish to teach certain basic woodworking operations. A small wood tool box is considered as a potential project, as shown below, with a list of the doing content or operations involved and the order in which they should be taught.

A similar approach can be taken in any subject in which tools and materials are used. Some electronics can be taught through the building of radio receivers. Certain elements of aviation can be taught through the construction and

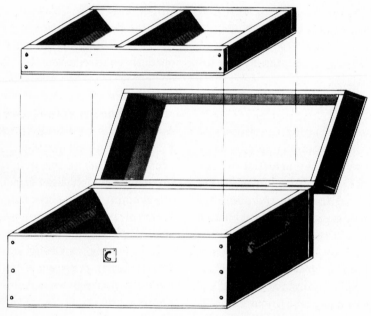

HAND TOOL OPERATIONS	ORDER OF PERFORMANCE ELEMENTS BASED ON THE ORIGINAL LISTING	INSTRUCTIONAL ORDER OF OPERATIONS BASED ON A SPECIFIC PROJECT
Measure with a rule or square	1	1
Cut to line with cross-cut saw	2	2
Cut to line with rip saw	3	3
Assemble and adjust hand plane	4	5
Square stock to dimensions	5	6
Sharpen plane iron and chisel	6	4
Lay out with dividers	7	7
Drill holes	8	10
Counter sink holes	9	11
Set screws	10	12
Drive and draw nails	11	13
Make cuts with chisel	12	9
Lay out and cut dado point	13	8
Fasten with dowels	14	Not required by project
Clamp with handscrews and clamps	15	Not required by project
Sand wood surfaces	16	14
Fit butt hinges	17	15
Place and fasten handles and hasp	18	16
Apply enamel	19	17

A potential project with a list of the doing content.

operation of model aircraft. Mathematics, physics, and chemistry lend themselves to various types of projects.

Photography, printing, mechanical drawing, painting, all of the building and metal working trades, and other subjects in which design is important are almost always taught most effectively through the use of projects.

Field trips. Field trips are very important in assisting students to see beyond the classroom and in understanding the world in which we live. The trips will also help you to keep your instruction up-to-date and interesting. As examples: woodworking classes may visit a specialized woodworking plant; metalworkers may visit plants to see certain types of work such as metal spinning, drop forging or electroplating. Design classes can learn from museums, special exhibits, large retail stores; photography students should see newspaper-type photographic processes including highspeed development, printing, and engraving.

Companies and industrial plants are pleased to have serious visitors. Arrangements should, of course, be worked out carefully in advance and students should be given a thorough briefing including certain things to look for and observe, as well as the proper behavior while they are guests. Your host should know something about the class and what types of experiences that will be of particular value during the visit. If possible, a schedule of events during the visit should be arranged in advance.

Students should be given the opportunity, on their return, to discuss things they have seen so that each may add to the other's understanding. It is appropriate to send a letter of appreciation to your host after the visit.

Outside Speakers. Listening and observing are important learning activities. Bringing persons from the "real" world of work into the classroom often provides valuable instruction as well as motivation to students. In many locations, highly skilled individuals are available for special instruction. Technical specialists, scientists, authors, designers, and hobbyists are frequently willing to put on a special demonstration or illustrated lecture in their fields. These can add variety, realism, and motivation to any class. In making arrangements, be sure that the special demonstration is consistent with your objectives and can be provided at the right time.

Since most potential speakers are quite busy, every effort should be made to facilitate their participation in your course. Transportation and the time schedule should be arranged carefully. A capable student may be assigned to assist the speaker with all details of setting up the demonstration. The class should look for appropriate means of showing its appreciation.

Outside Reading. Outside reading assignments in addition to regular text assignments are a part of all technical courses of study. General reading of a semi-fiction or historical nature is of value for motivation and the development of interest. It might be difficult to prove that reading the history of submarines in World War II would make a man a better sailor; however, such reading should be encouraged because it helps to develop desirable attitudes.

The instructor can facilitate this worthwhile activity by showing an interest in it and by making reading materials easily available. An occasional reference to a book, current article, or an appropriate movie is frequently all that is necessary to start alert students toward an expanding interest in the "nice to know" material related to the course of study.

The Teaching Plan

As previously mentioned, the purpose of this chapter is to describe an organizational framework whereby the instructor might plan more effectively for instruction. The course of study is a proven organizational scheme although it certainly is not the only system.

Even though most of the course of study may be prepared in advance of instruction, the revision and updating process is never completed. The course of study must be viewed as a dynamic document that is continually changing. Effective instructors make frequent changes in their resource materials, teaching-learning aids and student activities, even though the course objectives and content may be relatively stable.

After the instructor has all or most of the components listed on page 72 prepared, at least in preliminary form, the teaching plan, may be prepared. The teaching plan becomes the instructor's guide as it identifies the various items within the components and places them in instruction order or sequence. The format suggested here for a teaching plan involves a series of columns which permit the instructor to list (1) each major *subdivision, large unit* or *block* with the amount of time in weeks, days or hours, (2) the *student learning activities* for the unit, (3) *demonstrations* to be provided by the instructor, (4) *informational* content to be learned in the unit, keyed to textbook or other resource, (5) *supplementary aids or activities* which allow the listing

of instructional aids to be used such as field trips, films, as well as evaluative activities such as performance tests, rating scales, written examination.

As can readily be observed, the teaching plan provides the skeletal framework for the entire course; however, it does not provide sufficient detail for the successful execution of instruction on a day to day basis. A further step in the planning process is required which is referred to simply as *lesson planning*.

Planning the Lessons

Consistent with the purpose of this chapter, this section on lesson planning seeks to acquaint you with the final link in the instructional planning process. In simplest terms, a lesson plan provides the instructor with detailed directions for carrying out the instructional process for one or more class period which focus on a given topic or theme.

The length of a lesson is a variable which might be as short as 30 to 40 minutes to as much as 4 to 5 hours. The content, the age and maturity of students, the nature of the instructional program (amount of student application or practice) and other factors are the determinants of a lesson's length.

As sample lesson planning formats and examples of lesson plans are presented, it is recognized that you may not have a thorough knowledge of some of the instructional methods that are mentioned. However, your focus should be directed to the planning process with the recognition that you will learn a variety of methods for the execution of instruction through a study of Chapters 7, 8, 9, 10, and 11.

Elements of the lesson plan. Two elements are essential in all good lesson plans: what to teach and how to teach it.

The second element is often neglected. When we plan the content to be taught *and* decide the methods of instruction to be used, we have a lesson plan.

Some may feel that if they know the subject and have taught it, no further planning is necessary. They may recall instructors who did a good job without any written plan in evidence.

It is possible, of course, for a simple plan to be thought through and carried out without placing it on paper. However, for most of us a plan on paper is an absolute necessity if we are to do our best.

Purpose of the lesson plan. There are a number of specific reasons for the lesson plan. Prior to presenting the lesson it helps the instructor to "think through" or visualize the lesson as it will be taught. At this point the experienced instructor can anticipate learning difficulties and decide on ways to overcome them. The plan assists in the organization of tools, materials and aids needed to carry out the plan. A good lesson plan gives the instructor confidence while teaching, and helps to:

1. Provide needed motivation.
2. Give proper emphasis to the various parts of the lesson including those requiring student activity.
3. Insure that all essential information is included.
4. Provide for the use of instructional aids.
5. Insert questions at the proper time.
6. Stay on schedule.

Some skilled instructors write out a detailed plan as a means of preparing themselves and then reduce it to a few notes and a time schedule for use in the classroom. Others prefer to teach from a detailed outline. In any event, the plan should be designed to fit your needs for each lesson you are planning to teach.

Canned lesson plans or plans prepared by someone else may be of value, but they are seldom usable without modification.

SUGGESTED TEACHING PLAN FORMAT

MAJOR UNIT	LEARNING ACTIVITY	DEMONSTRATION	INFORMATIONAL TOPIC DISCUSSION, LECTURE, READING	SUPPLEMENTARY AIDS

TEACHING PLAN*

FUNDAMENTALS OF ELECTRICITY

Suggested Activities	Demonstrations	Topics for Class Discussion	Informational Assignments	Other Instructional Aids
	Solve problems with Ohm's Law.	Increased use and decreasing cost of electricity. Nuclear structure and electron theory. Ohm's Law.	1	Film: "What is Electricity"
1. Wire a series circuit.	Read an ammeter. Read a voltmeter. Read an ohmmeter. Read a VOM. Wire meters in circuits.	Construction, use, and precautions with meters. Characteristics of D.C. series circuits.	2	Film: "Series and Parallel Circuits"
2. Construct a voltage tester. 3. Wire a parallel circuit.		Characteristics of D.C. parallel circuits.		
4. Calculate electric power.	Measure power with wattmeter, voltmeter, and ammeter.	Electric power in D.C. circuits. Rate structures. Power unit conversion efficiency calculation.	3	Rate cards from power distributors.
5. Operate overcurrent protective devices.	Overload a fuse.	Overcurrent protective devices. Safety precautions with electricity, first aid. Grounding considerations. Open and closed circuits. Electrical and electronic schematic symbols.	4

5 | Start a file on newspaper clippings dealing with electric shock.

Make a demonstration board with the various sizes and types of fuses.

Films: "Electrical Safety in the Home" "How to do Rescue Breathing?"

Chart of symbols: available from Eico.

Architectural plans with wiring diagrams and schematic circuit drawings. |

*University of Missouri. Applied Electricity. Instructional Materials Laboratory: Department of Practical Arts and Vocational-Technical Education and Missouri State Department of Education, Division of Career and Adult Education, 1963.

Each instructor needs a "customized" plan, which may be developed from scratch or may be a modification of an existing plan to make it useful for a specific group of learners at a given point in time.

Points in lesson planning. Here are a number of points to consider in lesson planning:

1. The objective or reason for the lesson—what you expect students to know and be able to do as a result of the lesson.
2. Tools and equipment.
3. Publications and instructional aids or devices.
4. The content or subject matter to be included (from the analysis).
5. The methods to be used in presenting each part of the lesson.
6. The points where you should check for understanding.
7. The time schedule.
8. What tests are appropriate.
9. Ways of providing for student application of the content presented.

Typical Lesson Plan Elements

As previously indicated, a lesson plan may be prepared for a period in the course or it may be designed to cover a subject that extends through two or more periods of the course. Most good lesson plans will contain the following elements.

Title. The exact title of the lesson should be given. For example, the title "Micrometer" is not as good as the title "How to Read a Micrometer," if that is the real objective of the lesson. The title of a lesson plan usually comes from the list of knowing and doing content elements in

A good lesson plan includes a timetable.

the analysis. A lesson plan, however, may include less than one or more than one doing or knowing element from the analysis, in which case an appropriate title encompassing several content elements should be chosen. The length of the school periods and the content being taught must be considered.

Objectives. State the objective or reason from the point of view of the student. For example: "To develop a general understanding of the types of house paints," or "To develop skill in applying outside paint." The objective of the lesson sets the goal toward which the activity during the lesson should be directed. The lesson objective should be specific, realistic, to the point, and clearly consistent with the objectives for the course.

Instructional Aids. As the lesson is planned, the instructor should list the charts, models, films, and other aids that will facilitate learning. This list serves as an inventory when preparing to teach, and is of great help the next time the lesson is taught. The analysis of the proper use of aids in Chapter 10 may be used as a reminder in selecting aids for a lesson.

Texts and References. Be sure to identify and write down specific knowing and doing elements of content from the analysis to be included in the lesson. References to text material that have been used for information in the preparation of the plan should also be listed. If the plan is to be used over a period of time, space should be left to facilitate adding new references as they become available. All instruction sheets and text material to be used by the students should be listed. References should include page numbers, not just the book title.

Introduction. An enthusiastic and well planned introduction will help to develop interest and motivate the student to want to become involved with the subject. The introduction is so important that you may want to write it out in full. A good introduction may include:

1. What the lesson is about.
2. Where and when the students can use what they will learn in the lesson.
3. How the lesson will be taught.
4. What will be expected from students during and after the class.
5. A review of previous lessons.

Repetition is always necessary for effective instruction. The procedure used, however, should not be repetitious. Essential information may be emphasized through many different approaches, one of which is to review the previous lesson as a part of the introduction to the current lesson.

You may find it helpful to think through previous lessons and jot down in your plan certain key points that need re-emphasis or re-teaching before the current lesson can proceed smoothly. The review should not be long and involved. Don't waste time. The question and answer approach may be the most effective for a certain lesson, or you may simply remind the students of key points previously discussed.

Presentation. This is the core of the lesson. It contains two interwoven elements: (1) An outline complete enough to reveal the exact content to be taught and the order in which it will be taught, and (2) notes to yourself about ways to teach the various parts of the lesson. For example:

"Ask the following questions . . ."

Preparation: Planning the lesson.

Introduction: Instructor describes the lesson.

"Through discussion develop the reason for . . ."

"Introduce the film and run first 11 minutes only."

"Discuss the following points before showing the remaining part of the film."

"Ask Bill Jones to show how this is done at his plant."

In planning the presentation step, we draw on the analysis for content to be taught and on the techniques of lecturing, discussing, demonstrating, and questioning as ways to teach each step or part of the lesson.

Some instructors prefer to draw a line down the center of the page and to place the outline of content on one side and notes on teaching techniques on the other side.

Make sure all parts of the presentation follow each other in logical order and that there are no awkward gaps. Estimate the time required for each part of the lesson.

Summary and test. The summary of a lesson may be organized in several ways. One good way is to review the main points to emphasize them and to help students organize the content in their minds. This is often followed by oral questions to assure that the students can apply what they have learned and to check on their understanding.

Short tests covering the main points in the lesson are a valuable teaching device because they motivate the students to learn and analyze the content being learned. They are also valuable as an indication of the parts of the lesson that have been taught well and the parts needing clarification or re-emphasis. Marks or grades may be given if desired; however, it is more important to use the test as a teaching device than for the purpose of giving grades.

Application. Application occurs whenever, either mentally or both mentally and physically, the student applies the

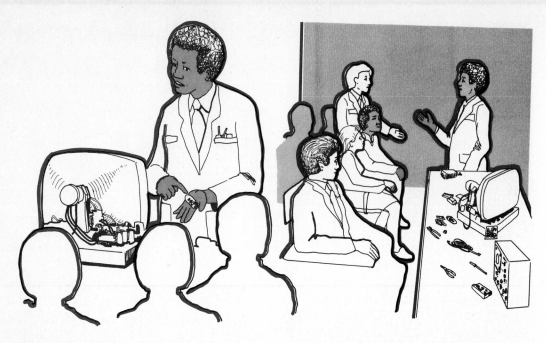

Presentation: By lecture, demonstration or discussion. Discussion: Questions and answers on key points.

Application: Students apply what they are learning.

Examination: Performance and written tests.

learned content to some type of problem. Application occurs all through the lesson if the student understands and mentally applies the content being presented.

Questions, illustrations, problems, examples and exercises, when properly used, cause the student to apply abstract concepts to specific and practical situations.

Application may be performed through the use of instructional aids and devices.

This application is essential for full understanding of basic concepts and for learning to transfer the basic theory to a variety of specific tasks.

In many good lessons, we find a part of the time reserved for application. When good application occurs, it is the result of the instructor's planning. The stage must be set and materials and tools must be available. In many situations, assignments to individuals in the group must be made and a schedule provided for the use of equipment. Individual instruction sheets and other written materials must be made available when needed. The in-structor must be free to observe and guide individuals as they work through the assignment.

Assignment. When an assignment for work outside the class period is to be made, it is not enough to say, "For tomorrow, read Chapter 5." It pays to tell the student what to look for, what to read for general understanding, which parts to study, what questions to answer and how. A good assignment:

1. Is thought out and planned in advance so that when given it is easy to understand.

2. Contains specific instructions regarding the method of approach. Anticipated difficulties and problems should be discussed. Specific problems, questions, and methods should be listed and emphasized.

3. Is given slowly so that notes may be taken. This suggests giving the assignment at the beginning of the period when there is less chance of running out of time, unless the students need today's lesson in order to understand tomorrow's assignment.

4. Includes questions by the instructor to make sure everyone understands the assignment, and time for the students to ask questions.

In some cases the instructor may allow time to start the work on the assignment so that misconceptions may be noted and corrected.

Sample Lesson Plans

Following is a doing or performance element from the analysis and a lesson plan. As you read the plan, refer to the analysis to see the relationship of the analysis to the lesson plan.

This performance element or operation is complete in content, but the analysis gives no indication of how it should be taught. The sample lesson plan which follows shows the unit after it has been developed into a plan for teaching. All of the content from the analysis or outline has been retained, but the "how" of teaching has been added. A description is given of how to present each point. Reference is made to instructional aids. Questions are thought out and written into the plan. Remarks which are directed to the instructor can be underlined with red pencil.

DOING CONTENT: HOW TO TIN A SOLDERING COPPER

1 Heat the soldering copper.
Copper should be only hot enough to melt solder readily.

2 Clean the copper.
Wipe copper on damp rag.
Rub all sides of the point on sal-ammoniac block. This will clean off the oxidized copper and prepare the metal for the tinning.
CAUTION: Don't breathe fumes. Fumes from hot sal-ammoniac are harmful to the lungs and cause headaches.

3 Apply solder to point.
This may be done by placing a small drop of solder on the sal-ammoniac block and rubbing the copper over it.

4 Reheat the copper.
Copper should be only hot enough to melt solder readily.
More heat will burn off the tinning.

SAMPLE LESSON PLAN
Lesson Plan No. 17
Course: BASIC SHOP PRACTICE

TITLE

How to Tin a Soldering Copper

OBJECTIVES

1 To develop an understanding of how to tin a soldering copper
2 To develop a measure of skill in tinning a soldering copper

INSTRUCTIONAL AIDS

1 Three soldering coppers, standard or electric. One copper should be properly tinned, the other two in need of tinning
2 Sal-ammoniac block
3 Soft solder (half-and-half)
4 Small pieces of galvanized iron
5 Damp rag

REFERENCES

1 Use of Tools, Basic Navy Training Course, p. 128
2 Modern Metalcraft, J. L. Feirer, p. 227
3 Metalwork Essentials, Tustison and Kranzusch, page 17

INTRODUCTION

Tinning a soldering copper is an operation that often has to be done on the job. The purpose of a thin coat of solder (called tinning) on the tip of a soldering copper is to aid the heat to pass from the hot copper to the solder and the work. Without this coat of solder on the point, copper oxides would form and act as an insulation to hold the heat back. It is impossible to solder if the copper is not properly tinned.

During this class, I will show you how to tin a copper and someone in the group will be called on to tin a copper while the rest of you watch. All of you will be using soldering copper during your shop work. The job is quite simple, but must be done exactly right or the tinning will not stick.

PRESENTATION

1 Illustrate by means of the two coppers
  a Appearance of good tinning job
  b Appearance of copper in need of tinning
2 Attempt to solder galvanized iron with poorly tinned copper—point out:
  a Difficulties
  b Appearance of solder job
  c Comparison with good job
3 Show same operation with well tinned copper—point out:
  a Ease of doing a first-class job
  b Appearance of first-class job
    (1) Why do we need to know how to tin a soldering copper?

(2) How can you recognize a good tinning job?
4 Tin the copper
  a Heat copper only enough to melt solder
(Step 1 in analysis) (1) Show how to judge temperature
  (2) Emphasize the effect of too much heat
  b Clean point of copper
(Step 2 in analysis) (1) Use damp rag
  (2) Rub point on sal-ammoniac block
  CAUTION: Do not breathe fumes. They are poisonous and cause headaches.
  c Apply solder
(Step 3 in analysis) (1) How much and when
  (2) Movement of copper over block
  d Reheat copper. While copper is heating, ask questions
  (1) How can we judge temperature of copper?
(Step 4 in analysis) (2) What is the effect of too much heat?
  (3) What will too much solder do while tinning?
  e Solder a seam with copper to show that it is now in good condition

APPLICATION (25 MINUTES)
1 Take the third copper in need of tinning and call on one student to go through steps of tinning (If the copper has been heated with the others, some time can be saved)
2 Point out key points in the process (Further application comes during later shop work)

DISCUSSION AND TEST (15 MINUTES)
1 Ask each student to list the steps in tinning a copper
2 Exchange papers and give correct answers

ASSIGNMENT
Read Operation Sheet No. 12 and answer questions 4, 5, 6, and 10. Keep answers in notebook for spot inspection. Comment: "During the course, you will all use a soldering copper. All students will at some time be marked on the condition of the coppers found in use. Be sure to keep yours in first class condition."

Lesson plans that do not involve tools and materials are similar in appearance but vary in their content. Here is a lesson plan based on the theory of transfer of training from Chapter 2 which might be used in an instructor training program.

The plans used as illustrations can be improved. The check list in the Appendix will help you evaluate these plans and others you make for your own use.

SAMPLE LESSON PLAN

TITLE
      Transfer of Training

OBJECTIVE
      To develop an understanding of the nature of transfer of
      training, when to expect transfer and how to facilitate
      transfer when teaching

REFERENCES
      1 Rose and Miller: Instructors and their Jobs, Chapter 2
      2 Witherington: Educational Psychology, pages 370–380

INSTRUCTIONAL AIDS
      1 Chalk board
      2 Flip chart with lists of identical elements in two or
        more subjects

INTRODUCTION
      Many people still believe that the mind is developed like
      a muscle. They think that by mastering difficult subjects the
      mind can be strengthened and hence become more able to
      learn or deal with any subject. The concept that the mind
      can be strengthened by the studying of certain subjects and
      thus be more capable of dealing with all other subjects has
      not been generally accepted by psychologists for many
      years, nor do carefully controlled experiments support the
      theory. We do not learn very much about solving prob-
      lems on human relations through the study of geometry,
      nor does the study of human relations help us to learn
      geometry. We have all seen examples of highly competent
      people in their specialty who are extremely inept in other
      fields.

      Let's examine the matter further. Does the learning of cer-
      tain specific subjects help us learn other specific subjects?
      If this is so, why is it so in some cases and not in others?
      Of what value is this to the instructor? Since it should be
      obvious that no training program can provide every specific
      detail required by the individual in all the situations he
      will meet thereafter, it becomes important for us as in-
      structors to teach that which is fundamental, which under-
      lies specific procedures, and which will transfer from one
      situation to another.

PRESENTATION
      A Transfer of identical elements
          1 What are identical elements?
          2 What transfer would we expect from driving a car
            to driving a truck?
          3 What other training would have to be given?
          4 Is there transfer from driving a car to handling a
            boat in the water?
          5 What transfer would you expect of woodworking to
            sheetmetal working? Use flip chart to make this
            concept clear

It is possible that certain habits developed through the study of one subject may transfer to another. For example, study habits of having a regular schedule and place to study, of turning off the radio, keeping reference books, papers, etc., needed for effective study handy, of giving priority to study over other things, may transfer from one subject to another. Do they always transfer? Why?

Now we can draw this conclusion: we get transfer of training from one subject to another when identical elements of knowledge and procedure are found in both subjects and the student recognizes these similarities.

B Transfer of basic principles
1 What are basic principles?
2 Give examples in your subject
3 To what specific procedures is each principle related?
4 Will the principle change with time?
5 Has the procedure changed in the last ten, five, two years?

We can draw this conclusion: the occupation is continually changing, many jobs are just a little different from other jobs and therefore the worker must use judgment, knowledge of the basic principles and common elements gives the worker confidence because he understands the "why" of the specific job. Furthermore, no school or training program can cover everything needed later by the student. He must understand principles so that he can change methods and use judgment and continue to develop his skill without further training.

C What is negative transfer?
1 Give example
2 What would happen when a simulator gets out of adjustment?

D Facilitating transfer
1 Let student know when to expect transfer, its advantages, and the reasons for emphasizing basic concepts and theories
2 Use projects, experiments, problems, discussions, and leading questions to develop skill in the transfer of the basic theory to practical use
3 Give attention to how the student learns as well as to the results

APPLICATION

Have each student make a short list of the identical elements in two or more related subjects. Have each student state a basic principle and how it can apply to a practical situation. For example, if the hypotenuse of a right triangle is 10 inches, the other two sides will measure 8 and 6 inches. How could this be used in laying out a foundation of a building? Use chalkboard to illustrate.

SUMMARY

The mind is not trained like a muscle. Transfer is important in all training. Teach principles so that they will transfer to practical situations. Evaluate how the student makes use of the principles in his work.

Lesson Plan Format

The Lesson Plan Format[1] as shown below, consists of four color-coded pages. It provides for the recording of informa-tion which will assist the instructor when preparing for and performing the responsibilities of teaching and evaluating students.

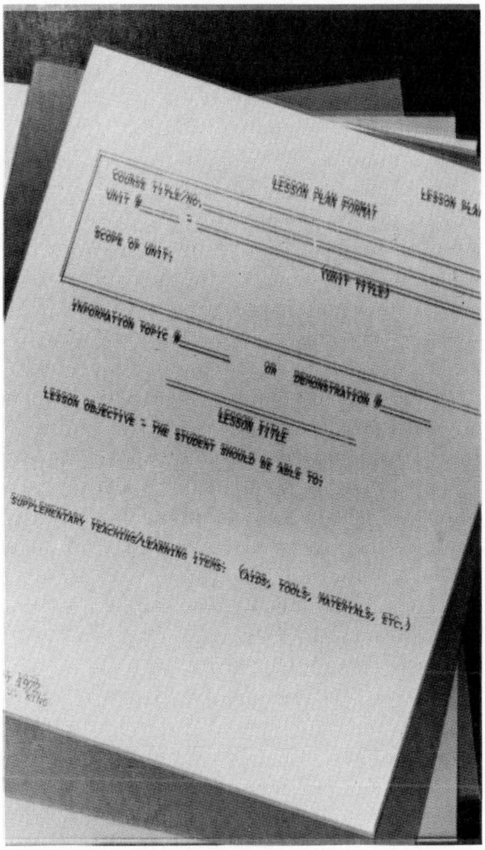

Lesson Plan Format

The development of this Lesson Plan Format was based upon an analysis of common instructional problems. The final specifications for the plan called for a lesson plan that was a complete unit. This meant that it must be comprehensive, usable, reusable, practical, and in a functional form. The placement of each item on the plan was decided by the order of usage.

Providing a space for recording the lesson plan number solved the problem of identifying and keeping plans in a sequential order. Further, by simply numbering a lesson plan the problems of filing, retrieving, and refiling lessons are solved.

Page one of the plan, color-coded white, provides for identifying the course and unit in which a particular lesson will be taught. The instructor may also record the type of lesson to be taught (informational or skill-type) along with the lesson title, objectives and the items needed to supplement the teacher-learning process. The reverse side of page one is utilized to record student information assignments, reference data and space to write an introduction to the lesson.

[1]Copyrighted, 1972, by Dr. F. J. King, Coordinator of Industrial Education, University of Missouri-Columbia. Used by permission. Available from Instructional Materials Laboratory, 8 Industrial Education Building, University of Missouri-Columbia, Columbia, Missouri, 65201.

Page two of an information-type lesson is color-coded yellow. This sheet is used for the instructor to record an outline of the lesson content. If needed, the reverse side of the page may be used to complete the outline.

When a skill-type lesson is taught by the demonstration method, the second page of the plan is color-coded green. The lesson content is recorded as the demonstration will be taught in a step one, two, three sequential order.

The reader should now be aware that the four-page lesson plan format has a yellow second page for informational lessons and the skill-type lesson has a green second page. The other three sheets are identical for each type lesson.

Page three of the plan is color-coded blue. It provides space to write interac-tion items and to record classroom, labo-ratory or other activities the instructor designs to supplement the learning based upon the lesson content.

The fourth and final page of the lesson plan is color-coded pink. This page is for recording the evaluation items designed to gather the evidence which the instructor desires to make a judgment about whether or not the lesson objectives have been accomplished.

Completed lesson plans accumulate to form an important part of a course of study. The instructor should exercise initiative in both preparing the lesson plans and then filing them in notebooks or file drawers with appropriate unit numbers and titles in order to conserve time and effort when preparing for a class presentation.

QUESTIONS AND ASSIGNMENTS

1. What are the reasons for a course of study?
2. How is it related to the analysis?
3. Why do inexperienced instructors need a lesson plan?
4. Why do experienced instructors need a plan?
5. What are the advantages of each instructor preparing his own plan?
6. What is the Teaching Plan for a course?
7. What are some of the things to consider in planning a lesson?
8. What are the major elements of a plan?
9. When would you list the tools, materials, and training aids needed for the plan?
10. What two features are found in the presentation step?
11. What are some characteristics of a good assignment?
12. What are the advantages of using projects in the course of study? Are there any disadvantages?
13. Lay out a short course of study to meet predetermined objectives by: (1) stating the objectives, (2) selecting the knowing and doing content and (3) arranging them in a good learning sequence.
14. Design a project and list the knowing and doing content that can be mastered by the student in completing the project. Can the design be changed to give the best possible emphasis to the content to be learned?
15. Under what conditions would you use an instructional film? A display? An opaque projector? A chalkboard?

Written Instructional Materials

Written materials in a variety of forms are essential to the success of instructional programs. However, like all other aids to learning, they must be carefully prepared or selected and skillfully used if their full value is to be realized. Our objective in this chapter and in Chapter 11 is to describe and illustrate the various types of instructional materials. Common technical and laboratory subjects are used as examples in Chapters 6 and 11. This is done because these subjects are easily understood by a wide range of readers, and because graphic illustrations help to convey the basic concepts of effectively written instructional materials. The use of these examples should not suggest that the concepts are limited to technical and laboratory subjects. Examples are found in all types and levels of instruction. An analytical approach is necessary if we are to use written materials effectively.

Manuals and Textbooks

A good textbook in the hands of the student is, with few exceptions, a basic requirement of every substantial course of instruction. The purpose of a text, however, varies with the nature of the subject and the objectives of the course being taught. In some programs, the main value of the text is to provide general or supplementary background reading; to develop a broad understanding of the subject being studied. In this situation, specific procedures or technical content is taught by the instructor in the shop, classroom, or laboratory using a variety of instructional procedures.

In other courses, the text provides the bulk of the detailed information on the subject for which the students can be held responsible. This leaves the instructor free to illustrate and elaborate on the most important material while in direct contact with the students. This use of a text is, perhaps, most common in college level courses in the less technical areas.

Some texts used in technical instruction are like a set of individual instruction sheets bound in one volume for convenience. Such a text can be of great value to the student for detailed step-by-step guidance, as certain experiments are performed, and skill is developed.

When planning a course of study, the potential value of a book can be judged by how well it presents the procedures and information which are consistent with the objectives and content of the course. An excellent text for one course may be inferior for another. For example, a book on mechanical drawing which provides three different levels of problems for each assignment would, perhaps, be ideal at the secondary school level where there is a need to provide for a wide range of ability in the student group, and yet teach certain fundamentals. In an adult level technical school, with a somewhat more selected or homogeneous group of students, a different type of text would be more suitable.

In selecting a text for a particular course, consideration should be given to all aspects of the course including course objectives, equipment, level of competence of individuals in the group, and type of student activity desired. It seems obvious that in selecting a book, the reputation of the publisher in the field represented by the book and the qualifications of the author should be carefully considered.

Short Articles and Clippings

Written material, in the form of short articles and clippings, is likely to be current, well illustrated, and has potential value in most educational programs. It can be used to reinforce and emphasize the value of skills and knowledge covered in the program, and to provide additional related information of both factual and motivational nature.

Several methods can be used to display or circulate the materials. One way is to use a bulletin board. An attractive, well organized bulletin board, and one that displays only current and useful information, will be noticed. The location of the board is important. Generally, it should be in a clean, well-lighted area, and in one that is relatively free of heavy traffic. The material should be removed when it has served its purpose, and the board should be kept fresh looking and attractive. A little color helps. A system of initialing may be used to assure that the important material is read by each person.

Materials that run to several pages are best circulated by some type of routing slip addressed to each intended reader. In order to keep the material moving, it is usually necessary to set time limits for each reader and to provide a control system to prevent delays in routing. When cost is not a limiting factor, copies for each member of the group should be provided.

Individual Instruction Sheets

Instruction sheets can be described as short, written instructional units which are designed to be used by the individual student when needed. There are advantages in having each unit in sheet or loose leaf form as:

1. Additional sheets may be added, as needed, without disturbing the others.

2. Sheets may be modified, improved and replaced at will, and thus, the course of instruction is more easily kept up-to-date.
3. Sheets may be designed for the most practical use, as determined by the objective and content of the course, and within the limits of equipment, material, and the time schedule.

Instruction sheets have had special significance in programs of practical arts, vocational and technical education for many years. Specialists in the broad field of practical arts, vocational and technical education have reinforced the need for, and use of, individual instructional materials. Special credit is due Fryklund[1] and Emerson[2] for their insights and contributions on the preparation and use of instruction sheets.

With the current increase in both the quality and quantity of text books, individual instruction sheets can be used to best advantage in many courses as supplements to the standard textbooks. Instruction sheets may be used for the following reasons:

1. Methods have been developed or materials marketed after the text was published.
2. Text is too technical for experience level of students. Needs simplifying in certain spots.
3. Text is too general in spots; not specific enough for your purposes.

4. Too much reading required to "dig out" a few essential facts.
5. Desirability of having tables and other "handy" information in a form which can be kept in the student's notebook or tool-kit.

Instruction sheets have greatest potential value when:

1. The instructor cannot spend much time with each student because of class size.
2. There is a considerable time lapse between demonstrations and the related shop and laboratory work. Written materials are useful for individual review of material taught some time previously.
3. Additional work and study is required of the student outside of class.
4. Students must work on a variety of assignments at any one time because of the scheduling of limited equipment or for other reasons.
5. A wide range of ability and experience exists among individuals in the class. Instruction sheets are invaluable in compensating for individual differences.

Instruction sheets, like textbooks, are not normally intended to carry the full load of instruction. They provide a practical means of supplementing and reinforcing instruction which has been given by other means, such as demonstration, lec-

---

[1]Verne C. Fryklund, *Occupational Analysis: Techniques and Procedures* (Milwaukee: Bruce Publishing Co., 1970) Chapter 12.

---

[2]Lynn A. Emerson, *How to Prepare Instructional Manuals.* (New York: State Ed. Dept., 1952), pp. 58–64, 260–303.

TYPES OF INSTRUCTION SHEETS

JOB SHEET
Instruction on how to do a complete task or job. Contains all details needed to complete the job. Based on a list of doing content of the analysis.
Sample titles
1. How to make a drift punch.
2. How to construct a tripod.
3. How to type a manuscript.

OPERATION SHEET
Instruction on how to perform a standard operation. Based on doing content of the analysis.
Sample titles
1. How to turn a taper with taper attachment.
2. How to harden and temper carbon tool steel.
3. How to prepare hard wood for finishing.
4. How to type a footnote.

INFORMATION SHEET
Information related to occupation or subject. Based on knowing content of analysis and is self contained.
Sample titles
1. Types of tool steels.
2. Characteristics of American cabinet woods.
3. Opportunities in the auto repair business.
4. Principles of the gyroscope.

INFORMATIONAL ASSIGNMENT SHEET
Specific instructions regarding the references to be read and studied. Includes study questions and problems.
Sample titles
Titles must be same as those shown for Information Sheet. The Informational Assignment Sheet is not self contained as it refers the student to various resources for the information.

JOB ASSIGNMENT SHEET
A modification of the Job Sheets. Most often used for production and service tasks. Usually contains drawing or diagram, as well as steps of procedure for completing a task or job. It differs primarily from the job sheet in that it is not self contained. The steps of procedure are brief and refer the student to a reference for details of performance.
Sample titles
Titles may be same as those shown for Job Sheet.

Five basic types of instruction sheets.

ture, and conference.

The five basic types of instruction sheets (operation, information, job sheet, job assignment and informational assignment) are consistent with the analysis method, and are directly related to it. Each type will be discussed briefly.

Operation Sheets

This type of sheet is based on a doing, or performance, element of the analysis. The title of the operation sheet should match that of the corresponding doing, or performance, element.

An operation sheet provides step-by-step instructions for performing the unit along with brief explanations as needed; it is usually provided with graphic or pictorial illustrations. As you will want to use readily available printed material and not attempt to write all of your own operation sheets, your main concern will be to identify usable materials in any form and organize them to facilitate their use. One way is to place the title of each doing, or performance, element on a card, after which the appropriate references are listed by page number. From this

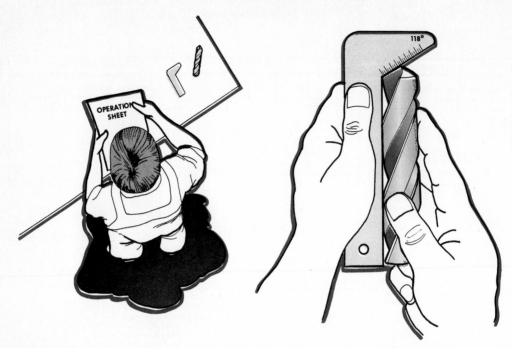

Operation sheets give step by step instructions with illustrations. Shown above is: Step 1: Measure the angle of the drill point.

organization of resources, you can draw content to prepare an operation sheet, or refer a student to the performance element, or operation, that already exists in a text book or reference. Examples are shown on pages 101 and 102.

The student using an operation sheet must perform each step before going to the next. In contrast with an information sheet, operation sheets require the use of tools, equipment, and materials. Appropriate checks and standards should be included so that students know when they have performed each step properly. Normally an operation sheet should contain the following elements:

1. Title—to properly identify the procedure on which the sheet is based.
2. Introduction—to describe the procedure and how it is used on the job.
3. Tools and materials—a list of the tools, equipment, and materials needed to perform the operation.
4. Steps of procedure—a list of the steps of procedure with pictorial illustrations and very brief written explanations of how to perform each step, including notes on safety.
5. Performance checks and/or standards—to let the student know how he is progressing.
6. Questions—to direct the student's attention to the key points and basic concepts behind the specific steps of procedure. This has important transfer of training value.
7. References—a list of sources of further information. May include other instruction sheets as well as textbook material.

OPERATION SHEET

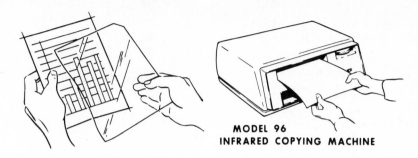

MODEL 96
INFRARED COPYING MACHINE

3M BRAND INFRARED TRANSPARENCY FILMS

TYPE NO.	DESCRIPTION	CHARACTERISTICS	OPERATING TIPS
125	Heavyweight. Positive - clear background.	Etched white image. Image can be colored with 3M Brand coloring pencil. Excellent overlay film.	Expose 1-2 numbers slower than Type 11 Standard Buff. Under-expose if you intend to add color. Over-exposure will result in curling or buckling.
127	Heavyweight. Positive - clear background.	Black image. Easily read on projector stage. Good lay-flat quality. Excellent diazo master or master for 3M Brand Type 131 color positive.	Expose 1-2 numbers slower than Type 11 Standard Buff. Over-exposure results in letters filling in.
129	Medium weight. Positive- tinted background. Available in red, blue, green and yellow.	Similar to Type 127 but tinted back- ground. For change of pace and easy reading on projector stage.	Same as Type 127.
133	Medium weight. Positive - clear background.	Black image similar to Type 127. Available in economy 500-sheet pack only.	Expose 1 number faster than Type 11 Standard Buff. Over-exposure makes image appear dotted with pinholes.
128	Heavyweight. Negative. Available in silver, red, blue, green and yellow.	Clear or colored image on a dark background. Excellent for "impact" situations.	Expose 3 numbers slower than Type 11 Standard Buff. Type 720 colored adhe- sive on silver makes multicolor negative.

HOW TO MAKE TRANSPARENCIES
FOR THE OVERHEAD PROJECTOR WITH 3-M BRAND INFRARED FILMS*

The originals to be copied by this method must be compatible with the in- frared process. Black printers ink, graphite pencil (No. 2 is best), carbon containing typewriter ribbon, and india ink are suitable image materials.

Infrared films may be developed in about four seconds on infrared copy machines. The films remain dry.

PROCEDURE

1. Place the film on top of the original to be copied.

2. Set dial of machine at the appropriate position for the type of film being used. Suggested dial setting are shown in the chart at the end of this sheet.

Note: The cut corner of film, must be in upper right hand corner as shown here. Material on reverse side of original is not copied.

3. Pass film and original through the machine with film up.

*Adapted from manufacturers instructions. Minnesota Mining and Manufacturing Company.

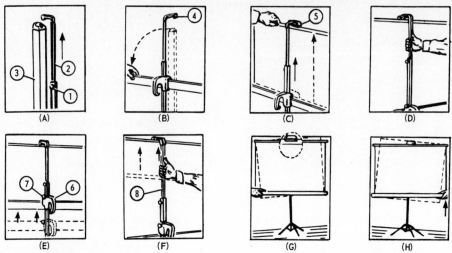

(A) (B) (C) (D)

(E) (F) (G) (H)

TO SET SCREEN UP

1. Open the legs of tripod. Grasp the unit firmly just above the handle and raise the unit slightly off the floor. Pull out on one leg and push the leg assembly downward, this will position all three legs to support the unit.

2. Swing case into position. Grasp the extension rod, item 2 in example (A), with your right hand and with the left hand pull out on the upper plunger button, item 1. Raise the extension rod to the next hole. Swing the case, item 3, to a horizontal position as shown in example (B).

3. Extend and fasten screen. Lower the extension rod as far as possible. Pull the screen out of the case and place the screen leveler, item 5, example (C), over the hanger hook, item 4, example (B). Now raise the extension rod until the screen is fully extended as shown in example (D).

4. Set screen height. Grasp the handle, item 6, example (E) with your right hand and with the left hand pull out the plunger button item 7, on the handle and set the screen case to the desired height. Raise or lower the extension rod as shown in example (F).

5. Level the screen to desired height. If the floor is uneven, level the screen by pushing up on either side of the screen as shown in examples (G) and (H).

TO TAKE SCREEN DOWN

1. Adjust height of case, to the second positioning hole from the top of the extension rod, item 2.

2. Lower the extension rod, as far as it will go.

3. Remove the screen leveler from the hanger hook, item 4, and slowly roll the screen back into its case.

4. Swing the screen case to a vertical position.

5. Raise the extension rod until the hanger hook is above the end of the screen case, then lower it until it engages into the end cap.

6. Close the legs of the tripod.

Information Sheets

This type of sheet is directly related to the knowing, or related information, content of the analysis. The title of the sheet is usually the same as the knowledge element on which it is based. For practice, you may wish to prepare some information sheets. On basic topics it is less time consuming to use material available in textbook or other written form. (Copyrighted material, however, should be used in its original form. It is a violation of copyright laws to reproduce or copy such material without permission from the publisher.) The system of using cards to identify sources of information as suggested for operation sheets is recommended. An information sheet should contain the following elements:

1. Title—from the analysis or appropriate to the content covered.

2. Introduction—a brief description of the content, its value to the learner, and a sentence or two to create interest.

3. The body—information the student must know, in paragraph form, and with graphic illustrations where needed.

4. Questions—a few questions should be included to cause the student to read carefully and mentally apply the information presented.

5. References—since a good information sheet is usually in condensed form, references to the material in more detail are often desirable.

These are the characteristics of a good information sheet:

1. Does not deal with material which is adequately covered in available texts.

Information sheets give information the student must know. Above: Add acid to water, NOT water to acid.

INFORMATION SHEET FOR THE SEQUENCE OF INSTRUCTION ON A COMPLEX JOB OR TASK

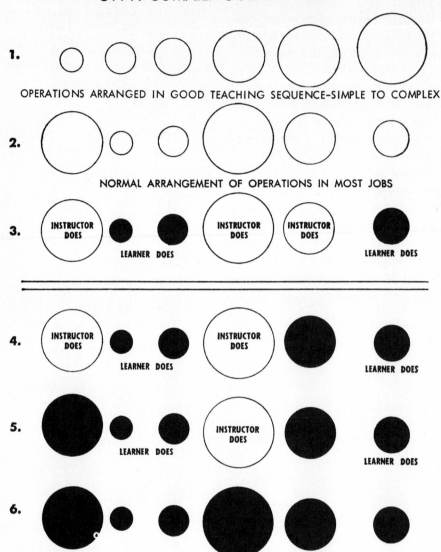

1.

OPERATIONS ARRANGED IN GOOD TEACHING SEQUENCE—SIMPLE TO COMPLEX

2.

NORMAL ARRANGEMENT OF OPERATIONS IN MOST JOBS

3. INSTRUCTOR DOES   LEARNER DOES   INSTRUCTOR DOES   INSTRUCTOR DOES   LEARNER DOES

4. INSTRUCTOR DOES   LEARNER DOES   INSTRUCTOR DOES   LEARNER DOES

5.   LEARNER DOES   INSTRUCTOR DOES   LEARNER DOES

6.

LEARNER DOES ALL OPERATIONS—SUPERVISOR CHECKS CLOSELY

If a job can be taught by proceeding from the easy steps to the difficult, teaching becomes easier. Few jobs, however, have their working sequence arranged in an order of increasing difficulty as shown at the top of the chart. Instead, the difficult parts of the job are usually mixed in with the easy ones, like the second line on the chart. These steps have to be done on the job in the correct order, and therefore, they should be learned in that order. What can the supervisor-instructor do? He can keep the job in proper sequence and still teach the easier parts first by setting up his teaching plan as shown by the dark spots in each row of the chart. The instructor does the difficult or white spots while the worker does the easy or black spots, thus maintaining a learning sequence even in a difficult or long operation—U.S. Air Force

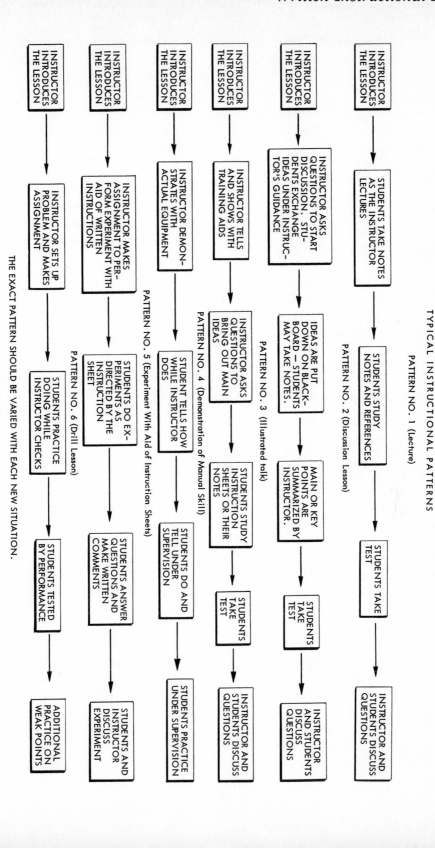

TYPICAL INSTRUCTIONAL PATTERNS

PATTERN NO. 1 (Lecture)

INSTRUCTOR INTRODUCES THE LESSON → STUDENTS TAKE NOTES AS THE INSTRUCTOR LECTURES → STUDENTS STUDY NOTES AND REFERENCES → STUDENTS TAKE TEST → INSTRUCTOR AND STUDENTS DISCUSS QUESTIONS

PATTERN NO. 2 (Discussion Lesson)

INSTRUCTOR INTRODUCES THE LESSON → INSTRUCTOR ASKS QUESTIONS TO START DISCUSSION, STUDENTS EXCHANGE IDEAS UNDER INSTRUCTOR'S GUIDANCE → IDEAS ARE PUT DOWN ON BLACKBOARD—STUDENTS MAY TAKE NOTES. → MAIN OR KEY POINTS ARE SUMMARIZED BY INSTRUCTOR. → STUDENTS TAKE TEST → INSTRUCTOR AND STUDENTS DISCUSS QUESTIONS

PATTERN NO. 3 (Illustrated talk)

INSTRUCTOR INTRODUCES THE LESSON → INSTRUCTOR TELLS AND SHOWS WITH TRAINING AIDS → INSTRUCTOR ASKS QUESTIONS TO BRING OUT MAIN IDEAS → STUDENTS STUDY INSTRUCTION SHEETS OR THEIR NOTES → STUDENTS TAKE TEST → INSTRUCTOR AND STUDENTS DISCUSS QUESTIONS

PATTERN NO. 4 (Demonstration of Manual Skill)

INSTRUCTOR INTRODUCES THE LESSON → INSTRUCTOR DEMONSTRATES WITH ACTUAL EQUIPMENT → STUDENT TELLS HOW WHILE INSTRUCTOR DOES → STUDENTS DO AND TELL UNDER SUPERVISION → STUDENTS PRACTICE UNDER SUPERVISION

PATTERN NO. 5 (Experiment With Aid of Instruction Sheets)

INSTRUCTOR INTRODUCES THE LESSON → INSTRUCTOR MAKES ASSIGNMENT TO PERFORM EXPERIMENT WITH AID OF WRITTEN INSTRUCTIONS → STUDENTS DO EXPERIMENTS AS DIRECTED BY THE INSTRUCTION SHEET → STUDENTS ANSWER QUESTIONS AND MAKE WRITTEN COMMENTS → STUDENTS AND INSTRUCTOR DISCUSS EXPERIMENT

PATTERN NO. 6 (Drill Lesson)

INSTRUCTOR INTRODUCES THE LESSON → INSTRUCTOR SETS UP PROBLEM AND MAKES ASSIGNMENT → STUDENTS PRACTICE DOING WHILE INSTRUCTOR CHECKS → STUDENTS TESTED BY PERFORMANCE → ADDITIONAL PRACTICE ON WEAK POINTS

THE EXACT PATTERN SHOULD BE VARIED WITH EACH NEW SITUATION.

A typical job sheet.

2. Well organized. Presents material in a smooth and progressive manner.
3. Uses common words, simple sentences with easily read paragraphs. Covers only a few ideas, but does it thoroughly.
4. Asks questions occasionally to stimulate thought and to check on understanding.
5. Uses good analogies; ties new content to former experiences.
6. Uses diagrams, drawings, illustrations.
7. Is technically correct.
8. Underlines or CAPITALIZES safety points and other important words and items.
9. Is not too lengthy.

Job and Job Assignment Sheets

There is some confusion in these terms because they have frequently been used to include all types of instruction sheets. The backbone of a true *job sheet,* however is a list of the doing or performance elements required to complete a specific task. The doing content of an analysis can be organized in any way to indicate the steps necessary for a larger task (each element, or operation, then becomes a step). A list of doing elements (also referred to as operations) necessary to build a small tool box is given in Chapter 5, page 78. This list of doing elements supplemented by the drawing, a bill of materials and the detailed procedural information needed by the student or trainee, becomes a job sheet.

Job sheets are frequently prepared by the instructor in the early stages of the instructional program. In later stages students and trainees who have developed competence with the doing, or performance, elements are required to plan their own job sheets. This is essentially what they must be able to do on the job, although not necessarily in detailed written form. A job sheet contains the following elements:

1. Title—to properly identify the job, or task, on which the sheet is based.
2. Introduction—a description of the job, or task, what it includes, and why it is to be done.
3. Tools and materials—a list of tools and materials needed for the entire job, or task.
4. Blueprints, drawings, photographs, and sketches to set standards for the completed job.
5. Procedure—a list of the operations, or doing elements, in their proper order with sufficient detail to permit performance.

In recent years, with the development of excellent references in most fields, the job sheet is seldom used in its "pure" form, but rather, it is modified by refering the learner to the proper operation sheets and related references as needed. Job sheets consist of several major steps, each one of which may be the subject of a single operation sheet, or be covered in more detail in the text. A specific operation sheet may represent a single step in several different job sheets. A reference to the appropriate operation sheets and pages of the text may be included after each operation, or doing element. This modification is referred to as a *job assignment sheet*. A typical job sheet including a number of basic operations, is shown on page 107.

HOW TO MAKE FLANNEL BOARDS AND FLANNEL GRAPHICS

A satisfactory board for use can be designed and easily constructed from common and inexpensive materials.

Materials Required:

1. Sheet of 1/4" plywood or composition-type board about 34" x 46" or larger
2. Sheet of flannel material 36" x 48" (must be two inches larger than board in both directions).
3. Rubber cement.
4. Stapler

The flannel material may be felt or any cotton flannel. The type of material used for quilt backing is satisfactory and is generally available.

Steps in making a flannel board:

1. Spread rubber cement over the entire surface of the plywood.
2. Place the flannel over the cemented board, smooth, and press down. Make sure that the flannel overlaps the board on all four sides.
3. Bend overlap on to the back side of the board and staple in place.

Flannel graphics can be made using show card board or any stiff cardboard. Flocked paper with adhesive backing to adhere to the cards can be purchased from school supply houses. As an alternative procedure, flocking material can be sprayed on the cards. A description of this method follows:

Materials Required:

Flannel board cards
Flocking (in tube container)
Clear enamel (in spray can)

Steps in flocking:

1. Spray enamel on back surface of card.
2. Spray flocking over enamel.
3. Spray flocking lightly with enamel to make flock stand up.

The cards may be cut to desired shapes and lettered, using magic markers or any other conventional lettering equipment.

A typical job sheet.

Assignment Sheets

This type of instruction sheet, as the name suggests, gives specific directions as an assignment to the student. It generally refers the learner to a resource and assigns certain pages to be read and problems to work or questions to answer. Assignment sheets are used in application steps of lessons in science subjects, mathematics, and drawing, and for related reading assignments in all studies. They are frequently referred to as informational assignment sheets to distinguish them from the modified job sheet, or job assignment sheet. An assignment sheet should contain these elements:

1. Title—a short statement of what the assignment includes, the amount of time it should take, the value of the assignment to the student and a sentence or two to stimulate interest.
2. Directions—a statement which makes the specific assignment and tells the student exactly what to do. For example: "Read pages 289 through 295 of *Fibers Into Fabrics* by D. D. Martin and answer the following questions."
3. References—others as needed.

Dr. Robert Wooldridge reports that he has used the assignment sheet on page 109 with good results in the development of skill in the use of the architects scale.[3]

Habits of accuracy and neatness are also stressed. The assignment takes about 30 minutes. The results are easy to check by observation or transparent overlay. This type of assignment sheet may also be used as a performance test as described in Chapter 12.

In addition to providing for application and practice, assignment sheets may be used to develop problem solving and creative abilities. A good example of this use of an assignment sheet prepared by Edward H. Conway is shown on page 110.[4] (See also pages 111 and 112.)

Combined Sheets

Instructional content suitable for information, operation, and assignment sheets are often combined. This is a practical approach when the information contained on the sheet is related to only one operation in the course. When material for an information sheet is related to several operations and assignments a separate information sheet is more suitable. An example of a combined sheet is shown on pages 113, 114, and 115.[5]

Instruction Sheets Aid Scheduling

Operation, job, and assignment sheets have a unique and important use when it is necessary or desirable to provide for flexibility in scheduling tools and equipment. The job sheets on the following pages illustrate this principle. (To save space only the first job sheet is reproduced in full.) Here waiting lines for tools and equipment were avoided by scheduling

---

[3]Published in *School Shop,* March 1965. p. 25.

---

[4]Published in *Industrial Arts and Vocational Education,* LIII, June, 1964.

---

[5]Joseph S. Umowski, *Ferrous Metallurgy Laboratory Manual* (Chicago: American Technical Society), pp. 9ff.

ASSIGNMENT SHEET

An Exercise in Measuring with the Architect's Scale

Directions: Read these instructions carefully and follow them exactly. Do step No. 1 first, then No. 2, and so on in succession. All lines are connected to form a continuous line. You will need a T-square, 45° triangle, scale, 2-H pencil, and one sheet of bond white paper (typing).

First: Fasten paper to drawing board and then establish a point 1″ down and 1″ to the right of the upper left-hand corner of the paper. Make *NO* border line. After this point is established, draw a continuous line according to the following directions:

Step	Scale	Length	Direction
1	¼″ = 1′ − 0″	27′ − 6″	Horizontal
2	1″ = 1″	6 13/16″	Vertical (down)
3	¾″ = 1′ − 0″	9′ − 6½″	Horizontal (left)
4	1½″ = 1′ − 0″	4′ − 3¼″	Vertical (up)
5	¼″ = 1′ − 0″	25′ − 10″	Horizontal (right)
6	¾″ = 1′ − 0″	6′ − 9″	Vertical (down)
7	1″ = 1′ − 0″	5′ − ¾″	Horizontal (left)
8	⅛″ = 1′ − 0″	30′ − 8″	Vertical (up)
9	½″ = 1′ − 0″	7′ − 9½″	Horizontal (right)
10	3/16″ = 1′ − 0″	15′ − 5″	Vertical (down)
11	3″ = 1′ − 0″	1′ − 1½″	Horizontal (left)
12	⅜″ = 1′ − 0″	6′ − 11″	Vertical (up)
13	½″ = 1′ − 0″	4′ − 9″	Horizontal (right)
14	1″ = 1′ − 0″	2′ − ¾″	Vertical (down)
15	3/32″ = 1′ − 0″	60′ − 0″	At 45° slanting upward toward the starting point

When completed, the last line should connect with the starting point; the series of lines should look like the drawing appearing at left, which has been reduced considerably for reproduction here.

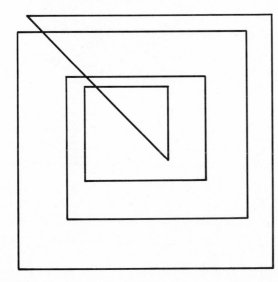

This assignment sheet for mechanical drawing has the advantage that it not only tests the student's skill but it is also self-checking
—School Shop

DESIGN ASSIGNMENT: To Design a Circle Scriber

The instrument must: (1) draw a circle of 5 ft.; (2) hold a pencil; (3) be adjustable; (4) have aesthetic appeal; (5) be made in school shop with as many purchasable items as desired.

The solution to the problem must be on a 12 by 18 sheet of vellum. It must include (1) a detail drawing and dimensions of each specially made part, (2) an isometric showing the assembled tool, (3) a title block and parts lists, and (4) an area for notes describing special operations.

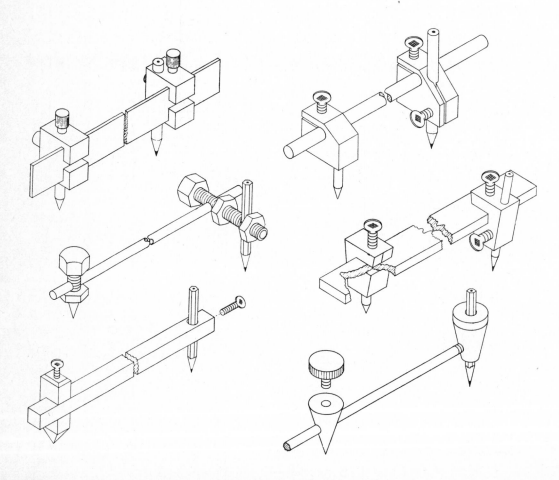

ASSIGNMENT SHEETS

ON-THE-JOB TRAINING TECHNIQUES COURSE

ASSIGNMENT #1

List the on-the-job training tasks that may be a part of a supervisor's job.

Be as specific as possible. Do not include what he must <u>know</u>, only what he must be able to <u>do</u>.

It is anticipated that you will list not less than 12 specific tasks.

Number each task as you list it.

Example:

\# _____ Interview employees

to obtain information on

training needs.

ON-THE-JOB TRAINING TECHNIQUES COURSE

ASSIGNMENT #2

Combine your list of tasks from Assignment 1 with the attached Master List as follows:

For each task listed by you that is essentially the same as one on the Master List, place the number of your task item to the left of the appropriate item on the Master List.

If one of the tasks on your list is a part of one of the Master List tasks, write your task under that Master List task.

At the end of the Master List, add those tasks from your list which you feel should be included to complete list of on-the-job training tasks.

ON-THE-JOB TRAINING

MASTER LIST

What the supervisor must be able to do:

_____ 1. Make an operation analysis including a detailed list of skills and knowledges required in each job under his supervision.

_____ 2. Assess the present performance and ability of employees and identify training needs in terms of specific skills and knowledges.

_____ 3. Determine the most effective and economical methods and techniques for providing required training.

_____ 4. Prepare plans and schedules for providing required training.

_____ 5. Obtain and organize training materials including texts, instruction sheets, training aids, and special equipment.

_____ 6. Implement training plans through direct instruction, motivation, and leadership.

_____ 7. Give demonstrations for the purpose of instruction and setting performance standards and to assure the use of safe procedures.

_____ 8. Provide for participation of those supervised in planning and organizing the work to be done.

_____ 9. Develop sound human relations and good communications with workers.

_____ 10. Evaluate workers' performance and progress toward the development of required ability.

Add items from your analysis that can not be included in one or more of the above.

SAMPLE ASSIGNMENT SHEET

TOPIC 2—SHRINKING

Assignment : 1. Sargent, Sheet Metal Repair, pp. 109-136.
2. Venk, Collision Work, pp. 157-162.

Introduction

- Can metal be shrunk and stretched like knitted wool?
- Can steel be shrunk without using heat?
- Must a furnace or oven be used for hot-shrinking large panels?
- What is quenching? What effect has it?
- Is shrinking done by heat alone?

Hot shrinking is the process of restoring stretched metal to its original form by controlled heat and proper dinging. This process is used when stretched metal cannot be worked back into shape by hammering alone.

Metal is usually stretched as a result of an accident, but occasionally it is purposely stretched by the repairman. Often he finds that it is easier to bring a badly damaged fender into shape by stretching the metal. At times, however, he accidentally stretches the metal through his carelessness or because he does not know the fundamentals of metal straightening.

Quenching is a part of the hot shrinking process. It consists of rapidly cooling the heated metal by the application of water, usually by means of a sponge.

Checkup

It is best to do most or all of the shrinking before the roughing-out process.	1.	T	F
Never quench a red hot spot.	2.	T	F
Whenever a panel is stretched by damage, both length and width will be increased.	3.	T	F
A perfect hot-shrink is always possible on a hood panel because of its low-crown contour.	4.	T	F
Shrinking over a pry rod is a very slow operation because it is done to close tolerances.	5.	T	F

A(n) __6__ __7__ should be used for heating stretched metal.

The hot-shrinkage process does not w̶ ...

__8__ .   ...tched condition   13. _____

Stretched m̶ ...

... too great a degree will have a gathering ... on the __14__ surface.   14. _____

In one method of cold shrinking a dolly is used to make a(n) __15__ through the stretched area.   15. _____

From blue color temperature to bright red, the softening effect of heat is proportional to the __16__ in temperature.   16. _____

UNIT I: PHYSICAL TESTING

Spark Testing

> **OBJECTIVES** To identify steels and chemical elements present in steels by visual examination of a spark stream.

INFORMATION

The spark test is used in the identification of steels and certain elements in them by a visual examination of the sparks that are thrown off when a piece of steel is held against a high speed grinding wheel. Identification depends upon the experience and judgment of the observer, and thus cannot be expected to give the results that may be obtained in a chemical analysis. Spark testing is, however, a fast, convenient, economical method, and gives fairly reliable and accurate results within its limitations.

When any type of iron or steel is held against a grinding wheel (see Fig. 1), small particles heated to red or yellow are released from the metal and thrown out into the air. Upon contact with the oxygen of the air they burn. The presence of carbon in the

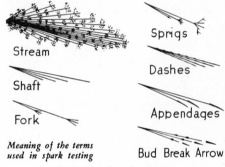

Meaning of the terms used in spark testing

Fig. 2. Typical spark test terms.

particles produces a rapid burning, resulting in a bursting of the particles.

For different steels, spark bursts vary in intensity, size, number, shape, and distance from the wheel at which they occur. Fig. 2 shows typical spark patterns. The burst is the characteristic spark of carbon. Low carbon steels show a sparkler effect of bursts on long shafts. Medium carbon steels show pronounced bursting. As the carbon content increases from a low to a high percentage, the intensity of the bursting increases.

Alloying elements have an influence on the spark picture. Different alloy steels of approximately the same carbon content are more difficult to distinguish, especially when the pressure on the wheel is too great. The best way to master this method of identification is to obtain a set of known samples and become familiar with each spark pattern. By

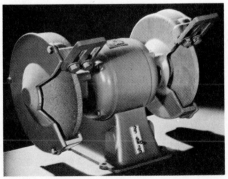

Buehler Ltd.

Fig. 1. Two wheel grinder for spark testing.

comparing the spark pattern of the unknown with the known steel, fairly accurate identification is possible.

REFERENCES A.S.M. Handbook, Spark Testing Chart, metallurgy library references, A.S.T.M. standards.

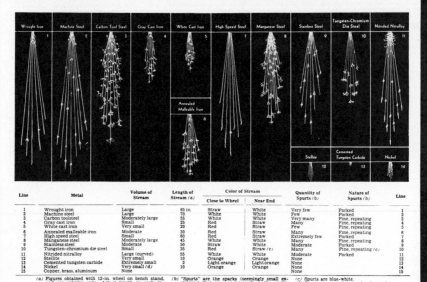

Line	Metal	Volume of Stream	Length of Stream (a)	Color of Stream		Quantity of Spurts (b)	Nature of Spurts (b)	Line
				Close to Wheel	Near End			
1	Wrought iron	Large	65 in.	Straw	White	Very few	Forked	1
2	Machine steel	Large	70	White	White	Few	Forked	2
3	Carbon toolsteel	Moderately large	55	White	White	Very many	Fine, repeating	3
4	Gray cast iron	Small	25	Red	Straw	Many	Fine, repeating	4
5	White cast iron	Very small	20	Red	Straw	Few	Fine, repeating	5
6	Annealed malleable iron	Moderate	30	Red	Straw	Many	Fine, repeating	6
7	High speed steel	Small	60	Red	Straw	Extremely few	Forked	7
8	Manganese steel	Moderately large	45	White	White	Many	Fine, repeating	8
9	Stainless steel	Moderate	50	Straw	White	Moderate	Forked	9
10	Tungsten-chromium die steel	Small	35	Red	Straw (c)	Many	Fine, repeating (c)	10
11	Nitrided nitralloy	Large (curved)	55	White	White	Moderate	Forked	11
12	Stellite	Very small	10	Orange	Orange	None	None	12
13	Cemented tungsten carbide	Extremely small	2	Light orange	Light orange	None	None	13
14	Nickel	Very small (d)	10	Orange	Orange	None	None	14
15	Copper, brass, aluminum	None						15

(a) Figures obtained with 12-in. wheel on bench stand, and are relative only. Actual length in each instance will vary with grinding wheel and pressure.   (b) "Spurts" are the sparks (seemingly small explosions) that occur at intervals on the carrier lines.   (c) Spurts are blue-white.   (d) Some wavy streaks may be observed

American Society for Metals

Fig. 3. Typical spark patterns generated for a variety of metals during spark testing.

MATERIALS, APPARATUS, PROCEDURE

MATERIALS   Selected samples of various types of unknown steels.

APPARATUS   Pedestal grinder
Coded set of spark-test specimens
Protective face shield

PROCEDURE   Obtain a coded set of spark test samples (see Fig. 4) and a number of unknown samples from the instructor. Protect your eyes with goggles or a face shield. Hold one piece of the unknown samples in contact with the grinding wheel and study the spark stream for forks and bursts. To see the spark stream more easily, grind the specimen in subdued light and place a dark colored background below the spark stream.

Grind the coded set in the same manner and select the one with the same spark stream. Recheck the known and the unknown to make sure. Identify the unknown specimen by comparison with the known labeled specimen. Record on the data sheet the number stamped on the unknown with the type of steel stamped on the coded set. Draw a sketch of the spark pattern in the space provided on the data sheets. Be sure to examine the full length of the spark stream.

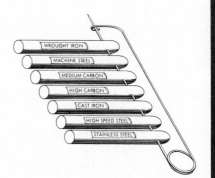

Fig. 4. Coded spark test specimen set.

PREPARATION AND INTERPRETATION OF DATA

DISCUSSION Discuss the spark test method, its use, advantages, theory, causes of the forks and bursts, and its limitations. Refer to Fig. 3 when discussing the matter of limitations.

CONCLUSIONS State your conclusions from the experiences and results of this test, with emphasis on the specific characteristics which identify a particular element in the steel.

FORMAL REPORT Submit a formal report according to the standard procedure for writing reports.

SAFETY List the specific hazards and the corresponding safety precautions necessary to avoid accidental injury in this experiment. Be sure to protect your eyes with goggles or face shield against flying particles. Do not permit others to watch you without these same precautions.

---

the work in three different ways. Each student eventually performed each operation in the job sheet, but the workload on tools and equipment was distributed more evenly throughout the instructional period than would be possible with a single job sheet.

Advantages of Instruction Sheets

1. Can be based on content of the occupational analysis and the course objective and thus provide for an orderly and consistent arrangement of the content for learning.
2. When properly prepared, they are more concise and accurate than oral instruction.
3. Are in permanent form and can be made readily available for review.
4. Reinforce learning and help develop feelings of security and self-reliance in students.
5. Can be based on the major concepts of programed instruction as illustrated in Chapter 11.
6. Permit students to progress at their own rate and thus provide for individual differences in the group.

Assist advanced students to do additional work.

7. Develop the ability and habit of using written instructions of all types.
8. Help to free the instructor of the need to repeat instruction and thus provide more time for special problems.

Some Problems with Instruction Sheets

Ready made sheets which are consistent with the content and organization of the course are frequently not available. This is especially true when the unit involves tools, materials, and equipment.

The preparation of effective written instruction, including graphic illustrations, is difficult for many instructors. Initial costs in terms of instructor time are relatively high. Duplication of the sheets in quantity is often a problem.

It follows that, although individual instruction sheets are of great value, it is not always practical to use them extensively. In some situations only the most key or critical areas of instruction should be covered by instruction sheets.

JOB SHEET AA   **BASIC SHOP PRACTICE**

OBJECT—To make a machinist's tool clamp

STATION No. 1

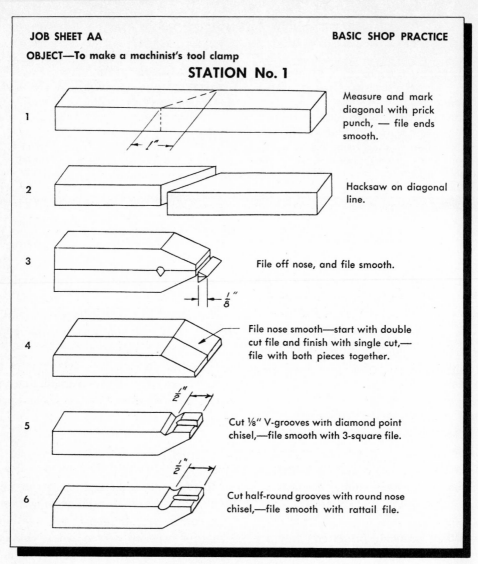

1   Measure and mark diagonal with prick punch, — file ends smooth.

2   Hacksaw on diagonal line.

3   File off nose, and file smooth.

4   File nose smooth—start with double cut file and finish with single cut,— file with both pieces together.

5   Cut ⅛" V-grooves with diamond point chisel,—file smooth with 3-square file.

6   Cut half-round grooves with round nose chisel,—file smooth with rattail file.

STATION No. 2

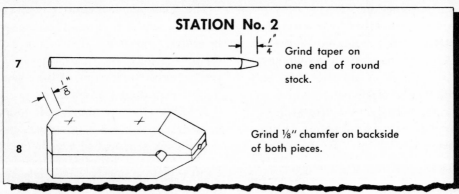

7   Grind taper on one end of round stock.

8   Grind ⅛" chamfer on backside of both pieces.

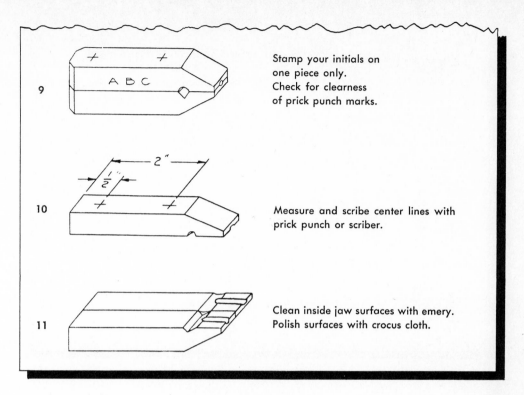

9 Stamp your initials on one piece only. Check for clearness of prick punch marks.

10 Measure and scribe center lines with prick punch or scriber.

11 Clean inside jaw surfaces with emery. Polish surfaces with crocus cloth.

STATION No. 3

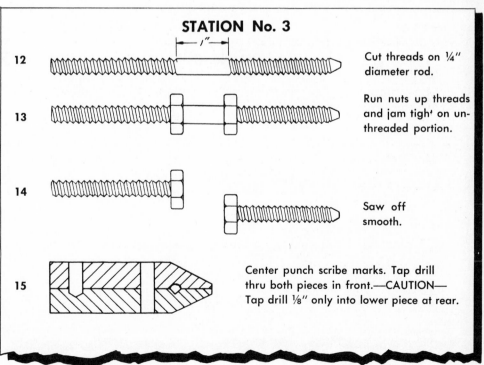

12 Cut threads on ¼″ diameter rod.

13 Run nuts up threads and jam tight on un-threaded portion.

14 Saw off smooth.

15 Center punch scribe marks. Tap drill thru both pieces in front.—CAUTION— Tap drill ⅛″ only into lower piece at rear.

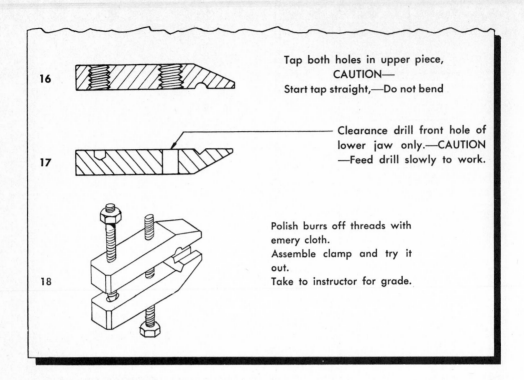

16   Tap both holes in upper piece,
CAUTION—
Start tap straight,—Do not bend

17   Clearance drill front hole of
lower jaw only.—CAUTION
—Feed drill slowly to work.

18   Polish burrs off threads with
emery cloth.
Assemble clamp and try it
out.
Take to instructor for grade.

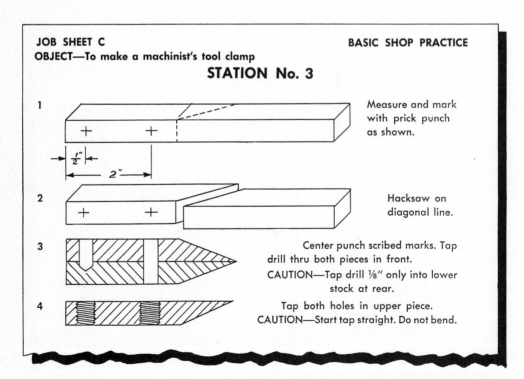

JOB SHEET C   **BASIC SHOP PRACTICE**
OBJECT—To make a machinist's tool clamp

STATION No. 3

1   Measure and mark
with prick punch
as shown.

$\frac{1}{2}$″   2″

2   Hacksaw on
diagonal line.

3   Center punch scribed marks. Tap
drill thru both pieces in front.
CAUTION—Tap drill ⅛″ only into lower
stock at rear.

4   Tap both holes in upper piece.
CAUTION—Start tap straight. Do not bend.

How to use Instruction Sheets

1. Locate instruction sheets or other written material for the unit you plan to teach.
2. Study these sheets to make sure they fit your needs exactly. If they do not, either supplement them with other material or don't use them. You may wish to write a few instruction sheets of your own.
3. Use a reference card on each operation and element of related information to facilitate the use of written materials.
4. Thoroughly explain the procedure for using the sheets. Remember, they only supplement other methods of instruction and do not take the place of the instructor.
5. Refer to specific steps in operation and job sheets while demonstrating, so that students know where to find material for future reference.
6. Make the written materials readily available and refer to them in such a way that students get in the habit of using them properly.

QUESTIONS AND ASSIGNMENTS

1. List the major types of instruction sheets.
2. Make up an assignment sheet to be used with one of the lessons you may teach.
3. Select one of the doing or performance elements of your analysis and develop it into an operation sheet.
4. Prepare an information sheet based on one of the related information items of your analysis.
5. List in the form of a job assignment sheet the operations required for a specific job.
6. Rewrite the procedure part of the combination sheet in Figure 6-16 by listing and numbering the specific steps required.
7. Prepare reference cards on one operation.
8. You wish to provide an employee with a general overview of the subject, and to develop his knowledge of the language and terms used prior to initiating formal instruction. Your objective is for the trainee to learn some facts, get a feel for the subject, and learn some of the terms so that classroom time can be devoted to a discussion of key information and problems. Describe how you might use a written instructional sheet to fill this requirement.
9. You have given a demonstration on an important procedure. You wish to give additional emphasis to related information and to the steps in this procedure. A text including necessary pictures dealing with the procedure is available. This is completely consistent with your demonstration and emphasizes the same key steps. What instructions would you give to a group of students? How should this be done?

10. Your trainees have mastered the information and skills required in a planned on-the-job educational program. This program has been provided under strict time limits which left little time for discussion and for supplementary information. How could written instructional material be used to motivate the trainees and provide them with timely information?

11. The instruction sheets shown in this chapter are from various programs. Rewrite selected sheets from this or other sources to bring them into consistency with elements and standards suggested for each type of sheet. Summarize the changes you have made.

The Lecture, Discussion, and Group Participation Methods

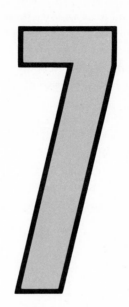

There is some truth in the old saying "telling isn't teaching." Good instruction always provides for two-way communication between instructor and student, and for this reason other methods such as the demonstration, are more effective than the lecture in many situations. Nevertheless, short talks and verbal explanations are common and necessary in all practical instruction.

In this chapter, we will consider ways by which instructors can make the lecture, the discussion and other group participation methods most effective. Even though the methods are presented separately for sake of clarity, it should be emphasized that a variety of methods are used by effective instructors and that one method would seldom be used exclusively during a given class session.

General Factors in Speaking

A good lecture is always tailor-made to the audience. The approach in speaking should vary with the subject matter, the class, and the objective of the presentation.

A common cause of failure in speaking and teaching is the assumption that one can present without preparation if he or she is thoroughly familiar with the subject. The poor speaker may be thinking out loud with his thoughts on the subject and little or no thought given to the audience. To avoid this, careful preparation must be made. This preparation, in addition to study of the subject, calls for the use of a well-organized but flexible plan. The content must be organized to help members of the audience gain a clear understanding of the concepts or ideas being presented. This organization need not and probably should not be the same as the organization of the same content in the textbook, because a speaker can use many techniques not available to the writer. The speaker can take advantage of recent events, various abilities and experiences of members of the group, and the situation in which the presentation is given.

The quality of oral instruction depends upon the instructor's skill in the timely use of effective techniques. Techniques that catch and hold attention, the employment of illustrations to put over a point, the use of stories and humor and change of emphasis by increasing or decreasing the rate of speaking and the loudness of the voice are some of the factors to be considered. Let us look more closely at them.

The Outline

A good outline is extremely useful in keeping you on the subject and in helping you make the best use of your time.

The kind of outline you use should be determined by your objectives for teaching the subject, your knowledge of it, and your students' level of development.

The knowing elements or knowledge content from your analysis provide a guide with respect to the content to cover.

A little humor helps.

However, you will need to make further notes on the specific details to include, and you must give consideration to the method of presenting the subject. It may be helpful to review the section on *Learning by Doing* in Chapter 2.

It is not a good idea to memorize your material word for word. You may want to memorize the first few words of the talk just to get yourself started, but a canned speech is not what your audience wants. Chapter 8 on *Questioning* and Chapter 5 on *Lesson Planning* cover this topic in greater detail.

Catch and Hold Attention

Obviously, students will learn nothing during a talk if their attention is not held. What can we do about it? We should be enthusiastic about the subject. We gain interest through preparation. It is difficult not to be interested in something about which we know a lot, for the more we know about a subject the more uses we

A dull or uninformed instructor cannot hold attention.

can see for it, and the more enthusiastic we become. Without preparation and the resulting interest it is most difficult and often impossible to appear enthusiastic and to hold the students' attention. You earn the right to talk about something through firsthand experience and study; there is no substitute for experience and exact knowledge. Without these, the lecture is a phony. Who wants to listen to or read a book by one who has never done what he is telling us to do?

As with the subject matter, the more we know about the students the more interested we are likely to become. An instructor should learn and use the names of individuals in the group. Individuals should receive credit and recognition for work well done. Much of the pleasure in teaching comes through knowing and understanding individual students.

Use Conversational Style

The instructor should always use a normal conversational approach, not old-fashioned oratory. This calls for clear, simple language and for the logical explanation of ideas without any shouting or arm waving. A conversational approach is the best because it causes the student to forget that there is a teacher, and that he is being taught. It helps to eliminate resentment that occurs when individuals are forced to do something, and it makes it easy for the instructor to develop a friendly, natural relationship with students.

An instructor, or any other speaker, should attempt to judge the reactions of individuals in the group to the presentation. Boredom detected in the audience may indicate a need to use an analogy, to tell a story to illustrate some point in the subject or to switch from the straight lecture to discussion. However, unless you are sure that you can tell that funny story the way it should be told, don't tell it. It isn't necessary to be funny to be a good speaker but, of course, it may help to tell a good story that illustrates a point you are trying to make. The use of charts, posters, and other aids to instruction may also help. If you use charts, be sure that they are large enough and placed so they can be seen. Put them away when they have served their purpose.

Physical Behavior

A speaker's behavior either contributes or detracts. Body movement should be natural—neither too stiff nor too informal. There is no reason to stand with the hands straight down at the sides, but neither is there any reason to wave the arms about in meaningless gestures.

In one class, the instructor looked out of the window while he talked. The subject matter was well prepared and very logically organized. The instructor was able to speak smoothly and appeared to have a great amount of good information. The one bad factor in his talk was his persistence in looking away from the class. This was so pronounced that in changing his view from one side of the room to the other he either looked over the heads of the students or allowed his eyes to follow along the floor as he turned from one side to the other. Although this instructor had complete mastery of the subject, he was not as successful as he might have been because he had no way of estimating the reaction of the students to the presentation. It is much easier to speak effectively if we look at the audience. It may help to select individuals in the class and talk directly to them for short periods of time as is our habit in conversation.

You should place yourself where all can see you. If, by position or movement, it becomes necessary for students sitting behind others to first look on one side and then on the other of the heads in front of them, the distracted individuals are almost certain to give up and daydream.

· Seats should, of course, be arranged properly before the instruction is begun. However, regardless of the seating arrangement, instructors should guard against any movement which may be annoying to members of the class. In general, rather slow natural movements do not distract. Sometimes a few steps to one side or another will help to emphasize definite breaking points in a lecture.

Be sure that all can see you.

Stand tall in front of the class.

Many authors on the subject of speech-making recommend that the speaker stand up as tall as possible. Probably this is a good recommendation because in attempting to stand tall one naturally assumes a better posture and may provide a feeling of confidence and well being. Probably the best advice about movement is to avoid extremes.

We use *gestures* to reinforce our ideas, to point out something, to indicate that we are combining ideas, or to denote that there are other points of view. Gestures help in conveying meaning. A shrug of the shoulders, a glance at the ceiling, or spreading of the arms may convey more meaning than a dozen words. The timing of these gestures is as important as the gestures themselves. It is important not to overemphasize every point in the talk, since this makes it impossible to emphasize the key points successfully.

Mannerisms, on the otherhand, are movements of the body which are repeated without regard to the meaning they might convey. They tend to distract an audience and should be avoided. Such things as playing with coins in one's pocket, leaning over the speaker's stand, or placing the pointer exactly on the center of the toe of the shoe, are examples of mannerisms. Occasionally an instructor should ask someone who is capable of giving a frank opinion to identify mannerisms which are likely to be distracting to an audience.

Movement tends to release tension. At the beginning of a speech it may be advisable to move something, such as a chair or a chart, or to write something on the blackboard. This gives the speaker something to do, and relaxes both mind and muscles.

The facial expression of the speaker plays a part in the delivery. It is not desirable to force a smile unless it seems natural, but it is certainly desirable for an instructor to have a generally pleasant expression and to use other facial expressions when they occur naturally as they do in conversation.

The Voice

Every student in the class should be able to hear without difficulty every word said by the instructor. Here are some suggestions which may be useful to remember:

1. Relax.
2. Vary the volume of your voice with the size of the class and with the conditions under which instruction must be given. Be particularly attentive to this when you give instruction in the open air or in a room which has poor acoustics.
3. Watch the reactions of your students. You can usually tell it if they are having difficulty in hearing. If there is any possibility that the volume of your voice is not satisfactory, ask students at the back of the class if they hear you. In an unusual speaking situation, such as a classroom with a large fan or blower, a good idea is to arrange ahead of time with a person in the back row to signal you when more volume is needed.

The tape recorder is helpful in practicing to lecture. (Ampex Corporation)

4. For most people there is a range of tones which can be made without straining the voice. Whether you normally speak in a high or low pitch is not particularly important. Practice with a tape recorder if possible. Students find it monotonous to listen to the same pitch. The skillful speaker changes his pitch, from low, but audible and confidential, to loud and firm. Practice with a tape recorder may prove helpful.
5. Strive for variety.

Rate of Speaking

An average of approximately 100 to 150 words per minute is considered satisfactory for oral instruction. (Franklin D. Roosevelt spoke about 110 words per minute.) Even though many instructors can speak clearly at a faster rate than 150 words per minute, students ordinarily have insufficient time to think about and understand the ideas expressed if the rate of speaking is increased much above that point. Here are some suggestions to try:

1. Present simple materials at a fairly rapid rate.
2. Speak more slowly when presenting difficult matter.
3. Pause frequently. Give your students a chance to comprehend your remarks and to make any necessary notes.
4. If the time for a particular lesson is decreased, do not merely talk faster in an effort to cover the same material as before. Re-plan the lesson to fit the shortened time.

Articulation

The clarity of spoken words is more important than the production of sounds and syllables. Therefore, you should strive for good articulation each time you address your class. If you have an accent, be sure that students from all parts of the country will be able to understand you. Above all else, speak at a rate and with pronunciation that will enable students to distinguish the words you are using. We suggest:

1. Practice pronouncing each word distinctly and clearly. It may be necessary for you to speak more forcefully and deliberately when instructing a large group than when carrying on a conversation.
2. Be particularly careful in pronouncing words which may not be common to the vocabulary of your students. You will even need to spell out some words or write them on the board.

3. Do not slur or run your words together.

Thinking and Speaking

Before an instructor can express an idea clearly, the idea must first be thoroughly understood. Furthermore, thought must be given to the idea during the preparation stage, as well as during the presentation. The faulty choice of words which makes for weak expression is indicative of inadequate preparation. Some rules to remember are:

1. Use terms which are common to the vocabularies of your students. Consider the educational level of the group. It is better to oversimplify instruction than to run the risk of talking over the heads of your students.
2. Do not try to impress students by using words with which they are not familiar. Your purpose is to express ideas, not to display your vocabulary.
3. Use technical terms when they are essential, but define each new term the first time it is used. Remember, many words have several meanings.
4. Use short sentences for emphasis.
5. Eliminate unnecessary words and phrases.
6. Be specific. Whether your primary objective is to have your students acquire a general understanding or to learn detailed facts, make your statements exact and precise in meaning.

All ideas expressed must bear a positive relationship to the main idea of the lesson. Maintaining this continuity is

Use words according to the learning level of your students.

largely a matter of planning. In the actual presentation the instructor can maintain continuity by making careful transition from one point or sentence to the next. This may be done by using such terms as, however, nevertheless, consequently, furthermore, therefore, then, accordingly, in addition, finally. Do not overwork one word.

In order to make a transition from one phase of a lesson to another, you may introduce the new phase with a statement or two explaining the nature of the next concept to be taught next and also its relationship to the whole lesson. Lead the students directly from the summarizing or concluding statements of the phase just completed to the new content to be taught. Make sure that they follow you.

Use a variety of expressions for introducing the new materials. Avoid the monotonous repetition of such introductory remarks as, "Next we take up the," "Now we go into the."

Remember no verbal description of an object or process can make it possible for the student to reproduce the object or process exactly because words don't include all details. Other means of communicating including pictures, blueprints, tables, and charts are usually required.

Use Correct English

Some otherwise competent instructors fail to realize the far-reaching significance of a few bad speech habits. No one is perfect and most students will not condemn an otherwise skilled instructor who occasionally makes an error in speech. However, the habitual use of grossly bad English is a handicap few instructors can afford.

Suggestions: Ask a friend to tell you about the grammatical mistakes you make and practice the correct wording. Use the tape recorder. Listen carefully to those who have a reputation for speaking well. Consider signing up for some good instruction in speech or communication.

How to Prepare a Short Lecture

1. Identify the exact purpose. This should be specific enough to indicate exactly what you expect to talk about. Consider the knowing element of content from the analysis as the title.
2. Write out the introduction. This may be done in outline form or in full; however, since this is the sales talk for your ideas, it should be planned carefully and as interesting as you can make it. By writing out the introduction you will also set the aim of your lecture in your own mind so that you will be able to plan the major part of the lecture with more confidence.
3. Outline the body of the lecture. Start with the main points, which should seldom exceed ten. List under each of these points those facts and illustrations that will put them over. Always include questions. The outline should be sufficiently detailed to reveal the concepts or ideas to be presented. Some instructors prefer to make the outline very complete and to underline

with colored pencil the key points so that they may be located at a glance.
4. Prepare the summary. List the main points and the basic principles and/or make up questions that will cause the students to think through and use the information which has been presented.

Lecture: Points to Remember

1. Put some enthusiasm in your voice and speak a bit louder than you think is necessary. Use appropriate gestures.
2. Speak to a group as you talk to one person. Be conversational.
3. Use short sentences and simple language. It is more difficult to carry the thought if long sentences are used.
4. Explain new words. They probably seem as simple to you as ABC, but might have no meaning whatever to the student. Avoid using too much of the "short cut" or abbreviated language of the occupation with beginning students.
5. Watch your audience and, at the first sign of fatigue, do something. This may be the time to ask some questions or tell a story to illustrate an idea.
6. Use humor to hold interest. The only restriction here is that your humorous illustrations must add to and not detract from the lesson.
7. Move freely about the front of the room but guard against undesirable habits. There is no objection to the instructor moving about; however, avoid movement without meaning such as playing

Watch your audience to see if you are holding interest. (Delta Air Lines)

with chalk or periodically taking the glasses off and putting them on.

8. Keep eye contact. Look at individuals in the class just as you would look at them during ordinary conversation.

9. Use questions. Without questions, an instructor has no way of knowing if the class is still thinking along with him.

10. Always summarize. We do not learn much by hearing something only once. Repetition is necessary for effective learning. In a summary, the instructor states again the basic principles and main points that have been covered or asks questions to bring out these points through class discussion. The summary is important because it clears up misconceptions, emphasizes the main points and ties them together so that the student has a clearer understanding.

Directed Discussion

Directed discussion is different from the lecture in that the instructor causes the students to provide most of the information. That is, the instructor draws upon the experience of the group, while in the lecture the instructor directly relates ideas and information to students.

In a directed discussion the instructor acts as a conference leader and directs or redirects ideas and information produced by members of the class. Advantages of this method over the lecture are that it stimulates the students to think and tends to produce an informal situation in which learning may be facilitated. Since gaining the respect of the group is a strong desire of each member, the discussion method is far more effective in the development of attitudes.

The directed discussion may be used instead of a lecture whenever the students have some knowledge of the subject being discussed. It has a great advantage

Directed discussion provides for personal contact.

over the lecture in that students participate actively and the instructor can give some individual attention to each student. Personal contact between instructor and students is an essential part of any effective approach to learning.

The discussion method enables the instructor to find out how much the student has learned. The instructor, therefore, is in a position to judge when fuller explanation and review are necessary. Through discussion, the instructor can discover which students are developing good attitudes and making good progress in the subject and which ones need more attention or additional instruction. The directed discussion gives the instructor a chance to evaluate teaching success.

The directed discussion usually requires greater resourcefulness than the lecture because the instructor must allow maximum freedom, yet reach a predetermined goal. During discussion, the instructor must give constant attention to what is said that gives an insight into the level of knowledge and understanding of each student. Instructors must imagine themselves in the position of the learner and try to visualize the problems as they confront the student. Patience must be exercised with those who fail to grasp ideas which seem obvious to the instructor and he must at all times act with fairness and understanding.

The discussion consists of an orderly exchange of ideas with a goal in mind. It is not a "bull session." A good discussion helps to:

1. Arouse interest because the students take part and are challenged to think.

2. Bring out points of view from individuals that are helpful to the group as a whole in understanding the material.
3. Give the instructor valuable ideas as to the progress and ability of individuals in the group.
4. Locate misconceptions and give the instructor an opportunity to correct them and to strengthen teaching effectiveness.
5. Get students and instructor acquainted.

The discussion method is frequently quite effective as an introduction to a lesson. The instructor may start a lesson by asking questions to focus attention on the new content and its importance. Discussion may serve as a quick review with a gradual shift to the need for more information. Since we all learn new things in the light of our past experience, this is a sound technique.

A discussion provides a good means of application. When new content has been presented in a lesson, the instructor should provide ways for the student to apply this material as soon as possible. One way to do this is to start a discussion which causes the student to think through and use facts and principles presented in an earlier part of the lesson. This requires thoughtful preparation on the part of the instructor, but it pays dividends in terms of student progress.

Since students may learn facts and processes as taught in several lessons, without seeing the relationship of these to each other, some means must always be provided to integrate or tie these factors together in the proper relationship. Do not forget about *transfer of training*. A carefully planned discussion,

with leading and challenging questions by the instructor, provides the students an opportunity to grasp the full meaning and to gain deeper insight into concepts and principles presented previously.

Planning a Discussion

1. Decide on the outcome you expect from the discussion. In other words, do you want to find out the level of the students knowledge and understanding, or do you wish to reinforce ideas and concepts through group interaction? Keep your objective clearly in mind all through the advance planning and during the discussion.
2. Plan the introduction as in all other types of lessons.
3. List the main headings of the content to be covered.
4. Under each heading, write challenging questions that will focus attention on the information to be discussed.
5. Estimate the time for each step in the lesson and write this in the margin of the plan. Since a discussion may tend to get off the track, it is necessary for the instructor to set a time limit for each segment of the discussion and to stay on schedule in order to the lesson's objective.
6. List the main parts to be covered in the summary of the discussion. Since many ideas will be presented by the participants in a good discussion, the instructor must plan the summary to emphasize, organize, and tie together the essential points.

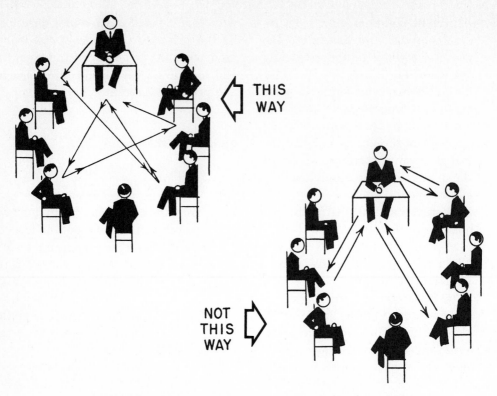

THIS
WAY

NOT
THIS
WAY

A productive discussion is more than a question and answer period.

Teaching through Discussion

Start the discussion. There are several ways to start a discussion. The method you use will depend on the type of content and the background of the students. One of the most practical ways is to announce the topic and indicate that you want each person to express their ideas on the subject. Then ask a challenging question and call on an individual to respond. Since the lead question should be challenging, you will usually get only part of the complete answer. At this point you may draw others in by allowing them to express their opinions.

Guide the discussion. As the discussion progresses, it may run off on a tangent or the students may focus attention on unimportant details of the topic. The instructor must then summarize what has been said and ask a leading question to bring them back on the topic. Should there be a tendency to spend too much time on one part of the lesson, the instructor may summarize what has been said, add a few facts to cover the necessary ground, and then ask another question to bring in the next part of the subject. In this way, the discussion can be kept moving in the proper direction and on the planned time schedule.

Use instructional aids. The chalk-board and the large chart pad are excellent aids to the discussion method. By recording significant facts as they are brought out, the discussion can be guided, the students can see the progress being made, and the proper relationship between facts and ideas can be established.

Summarize the discussion. During the discussion the individuals in the group will have interpreted the comments in their own way and in the light of their own past experience. It is, therefore, necessary that the instructor sum up the ideas discussed and emphasize the key points and their relationship. Do not fail to summarize. If students see that progress has been made and believe that they have taken part in the discussion and have contributed to it, they will tend to be cooperative and helpful in the next lesson.

Six Concepts for Leading a Discussion

1. It is easier to create favorable attitudes toward an idea or project than to change negative attitudes.
2. We are more inclined to accept new ideas from persons whom we respect in the field they represent.
3. We tend to accept ideas when we believe we have contributed to them.
4. We are more likely to accept new ideas which offer immediate and personal rewards. We respond favorably to praise. We tend to accept ideas which add to our prestige.
5. We are less likely to accept a new method if a number of procedures or skills must be mastered before the method can be put to use.

6. We resent being manipulated by selling techniques. Resentment of obvious selling techniques is likely to be strong among well-educated persons.

Other Group Participation Methods

Direct involvement or participation is generally recognized as essential to effective learning and is often referred to as "learning by doing." Participation can be provided in several ways: through discussion and questions, through the application step in a formal lesson, or through techniques which involve individuals as members of groups.

Where our objectives are to develop human relations ability, group participation methods are the most promising. These methods include the use of case studies, role playing and brainstorming.

The Case Study

The case study method makes use of written or recorded anecdotes, films or other media about specific real life problem situations. These presentations provide the essential facts for intelligent discussion of the case.

The group under instruction is asked to study the case, discuss all pertinent aspects, and suggest one or more solutions to the problems. In some situations, the group is divided into two or more smaller groups who attack the problem independently. This provides for competition and a greater range of suggested solutions and can lead to further discussion of the case.

Generally, it is not necessary and at times it is undesirable to have a standard or textbook solution to a problem. The

Direct involvement is important in learning.

objective is to stimulate an analytical approach in solving problems rather than to discover a single correct answer.

Most cases require several pages of case history in order to adequately describe the problem and state the relevant facts. Motion picture films are especially useful in cases used for management and human relations training. The film has an advantage over written materials because the attitudes and behavior of the people in the case come to life and thus the case seems more real. As a result, the group may be more motivated to discuss it.

Here is a very brief case history of a case, *An Instructor Training Problem:*

You are in charge of an instructor training program. The students in the school are skilled craftsmen and journeymen who have been selected to prepare new workers needed by an expanding organization. The course is intended to emphasize on-the-job rather than classroom techniques.

The program is new and only three groups have completed the 30 day training period.

Several students in the present group, all well qualified in their technical specialty, have asked to be taken out of the course and assigned back to their regular jobs.

The men have given plausible reasons for their requests but you suspect there may be other reasons, or at least you want to be sure that the reasons given are valid.

Would you talk with the trainees as a group in order to get at the real reasons? What other methods might you use?

If the real reasons are one or more of the following, what actions should you take?

1. The instructors are failing a high percentage of the trainees because of poor grades on written examinations.
2. Grades based on written examinations are sent back to each trainees' supervisor each week and at the end of the course.
3. Critiques following each role playing or practice teaching session have been severe and even sarcastic with little recognition of the progress and improvement being made.
4. Supervisors under whom the trainees will work when assigned as instructors have indicated that they see no need for training.
5. The instructional personnel in the school fail to "practice what they preach." Although well-qualified on paper, they are not effective instructors.

Role Playing

Role playing requires the participants to act as though they were involved in a real life incident. When skillfully used, the method is effective in giving individu-

als a better understanding of the emotions and behavior of others in similar situations. The method helps some people to better understand their own behavior, and to be more able to respond in a positive way to various human relationship situations.

The role playing approach to instruction is far from simple and may fail unless the stage is set properly. Some participants find it difficult to become deeply involved in the problem and consequently gain little in the way of new insights from the experience. This is especially true when the roles to be played are quite artificial or when the materials are hastily prepared. Many situations can, however, be acted out in such a way as to increase human relations skills.

In one sense, we are using role playing when we set up practice teaching sessions in a teacher education program. There can be no doubt of the value and necessity for this type of role playing for those learning to instruct, as they can try out different techniques and observe the effect they have on learners.

For example, a person acting the role of an instructor could try for motivation in a practice teaching session by giving the students a short test before teaching the lesson. During the discussion which follows the practice lesson, the use of such an approach can be analyzed with benefit to all participants.

In the more typical role playing session, each participant is given a description of the role to be played. This may be done by a written assignment sheet or by an oral briefing of each participant. In either case, the role players are not informed of any role other than their own. With oral briefing all individuals in the class, other than the role players, hear all briefings.

The role players are then brought into contact with each other and play their parts as they develop.

As participants have no previous knowlege of the role other participants are to play, the experience is far from cut and dried and can lead to better insight into one's behavior under stress.

The participants gain practice in listening and in detecting hidden meanings that lie beneath the surface. They may see more clearly the different points of view in most situations.

Participants may also learn that habits of speech or the use of a pet expression have an effect beyond that expected. For example, one supervisor had the habit of saying "for the simple reason that." The supervisor was unaware of the way others reacted to this statement.

In more advanced programs, an analysis of the reasons behind each individual's behavior is made by a qualified psychologist.

Here is a portion of a role playing scene staged in an instructor-student situation:

Instructor: (looking over the shoulder of student draftsman) Bill your dimension lines are too heavy. They should be about one-half the thickness of the lines forming the views.

Bill: I know but I'm trying to get the design worked out; I can clean up the lines later.

Instructor: It's better to keep your drawing clean and all the lines right as you go.

Bill: OK but I can't think about the thing I'm drawing if I have to worry about lines.

Instructor: The ideas are important, but so is the appearance of your drawing. Why don't you work out the idea with free hand sketches first and then draw it carefully.

Bill: I don't have time for that. I have a test in math tomorrow.

Instructor: I think you will find it takes less time to do it my way.

Bill: Maybe, but I don't want to start over now.

Instructor: I'm going to insist that you keep your work clean and. . . .

As each participant plays the assigned role, he becomes more and more involved. Emotions may dominate reason and the resulting actions may be surprising.

A careful analysis of actions and emotions should follow the role playing incident. The net result may give insights not easily available in any other way.

Brainstorming

This technique is useful in some types of problem-solving. It may also be used to obtain cooperation between individuals working in groups. Brainstorming is useful in dealing with human relation problems which do not lend themselves to an easy or obvious solution.

In brainstorming, the group is given a problem and asked to suggest as many solutions as they can in a given time. There is no "at the moment" evaluation of ideas as they are presented. An unusual or unique idea is as welcome as any other. The objective is to stimulate imagination and to encourage creative approaches.

It is recognized that many people are normally inhibited by their desire to conform, or the urge to look "good" in the group. As a result, many truly original and creative ideas are not expressed in groups where status and organization are overriding considerations.

Brainstorming puts the emphasis on the number of different ideas suggested by the group or by competing groups. The

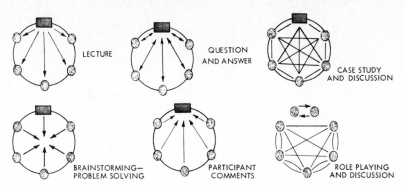

LECTURE

QUESTION
AND ANSWER

CASE STUDY
AND DISCUSSION

BRAINSTORMING—
PROBLEM SOLVING

PARTICIPANT
COMMENTS

ROLE PLAYING
AND DISCUSSION

Typical patterns of group interaction.

value of the approach lies in the participation and stimulation developed and in breaking away from stereotyped thinking.

After all of the suggestions have been recorded, they may be evaluated and grouped into categories for comparison and discussion.

The Instructor's Role in Group Participation

The role of the instructor or leader in group participation is to get every one actively involved in an effective and constructive learning situation. This is a difficult task. The fact that the leader does less talking than with some other types of instruction does not suggest less preparation. Just the opposite is usually the case.

Preparation in depth is necessary if the instructor is to set the stage, develop the problem to be discussed, act to guide the discussion when necessary without being too obvious about it, and to bring the session to a close with an adequate summary and a feeling of accomplish-

ment on the part of the participants. Above all, the instructor must be sensitive to individual responses as well as the feelings and attitudes of the participants.

A Few Suggestions

1. Set the stage. Explain the method to be used and the nature of the problem to be discussed. Use questions to get participants involved from the start. Make sure that everyone understands that the objective is to learn by experience and that no one will be criticized as they experiment with ideas and human relations behavior.

2. Assign the problem and discuss it sufficiently to be sure that it is thoroughly understood.

3. Start the discussion and keep it going. Be prepared to ask a question or suggest another facet of the problem whenever necessary to avoid any situation that tends to cut off free and open discussion. It is important to keep individuals out of too much trouble which may cause them to withdraw from any further participation. This can often be

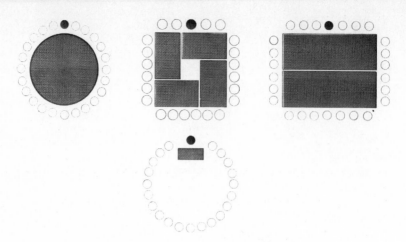

Four seating arrangements that gives each participant a clear view.

accomplished by giving a little credit where needed, by suggesting a short review of what has been said, or by asking a question to draw individuals back into the discussion.

4. Listen and think. Do not become emotionally involved in the problem or do too much talking. The leader's job is to draw out the thoughts and feelings of the group. Try to salvage something out of anything that is said.

5. Summarize the discussion and clear up any misconceptions of fact that may have occurred. This may be done on the chalkboard or by verbal comments and discussion.

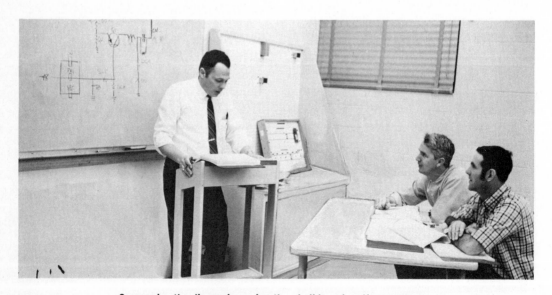

Summarize the discussion using the chalkboard and/or comments.

QUESTIONS AND ASSIGNMENTS

1. What advantage does the speaker have over the writer?
2. What kind of preparation would you make for talking about a new subject?
3. What advantage does the conversational style have over old-fashioned oratory?
4. What are the signs of boredom?
5. Under what conditions would you use the discussion as a method of teaching?
6. What are the advantages of discussion?
7. Why must a discussion leader know a great deal about the subject?
8. What part do questions play in a discussion?
9. How can a discussion leader stay on the time schedule during a discussion?
10. What would you do if a few students wanted to do all of the talking?
11. What would you do if arguments developed during the discussion?
12. Tell how you would use the chalkboard during a discussion.
13. Should students have study assignments before using the conference method?
14. Contrast the lecture method with the discussion method.
15. How may a shy person be encouraged to participate more freely in discussion?
16. Why use the chalkboard or chart pad during conferences?
17. Make an outline of a five minute lecture. If a tape recorder is available give the lecture, listen to it, make changes and record it again.
18. Make your short lecture in front of a mirror to check your physical behavior.
19. With a tape recording, determine your normal rate of speaking. This will help you in planning an oral presentation.
20. Have your recording transcribed and study the sentence structure. Can you say it more clearly in fewer words? Look for errors in English.
21. When would you use a case study in teaching your subject?
22. Prepare a simple case that could be used with your group.
23. When could you use role playing?
24. Prepare the written instructions for two or more parts in a role playing session.
25. List five topics that could be used in brainstorming sessions.

Questioning

8

As a piece of metal is turned in the lathe, certain sounds are made by the cutting action and the metal chips have a predictable color and shape. Through practice the machinist has learned to interpret these signs and to judge, with reasonable accuracy, how well the machine is working. The skilled instructor does something very similar. The expressions on the faces of students are observed; their questions are analyzed as the instructor becomes sensitive to indications of attention and understanding.

Skilled Machinist vs. Skilled Instructor

Both the skilled machinist and the skilled instructor are quick to see when things are not going right. They seldom miss a cue, whether it is the chatter of a piece of stock in the machine or signs of restlessness in a group in the classroom, shop, or laboratory. From time to time, however, the machinist stops the lathe, takes careful measurements with micrometer and rule, and checks the work against the blueprint. An instructor does not have such accurate measuring instruments, but skillful questioning can assess student comprehension with useful accuracy. Questioning students at intervals throughout the lesson is as much a part of the instructor's role as taking measurements is a part of the machinist's. Without careful checking the machinist spoils the job; similarly, the instructor fails to teach.

After each measurement is taken the machinist either continues with the cut or adjusts the machine. If the instructor finds that the students understand the content being presented, then the lesson can be continued or if they do not seem to understand, another teaching technique may be used, content may be repeated or more illustrations may be used.

The machinist makes a final check of the work by taking accurate measurements and checking all dimensions called for by the blueprint. The instructor does much the same thing. Near the end of the lesson, questions are asked which require the use of all the facts, concepts and steps of procedure covered by the complete lesson. Frequently, a written test is given or the students use the newly acquired knowledge on practical work. The chart below summarizes the comparison between the machinist and the instructor.

Questioning is closely related to the directed discussion method of instruction, but the questioning techniques should be used to some extent in all types of lessons. In our discussion of transfer of training in Chapter 2, we emphasize the value of questions. Questioning leads to a more interesting and effective lesson.

Effective Questioning

In spite of all the obvious advantages of questioning, inexperienced teachers and those who are interested primarily in the subject matter are prone to overlook this technique and rely too heavily on one way communication. Such instruction frequently results in exposing the student to the subject without much learning taking place. Perhaps one reason for this failure to use questions is the tendency to think of questions which require only the recall of facts presented. This "echo" approach places undue emphasis on pure memorization of facts. One way to avoid asking questions leading to the mere repeating of facts is to start each question with a word or phrase that calls for thought on the part of the student. Such words as *why, what, how, summarize, justify, trace, describe,* or *define,* tend to encourage thoughtful answers and productive discussions.

THE MACHINIST	THE INSTRUCTOR
Watches the color and shape of the chips, etc.	Watches the expressions on the students' faces.
Stops the work and makes accurate measurements at the proper times throughout the job.	Stops "telling and "showing" at intervals throughout the lesson and asks well planned questions to measure understanding.
Adjusts the machine and makes the next cut.	Repeats those points in the lesson that are not understood or uses other illustrations to help put the point over.
Checks the completed piece against the blueprint to see if it meets specifications.	Asks questions on the whole lesson to see if the students know and understand the facts and procedures.

The machinest and instructor follow similar procedures.

While questioning, we are interested primarily in stimulating the learner to make use of information, to put together facts which may not have been thoroughly understood or assimilated and to draw logical conclusions which become evident when the pertinent facts are interrelated.

The questioning technique is good if it is done at the right time, causes the student to learn by thinking and doing, and changes the student's role from passive listening or watching to thinking and applying while listening and watching.

Skillful questioning, like any other teaching technique, can be learned by any creative person. In planning for the effective use of questions we need to consider the characteristics of good questions, the types of questions that may be employed for different purposes, and the techniques of using questions.

We can divide questions into two main groups: (1) factual or recall, and (2) problem or application.

Factual questions are used to determine whether the student can remember or at least recognize certain specific facts. Problem or application questions cause the student to apply facts and principles in the solution of problems.

Factual Questions

Skill in the application of facts and principles is, of course, more significant than the memorization of facts. However, some factual questions are appropriate at any phase of the instructional program, especially if they are based on important elements that are used frequently. Factual questions are more common than others because they are much easier to ask, and it is much easier to decide whether the answer is right or wrong.

The following questions illustrate the factual type of question:

1. How many poles does a magnet have?
2. In an open electrical circuit how much power is consumed?
3. What are two systems of shorthand?
4. What American woods are used most commonly for high grade cabinet work?
5. For what type of material is the opaque projector used?
6. List three methods of learning.

Also note questions 1 through 4 at the end of this chapter.

Problem and Application Questions

Problem and application questions cause the student to use or apply information. The question may set up a problem involving a number of factors and perhaps some variable elements. This type of question challenges the student to make a sound application of knowledge to specific problems. The principles of *learning by doing* and *transfer of training* are used in questions of this type. Here are some examples:

1. You want to build a transformer to step down 440 volts to 110 volts. If 2,080 turns are used on the secondary coil, how many turns will be used on the primary coil?
2. In drawer construction, the bottom is usually held in grooves on the front and two sides but fastened with one or two small nails to the bottom of the back piece of the drawer. From your knowledge of how wood swells or shrinks with

moisture changes what was the original reason for this design? With plywood or hardboard bottoms is there still a good reason for the use of this construction at times? What is the reason?

3. We have said that one theory of transfer of training is that the learning of elements in one subject that are identical with elements in a second subject will help us learn the second subject. There is a similarity between the cutting action of a radial woodworking saw and the cutting action of a slitting saw on a milling machine. To what extent would we expect transfer of training from one to the other? What important differences exist between the two processes? Is there a possibility of some negative transfer? Explain.

Leading Questions

Factual or recall as well as problem and application questions can be used to assist the student in thinking through to the right answer. The instructor will occasionally notice that a student is groping for an answer to a question when it is known that the student has already learned the information necessary for the correct answer. In this case, the instructor may ask additional questions, using key terms or phrases to remind the student of this information. These are called *leading questions.* Here is an example:

Instructor: In using a T-square and drawing board, we only use one edge of the board. Why is this important?

Student: We use the T-square for horizontal lines, but we use a triangle on the T-square to draw vertical lines.

Instructor: In other words, we have no need to use more than one edge of the board. Suppose we wanted to draw a series of long vertical lines. Would it not be easier to use the top

WHY DO WE USE ONLY ONE EDGE OF THE DRAWING BOARD WHEN USING THE T-SQUARE?

Leading questions stimulate the student to communicate information.

edge of the board to guide the T-square?

Student: Yes.

Instructor: Do we know that the left edge and the top edge are exactly at 90° to each other?

Student: They seem to be but I'm not sure. I'm not sure either whether the head of the T-square and its blade are exactly at 90° to each other.

Instructor: If we use only one edge of the board is it important that the T-square head and blade be at exactly 90° to each other? Suppose they are at 91°?

Student: No, because the triangle will assure us that vertical lines will be at 90° with the horizontal lines.

Instructor: What would be the result if we draw lines from the left edge and also from the top edge of a board that is not exactly square?

Student: Vertical lines and horizontal lines would not be at exactly 90° angles to each other.

Instructor: And that's the reason for not using the left edge and the top edge for accurate drawings.

The metal working instructor might say to the student learning to operate a metal lathe, "What effect does friction have on temperature? All right, what does temperature do to the size of the stock held between centers of the lathe? Will that increase the pressure on the lathe centers? Now what is the total effect on the lathe centers because of the heat generated by the cutting action? How can you prevent burning the centers?" Such a series of questions, although suggesting the answers, are valuable because they cause the student to use facts and to think through the problem

and solve it more or less on his own.

Using leading questions skillfully helps to build confidence in the student and provides practice in using appropriate facts and concepts.

The leading question may be used to help the awkward student, thus preventing embarrassment. Eventually, of course, the student must be able to give the right answers without the help of leading questions although they are useful in the early phases of learning and in the application of information to practical problems.

Leading questions are not usually prepared in advance as each situation will vary from others. The use of leading questions calls for resourcefulness on the part of the instructor in stimulating and leading the student. Each question in turn depends on the response given to the previous question. The process cannot be mechanical. It must be adapted to each situation as it develops. We should think of this as the art of questioning. Perhaps no other technique is as vital to successful instruction.

Productive Use of Questions

For maximum effectiveness the instructor should prepare questions carefully and use them to:

1. Stimulate interest in the lesson.
2. Establish communication between the instructor and students.
3. Focus the students' attention on the major points or principles to be remembered.
4. Stimulate mental "learning-by-doing" by causing students to apply facts and principles as they analyze problems.
5. Help students develop a feeling of confidence and success which leads

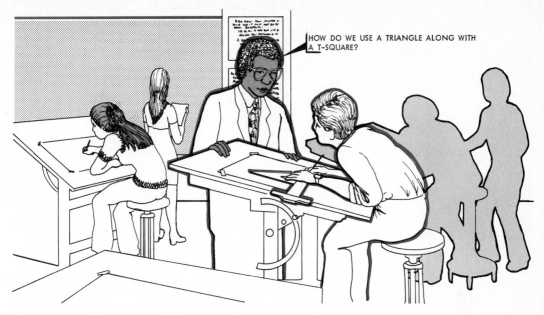

HOW DO WE USE A TRIANGLE ALONG WITH A T-SQUARE?

Use such key words as *why, when, who, what, where* and *how* when questioning to encourage specific answers.

to greater motivation, further study and experimentation.

6. Develop the ability to organize ideas and speak effectively.

7. Stimulate students to think for themselves rather than follow the pattern of the text or the thinking process of the instructor.

8. Build cooperation in the class through group activity and responsibility.

9. Provide for a democratic approach to learning.

10. Evaluate the effectiveness of instruction and provide valuable clues to better methods.

Key words for questions. Certain words used in questions tend to guide the question into the most significant form.

The table shown on page 148 gives a few of these key words.

Avoid questions that encourage guesswork. Use questions that include the words, *why, when, who, what, where,* and *how.*

Characteristics of Good Questions

Clear and easily understood. Questions should be stated in simple, straightforward language. They should be as brief as possible yet complete enough to assure understanding.

Composed of common words. Questions should be designed to measure understanding of the subject being taught. Trick or catch questions should be avoided in both oral and written form.

Thought provoking. Questions should

KEY WORD	SIGNIFICANCE
Explain	Requires the student to amplify and illustrate a subject.
Outline	Requires the listing of the main or key points in a logical order.
Define	Requires an accurate description of the limits of a subject.
Compare	Requires the identification of similarities and differences.
Illustrate	Requires the student to give examples of the principles or facts.
Trace	Calls for a step-by-step description of the growth or development of something, as the flow of electrical current, gases, or liquids.

A well worded question causes a particular response.

challenge the student to apply knowledge rather than repeat facts. Questions should not be answerable with 'yes' or 'no.' They should not be so easy that the answer is obvious to most students.

On major points of lesson. Questions should be built around the fundamental content of the lesson and should be asked at the proper place in the lesson to emphasize key points. If we wish to measure vocabulary, we should test for this alone rather than to make this an unknown value in each question.

Preparation of Questions in Advance

Good thought-provoking questions are not easy to construct and require more time than is available to the instructor during the class period. It is, therefore, sound practice to prepare questions while planning the lesson. One method is to identify the major or basic points to be included in the lesson, write out comprehensive questions and incorporate them at the proper place in the lesson plan. The Notes and Cautions that may have been identified with the doing or performance elements of your analysis often suggest questions. In asking the questions during the class period, it is not necessary or even desirable to read them. Having thought through and written out the questions the instructor should be able to state them with reasonable accuracy from memory after a glance at the lesson plan. These carefully prepared questions should not take the place of questions which may be asked on the spur of the moment whenever the instructor feels that a question is appropriate, but they should provide a satisfactory skeleton around which impromptu questions may be asked.

How to use Questions

Skillful use of questions comes with practice. However, a few basic ideas on their use can be set forth as guides.

The method of using questions in which the instructor asks questions and permits the whole group to answer in a chorus should not be used often or for very long. It may be used to stimulate a dull class and may encourage shy students to participate, but these good points are usually outweighed by inherent disadvantages. The group method decreases individual thought, gives the lazy student a chance to do nothing and develops a noisy class. A serious defect is that it gives the instructor no opportunity to evaluate an individual student's progress.

It is important in the questioning process to use appropriate pauses so that all persons in the group will have time to think about the question and to organize their thoughts. The instructor must judge the success of the question in stimulating ideas and the extent to which additional questions are needed to bring out other points. A pause after an answer or several different answers to the same question may be worthwhile in order to permit the class to think through the idea before a new thought is proposed by a new question.

The questioning procedure. For most questions, and for those prepared in advance around major points in the lesson, a definite procedure for asking the questions is recommended. This procedure requires mental participation on the part of all students and avoids the confusion that may result if the question is handled in a more formal fashion.

Of course, an instructor should state

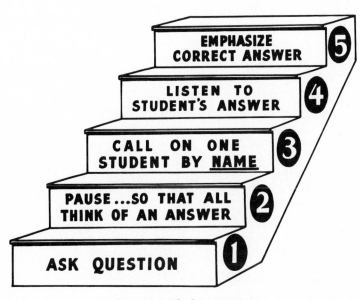

A good questioning procedure

the question as clearly as possible. To do this, the question must be well in mind before it is asked. If the question is complicated, it may be desirable to state it more than once, possibly varying the exact wording. It is important to state the question *before* naming the person to respond.

With regard to calling on individuals, some system should be employed to assure that everyone is called on with reasonable frequency. A number of systems which may appear feasible at first have serious drawbacks; for example, if members of the class are called on according to seating arrangement or in alphabetical order it is quite easy for an individual to estimate when the instructor will call on him. Thus, the lazy student will not think very hard about questions until he knows that it is about his turn to answer one. Some instructors have used cards with the names of members of the class on

each card. Shuffling of these cards results in alerting everyone but does not assure equal distribution of questions. Possibly the most practical approach is to call on individuals in a random fashion but record in some manner the number of questions each individual has been required to answer.

Match questions to individual. Some effort should be made to fit the questions to the individuals concerned. Because individuals in a normal class will vary considerably in ability and because it is a basic principle of teaching to recognize and provide for individual differences, it is appropriate at times to give the most difficult questions to the most advanced students. Probably it is undesirable to indicate the questions that you consider to be the most difficult, but a recognition of individual abilities and some effort to take them into consideration is desirable.

Student answers should be carefully

BILL, CAN YOU ANSWER THAT?

Match the question to the student. Call the student by name.

evaluated so that the individual understands how much of the correct answer was provided. Since individuals do not attach the same meaning to a statement, the instructor should restate the answer in such a manner as to leave no doubt in the students' mind. Do not form the bad habit of repeating, word for word, each answer as given. When the student responds to questions the instructor should be sure that:

1. Replies are given clearly enough so all may hear.
2. Any misconception or inaccurate

information revealed by wrong answers is corrected without arousing antagonism in the group.
3. The classroom atmosphere is such that students learn to evaluate and comment on each other's statements without resentment.

Good questions lead to good communication and understanding among students and between instructor and students.

Questions are essential teaching tools. Their skillful use is part of the instructor's role.

QUESTIONS AND ASSIGNMENTS

1. What are the two major types of questions?
2. List six key words used in questions.
3. What are four characteristics of good questioning?
4. List the steps that should normally be used in asking questions during a review lesson.
5. What effect does questioning have on student attention?
6. Give your opinion on the merit of: (1) asking the question first and then calling on an individual to answer, or (2) calling on one individual and then asking the question.
7. Under what conditions do you respond to a question from a student (1) by asking another question, (2) by calling on another student to answer it, or (3) by referring the student to the proper page in the text? Why?
8. What would you do about the student who wants to "show off" his knowledge by answering most of your questions or by answering the questions asked of you by other students?
9. Give an example of a thought-provoking question.
10. What use would you make of a seating chart in asking questions?
11. Give an example of a situation where oral questions are superior to written tests.
12. Analyze a paragraph of a text in the subject you teach and write questions that will cause the student to interpret the material.
13. Discuss how you would decide on the type of question to ask on a specific portion of a lesson.

14. Explain the system you would use to make sure all students in your class are called on to ask questions.

15. Sometimes a student after hesitating replies, "I know but I can't put it into words." How would you deal with this through the use of questions?

Demonstrating

Good instruction is always a matter of strategy in which the instructor plans and sets the stage by word and act so that students tend to learn the right things at the right time. The demonstration is the method of teaching in which sight rather than hearing is the major means of communication. Like other instructional methods the demonstration is usually composed of several elements including telling, showing, questioning, testing, and application. However, we use the word *demonstration* to identify the type of lesson that is characterized by *showing* on the part of the instructor and *observing* by the student.

Why Demonstrate?

Specific procedures including manipulative skills and many scientific theories and concepts can be presented more effectively by a step-by-step demonstration than by any other method. In fact, it is extremely difficult and wasteful of time and effort to try to teach skills and many units of information and concepts in most courses of study without skillful demonstrations. As in other methods, such as lectures and discussions, the presentation must always be followed by some form of application by the student.

When to Demonstrate

We cannot say that it is desirable to teach all of a certain subject by any particular method because the objective of each lesson, as well as the content to be taught at each point in the lesson, helps to determine the method or methods to use. If a class needs exact knowledge in order to work a particular problem in electronics, a chalkboard demonstration would be appropriate. If, on the other hand, one merely wishes to discuss new developments in a subject with the intention of giving only an overview of these developments to advanced students, a lecture or illustrated lecture rather than a demonstration may be more desirable.

Texts on teaching technical and advanced subjects emphasize the demonstration as a teaching method. Conversely, many simple skills, like shooting the free throw in basketball, require a demonstration. It is good practice to use a demonstration whenever possible. In general the demonstration is most effective for teaching:

1. Scientific principles and theories.

2. Movement or relationship of parts of tools and equipment.

3. Manipulative operations or hand skills.

The demonstration is generally effective in teaching science, mathematics, and mechanics, as well as the subject areas within the practical arts, vocational and technical education. These fields would include agriculture, business, distribution, home economics, health and industrial education. Learning about the

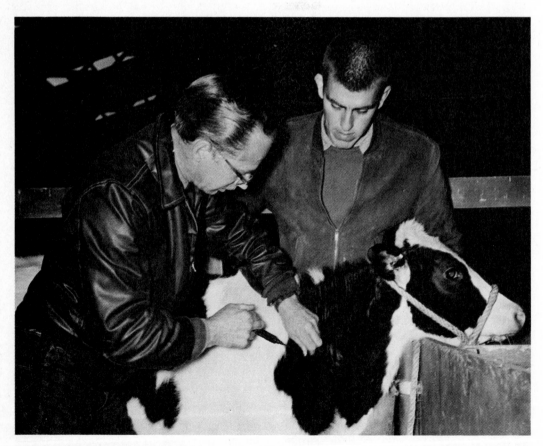

A vaccination demonstration as used in Vocational Agriculture.

movement of parts of a piece of equipment is made less difficult by seeing them actually move, perhaps with the aid of models or films.

The demonstration is the major teaching method in those subjects in which a high degree of accurate and skilled performance with tools and materials is required. Classroom instructors use the demonstration when explaining a principle, showing the steps of procedure of a mechanical operation, or illustrating ideas and relationships with the use of instructional aids and devices.

Careful planning is essential to all teaching. Some instructors, however, make the mistake of preparing less for a demonstration than for an equal amount of instruction to be given by some other method.

The remainder of the chapter deals with factors to consider in preparing for a demonstration.

Relationship of Demonstration to Doing Units

The doing or performance elements of the analysis (see Chapter 4) require the demonstration since they are composed of steps of procedure which usually must be seen to be understood. In Chapter 4 we emphasized that each doing or performance element should contain about the right amount of content for a demonstration. At times, however, it may be desirable to give a demonstration on less than the entire doing element, or to combine several doing or performance elements. This will depend on the level of the group being instructed, available equipment, the plan of instruction and the time available.

Many of the knowing elements can also

be demonstrated. For example, if you were to explain the principle of leverage, a demonstration would be the most effective method. With a simple table-top model, you could graphically show the factors of force, fulcrum and resistance while you are explaining the scientific principles or knowing elements.

Proper Time for a Demonstration

A demonstration gives best results when given at the time the students feel a need to learn the new content. It is quite easy to have a demonstration ready for a certain time. It is more difficult and under some conditions impractical to have all the students in a class "ready" for a demonstration at a certain time. Under such circumstances these alternatives are suggested:

1. The demonstration may be given to the entire group whenever a few of the advanced students are ready, and then be followed by individual or small group demonstrations as needed. This scheme may seem wasteful of teacher time; however, it provides for individual instruction which should be anticipated in any event. If written instruction sheets (described in Chapter 6) on the content demonstrated are available they can be used successfully for review by the individual student just prior to performing the operation or procedure demonstrated.

2. The students may be divided into groups of about equal ability and the demonstration repeated for each group when the individuals are ready for the instruction. This scheme is also useful in situations

where a number of different student activities are going on simultaneously under one instructor, as in shop or laboratory programs, where a limited amount of identical equipment is used.

As a general rule the knowledge content related to the demonstration should be taught first. However, it is wise to begin demonstrating and for students to begin doing as soon as practical. Students can more easily understand the value of a demonstration lesson and are more likely to be more interested in it if they know they will soon have a chance to use equipment or apply in other ways whatever has been taught.

Tools and Equipment

Most of us can remember demonstrations in which the instructor found it necessary to send for a tool or a piece of equipment because he had not taken the time to rehearse the demonstration, at least mentally, and lay out the necessary tools and equipment in advance. Such distracting interruptions to the demonstration can completely offset its effectiveness. All tools, equipment, and materials should be available and in proper working order prior to starting the demonstration. A list of equipment as a part of the written lesson plan is recommended.

Tools and equipment should be arranged so that they do not draw attention away from the process or concept to be learned. Ordinary tools and equipment which students have seen and worked with before are no problem, but a particularly interesting instructional aid, unusual item of equipment or a special instrument should, if possible, be brought into sight at the time it is needed.

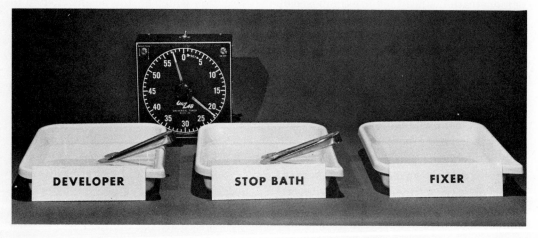

A well organized setup for a table-top demonstration for film processing.

DEVELOPER

A critical step in a demonstration. The tools, equipment and materials were ready in advance of the demonstration.

Occasionally a special arrangement or setup may be made to surprise the students and by this means cause an important element of the lesson to stand out. For example, an instructor might emphasize the light weight of balsa wood by having a large ball peen hammer made of the wood and stained to look like a real hammer. At the right moment a student is asked to hand the hammer to the instructor. The result may bring a touch of humor to the demonstration and contribute to its effectiveness.

Arranging the Students

A demonstration must be seen, yet arranging students so that all can see and hear is a frequently neglected aspect of teaching. The seating or standing arrangement will vary with the type of demonstration to be given. Chairs arranged in a semicircle may meet many requirements. In other cases where it is important that all students see the materials or equipment from a rather narrow angle or from one point of view bleacher type seats are desirable. Such

Here the students are arranged so that all have a good clear view of the instructor and the demonstration. (United Airlines)

seats are frequently used in shops and laboratories where a great many demonstrations are given and where equipment can be set up on a bench top in front of the entire class.

When demonstrating around stationary machines or equipment, it is necessary to prevent students in the front from walking forward and obscuring the view of others. This is a cause of horse play and discipline problems with young students and of boredom and inattention with more mature learners. Some instructors have found it helpful to use masking tape to make a line behind which observers should stand, or draw a chalk line on a tile or concrete floor around such equipment as lathes, milling machines, office equipment, tractors, and other large equipment. The perimeter of the chalk mark should provide standing space for at least half the group being instructed; the

other half can, of course look over the shoulders of those in front. A piece of rope or tape on the floor is also very effective in reminding those in front of the necessity for standing back if all are to see. Cooperation of the class can be obtained by a short explanation of the need for the line.

The habit of noticing whether or not all members of the class can see is important enough to warrant special planning and constant attention during the demonstration. The length of the demonstration, as well as the size of the class, the size of the equipment to be used, and the noise level created by the operation of equipment are all factors that must be considered.

Safe Work Habits

The most skillful way of performing a job is typically the safest way; safety is part of skill. It follows logically then that the teaching of key points of safety can

Safety rules and practices should be taught as part of the lesson. The instructor sets an example by putting on the apron before beginning a welding demonstration.

best be accomplished when taught along with the steps of procedure in performing the task. This helps the student to remember the safety precautions at the right time. Rules and regulations about safety and long discussions about safety, separated from the skills to which they are related, are often a waste of time. Certain safety instruction may well be the subject of special demonstrations, lectures, or conferences but, generally speaking, those things closely related to safe work habits can best be taught as the individual learns the exact steps in performing an operation. For this reason points of safety, as listed in the doing or performance elements of the analysis,

should be included in the demonstration and should be emphasized carefully and brought out in a clear manner at the point in the demonstration where they apply.

One Procedure at a Time

Frequently the instructor, skilled in the subject to be taught, will show several methods of performing an operation during a single demonstration. Obviously there are several acceptable ways to perform many operations. Sometimes a certain procedure has an advantage over others in specific situations. It is important, however, when showing how to do something, that one correct method be taught and understood before other methods are taught. Few things are more confusing to the student than changing from one procedure to another during a demonstration.

Demonstrations are often too long and the student is given too many ideas before he has a chance to try them out. Demonstrations should seldom exceed 15 to 20 minutes even for the more mature learner. Inexperienced instructors, unless they have made a careful analysis of the steps to be learned in a job, are likely to underestimate the difficulty which the student will encounter in remembering the complete process. The instructor, being very familiar with the skill, finds it simple, but to the uninitiated it may seem very complex.

Essential Information and Theory

Some information and theory should be given along with the demonstration. This is natural and effective. Basic theory or large elements of technical information based on the analysis and requiring considerable time to learn should be the subject of separate lessons, but small elements of informational content and particularly important key points as listed with the doing or performance elements of the analysis, should be included along with the demonstration. The instructor must, however, screen the material carefully to make sure that the information and concepts taught during the demonstration are essential and closely related to the steps being demonstrated. To stop in the middle of a demonstration and give a twenty minute lecture is generally not economical of student time and the use of equipment. The important point to remember is that information and theory given with the demonstration must be kept to a minimum and must apply directly to the steps of procedure being demonstrated.

Eye Contact

Of course it is important in any kind of instruction that the instructor look at the students. Such eye contact can be very helpful in judging whether or not the instruction is being understood. In giving the demonstration it is necessary to look at the equipment or at the blackboard, but the instructor must remember to look back to the students frequently so that he can judge their reactions, ask questions, repeat parts of the demonstration, or do whatever else is necessary to assure understanding.

Performance Standards

The instructor, in preparation for the demonstration, should actually go through the physical performance, work the problem, or manipulate the equipment effectively and skillfully to assure that there are no awkward gaps or mistakes. An insecure instructor may be

tempted to use the demonstration to impress students. While it is desirable that students know that the instructor has a high degree of skill in the subject, the demonstration, especially a demonstration on a basic point, should not be used to show the instructor's speed of performance. After the demonstration has been carefully and slowly presented, it may be desirable to repeat the performance steps another time at normal speed in order to set high standards of performance toward which the students should strive. This helps to give students an idea of the standards of speed and accuracy required of them on the job.

Instructional Aids and Substitute Materials

With the actual equipment present, it is not always necessary to use visual aids with the demonstration. On the other hand many demonstrations are made more effective with a combination of actual equipment and special instructional aids. Such aids might be used to show the

A combination display of actual equipment and printed diagrams.

An instructor may use several aids in a demonstration: chalkboard, simulator, actual equipment and an assistant. Note that all students have a clear view.

relationship of small or hidden parts of equipment, to blow up very small parts so that they may be seen, or to emphasize graphically the effect of improper heat in a cooking or baking process. A very common example of this is the use of a large facsimile of a slide rule even though the instructor and all members of the class have individual slide rules.

When demonstrating how to read a micrometer, a large scale demonstration micrometer is often used. It consists of a specially constructed micrometer built so large that it can easily be read from a distance of several feet. The overhead projector may also be used to project micrometer readings on a screen.

In demonstrating the principles of operation of an engine, the piston strokes, the valve operation, and the timing and firing cycle may be done easily and clearly by the use of a simple wooden model with moving parts.

Sometimes, it is expensive and wasteful to demonstrate with real materials. For instance, the clothing instructor will frequently demonstrate cutting and fitting with paper instead of cloth. Likewise drafting and sheet metal instructors often use cardboard for demonstrating sheet metal layouts and construction. If an article is to be made of brass, copper, stainless steel or other relatively expensive material a sample or practice piece may first be made of mild steel or other less expensive material. Cheaper materials may mean substantial savings and in many cases be as good for the beginner as the regular, more expensive material.

The Use of Assistants

Depending on the type of equipment being demonstrated and the nature of the subject matter, it may be wise to consider the use of assistants during the demonstration. Another instructor or an advanced student may be brought in to the demonstration to help. Variety may be added to a demonstration by having an individual who is particularly skillful in a certain part of the work present that part. This helps to create the desirable atmosphere of instructor and students working together.

The use of assistants may help to make demonstrations effective when the instructor, for physical or other reasons, is unable or does not wish to perform the demonstration personally. One of the most common examples of this is seen in athletics, where the head coach may no longer have the co-ordination and stamina to demonstrate.

Questions and Questioning

After each part or major step of the demonstration, the instructor should provide for questions. Students, however, may not ask questions for many reasons, including the fact that they may not know how to ask what they feel are intelligent questions. In these cases a stimulating question from the instructor will suggest questions to the students. The instructor must ask questions to make sure the demonstration has been understood and to emphasize key steps of

procedure, information and safety. *Never fail to ask questions on key points and safety precautions during a demonstration.*

The Follow-up

Presenting the content is only one step in the teaching process. Of equal importance is the follow-up or application step which normally occurs after each demonstration. This step provides for *learning by doing* as the student attempts to apply the procedures that have been demonstrated. Application may have the objective of merely helping the student to understand the material, or of developing a degree of skill. Without the application step a demonstration, even though skillfully presented, can fail to have a significant effect on the students.

Normally the first part of the follow-up consists of assigning work to the students, letting them start, and then correcting any errors or providing additional instruction on an individual basis. Such instruction should be given carefully and thoroughly. No student should be allowed to practice incorrect methods, and it is psychologically sound to have him succeed with reasonable effort from the start.

When giving individual instruction at the student's bench or desk, care should be taken not to take the job away from him. Occasionally an instructor will stop at a student's bench or work place, take the tools and equipment away from him, run through the process quickly, and then leave without making sure the student has understood. It is better at times to direct the student's attention to an error, but leave the tools and equipment in his possession, thereby assisting him to think through and perform the skill on his own.

The follow-up, or *learning by doing,* allows the student to apply the demonstration.

The Process of Skill Development

Although demonstrations are given to clarify concepts and reinforce informational content being learned, one of the primary uses of the demonstration method is to assist the process of skill development. The instructor will be well advised to keep the following key points in mind when planning demonstration lessons to facilitate skill development:

1. The learner must know the steps of procedure to be followed and the physical motions necessary to perform.
2. The learner should understand the purpose of each step and the relationship among steps that determine the sequence.
3. The learner should be guided through an initial performance correctly and successfully.
4. The learner must practice the physical-mental steps until the process becomes automatic.

When a high degree of skill is an objective of the instruction, considerable practice under supervision is necessary. Practice without supervision may be wasteful of time and materials and lead to the development of bad habits. After presenting the material you have only begun to teach. Much of the best instruction occurs through supervision and individual coaching as the student practices. The four levels of application are illustrated in Chapter 14, page 261.

Accuracy vs. Speed While Practicing

Whether a skill should be learned by practicing at high speed or not depends somewhat on the nature of the skill.

Some skills can be learned best by practice with emphasis on accuracy and the gradual development of speed. Other skills should be learned by performance at the required speed and with emphasis on the gradual development of accuracy. When learning to throw, one must concentrate on the proper arm and leg movements and use proper speed from the start. Accuracy comes with practice. When batting skills are being learned, the ball should not be thrown so hard that the batter cannot make contact. The speed must be adapted to the batter's hand-eye coordination and then gradually increased.

In learning such basic mental skills as spelling and arithmetic, we strive for accuracy first and develop speed with practice.

Steps in Giving a Demonstration

The actual steps of procedure in giving a demonstration will vary as the situation changes. We will consider four typical situations.

Situation number 1. Let us first take a small group of young students who are about to learn a simple but important skill such as how to multiply with a slide rule. The same procedure could be used in teaching skills in the shop, in sports, and on the rifle range. In such cases you probably have one piece of equipment for each student. Your teaching technique would be different, however, if you had only a few pieces of equipment. Suggested procedure:

1. Introduce the lesson and tell why the process about to be learned is important and how it will be taught.
2. Preview the steps once to give the

students a general idea of the task to be learned.

3. Have each person hold the slide rule exactly as you are holding the rule with which you are demonstrating. If possible, *face in the same direction as the students* and hold the slide rule high enough to be seen, or use a large working model of the rule.

4. Go through each motion of adjustment of the slide rule very slowly and have each student follow your movements. Watch your students. A few tips and suggestions may be made during this part of the demonstration but care should be taken not to talk too long and thus distract the student's attention from the steps of procedure.

5. Go through the steps again with all students duplicating your movements. This may be continued until everyone has begun to develop correct habits.

This technique is very effective where identical small equipment is available for all students to manipulate at the same time.

6. Have all students practice as you move about the group and check each student's work. Give such encouragement and help as seem necessary.

7. Ask questions and stress the need for further practice. The students must then practice under the instructor's supervision until all can do the operation with speed and accuracy.

This method may seem formal and dictatorial to some; however, it should be

remembered that students will usually appreciate an instructor who is firm and sure of the process. If skills are not taught so that students do the work correctly from the start many improper habits can develop.

The instructor's tone of voice and manner during the demonstration determine the attitude of the group more than the exact method used. *Be fair, firm, and friendly, not harsh, impatient and demanding.*

Situation number 2. In this situation we have a group of fifteen or more students and the instructor is going to show an operation such as how to clamp a cylindrical piece of material for drilling. Since there may be only one set of tools in the shop for this operation the students cannot follow along as in Situation number 1. Suggested procedure:

1. Place the tools and equipment used in the demonstration in the best possible position for all to see.

2. Introduce the lesson with illustrations of where the students will use the operation or skills in the lesson.

3. Demonstrate the whole process slowly and with proper yet short remarks. If the process is complicated (and most are to beginners) it may be well to repeat it a second time.

4. Call on a student to give the steps. Do each step as it is given. In some cases a different student may be called on to give each step as it comes up. Many inexperienced instructors give a demonstration but fail to check the students' understanding before they are allowed to practice.

5. Have at least one student do the

complete operation without help while the others observe and ask questions.

6. Provide a schedule so that each student can practice with the equipment as soon after the demonstration as possible. This is a part of your advance planning.

Situation number 3. In this situation you are demonstrating a basic principle. The purpose of this is to give the students basic facts and principles that will aid them in understanding processes and developing good judgment. No manual skill is to be developed and there are no steps of procedure to be learned. Let us assume that you are going to demonstrate the effect of passing a permanent magnet through a coil of insulated wire as part of a course in electricity. Suggested procedure:

1. Introduce the lesson with remarks relative to the principle about to be demonstrated and indicate where the knowledge of this principle will be useful.
2. Describe the equipment and material being used, such as permanent magnet, coil of insulated wire and galvanometer, and tell what each will do in the demonstration. Ask a question or two to assess the students' understanding of the equipment and materials.
3. Connect the apparatus and explain the hookup. Complicated equipment should be set up before class unless this is part of the demonstration and will be worth the students' time. This should be determined by your objectives for the demonstration.

4. Perform the demonstration step by step. Remember to:
   a. Make sure all can see.
   b. Work slowly and skillfully. Avoid quick movements and errors.
   c. Consider the class. Don't become so interested in the experiment that you forget you are teaching. Do *your* experimenting before the class comes in.
5. Ask questions to focus students' attention on correct steps and points of information.
6. Call on students to explain principle just demonstrated.
7. Repeat the demonstration and summarize the basic ideas to be remembered.

If questions are asked by the student during the demonstration you will need to use good judgment in answering them so that you do not get off the subject.

Situation number 4. In this situation a number of students are to learn exactly how to perform a difficult operation. The technique is effective in many situations ranging from teaching Cub Scouts how to set up their tents to rifle range instruction. It is a most applicable technique for on-the-job training situations. Suggested procedure:

1. Show and tell to the best of your ability, using appropriate instructional aids and devices.
2. Have students tell what to do *as you do it.* This is one form of application as each student must think through and indicate each step. With equipment or materials that can be dangerous to the student, this step is vital. For example: Do you pour the acid into the water or

the water into the acid?

3. Have students do each step as they state essential information, including safety precautions.

4. Put the students on their own but under supervision. Recognize that each student must learn at his own rate of speed to the level of skill required prior to performance without close supervision.

Following these simple four steps may save a great deal of time by reducing the need for much re-instruction. In some instances only the most important or most complex elements of a total demonstration should be taught in this way. This four-step procedure is worthy of serious consideration in many situations and can be highly effective. Parents with young children may find it especially valuable.

An Example

The following personal experience illustrates some of the points covered in this chapter. Several years ago while aboard a major combatant ship a talented chief petty officer was observed entertaining the ship's company during the evening "happy hour" by telling stories and acting as master of ceremonies for an amateur show.

On deck the next morning he was preparing to demonstrate the operation of a gasoline powered water pump known as a "handy billy" which is used aboard ship for a variety of purposes including fire fighting. As the chief had performed so well during the "happy hour", it was expected that he would provide a skilled demonstration.

The pump was moved to an open space on the deck. He next called to a group of young Naval Reserve sailors on their first cruise, and asked them to "move close enough to see the pump," which they did. Since about twenty-five men were involved only one man in five could really see the equipment. The chief didn't seem to notice.

Next, after a short explanation of the use of the pump, he attempted to start the engine only to find that it was inoperative. He then sent for another pump which arrived twenty minutes later. Twenty minutes × 25 men is 8.3 man hours wasted!

The second pump was in operating condition. After letting it run for a short time he took out the manufacturer's operating manual and read the steps for starting and stopping the engine and dismissed the group without a question being asked or answered.

Later when we were discussing the demonstration with the chief he agreed that he should have:

1. Made sure the equipment was in good working order.
2. Arranged the men so that all could see or given the demonstration to smaller groups.
3. Explained the starting procedure and asked questions so that the men would know what to look for.
4. Demonstrated one step at a time and emphasized the key points of procedure.
5. Had one or more of the men start and stop the engine as the others observed and were questioned.
6. Improved the demonstration by talking directly to the men, not by reading from the manual.

A good demonstration is not something

that can be given on the spur of the moment. The unprepared instructor is easily recognized when the steps of procedure are not clear, when the correct equipment is not ready, when the key points are not specified or when important safety precautions are not emphasized. When lecturing, the instructor may be able to switch to another related topic when realizing that there is a gap in knowledge and be able to fill in the gaps the following day, but in a poor demonstration, students become very much aware of the instructor's lack of preparation.

The demonstration is one of the most rewarding types of instruction because of the feeling of satisfaction that comes with knowing that students can perform, which is direct proof that the instruction has been effective and that students have profited from the time spent. The skillful instructor will find many opportunities to teach by showing.

QUESTIONS AND ASSIGNMENTS

1. What are the main advantages of the demonstration as a method of teaching?
2. What factors would you consider in determining a method of instruction?
3. In what type of learning situations would you use a demonstration?
4. What part do instructional aids have in a demonstration where actual equipment is used?
5. What should you watch for in the seating or standing arrangement?
6. Why teach only one procedure at a time?
7. How and when would you include safety precautions during the demonstration?
8. Why ask questions during the demonstration?
9. Under what conditions would you read material during a demonstration?
10. How would you determine the amount and type of information to include in a demonstration?
11. How fast should the instructor show the steps in performing a task?
12. What substitute materials might you use in a specific demonstration?
13. What advantages would substitute materials have?
14. What special problems may left-handed instructors and students have in presenting and learning from a demonstration?
15. Watch a demonstration on television and evaluate its effectiveness. What limitations and advantages do you see in TV demonstrations?
16. Prepare a simple demonstration of a procedure you have mastered and perform it for someone.
17. Describe a specific demonstration situation and tell how you would keep a group from crowding forward during the demonstration.
18. List the steps you would take in giving a specific demonstration.

Instructional Aids and Devices

10

Instructional aids have been used since primitive man drew pictures in the sand and on the walls of a cave. Pictures have always helped to illustrate and convey ideas. Modern instructional aids have evolved from primitive sketches to such complicated devices as working models, motion pictures, television, teaching machines, video and audio recording devices to name only a few.

Any subject can be taught more effectively through the appropriate use of aids, but there can be great waste as a result of improper use of these good tools. We should not accept without careful evaluation such statements as "85% of learning is through the eyes." Obviously the amount we learn through the eyes depends on the nature of the content being learned and the conditions under which we are learning. There are times when "one picture is worth a thousand words" but not always. One word may be as good as a thousand pictures at times.

The word "yes" to a proposal of marriage needs no picture to be understood.

The good instructor uses all the tools available to him in an expert fashion when they are needed. We should use aids when and only when they help to facilitate learning which is really the test of an instructional program.

Types of Instructional Aids

Before considering instructional aids in greater detail, it is necessary to agree on some terminology. For our purpose we shall consider an instructional aid to be any device, piece of equipment, graphic representation, sound reproduction, or illustration that helps the student to learn. Instructional aids may be divided roughly into four types:

Visual aids. Includes the chalkboard, posters, bulletin board, displays, models, motion pictures, slides, projected transparencies, projected opaque materials, and the flannel board.

Auditory aids. Includes radio and all types of recordings.

Audio-visual aids. Includes aids which make use of both sight and hearing, such as sound motion pictures, slides on sound and television.

Simulation devices. Includes devices built to simulate the action or function of the real device. They are frequently operated by the student. The prime purpose of this type of aid is to develop "feel" and correct habits. The electronic trainers used to simulate an airplane in the training of pilots are an example of this kind of aid. The football dummy and the punching bag used by the boxer are examples of simple aids that simulate to some degree.

Classes of Instructional Aids

On the basis of construction, it is sometimes convenient to classify instructional aids as follows:

Graphic aids. Includes all flat pictures, posters, graphs, charts, diagrams, and chalkboard illustrations.

Projected aids. Includes motion pictures, material for opaque projection, and transparencies for overhead, slide and strip film projectors.

Mechanical-electrical aids. Includes models, actual objects, cutaways, electronic trainers and the more complex teaching machines.

When the Instructor Needs an Instructional Aid

For obvious reasons, the real object under discussion is best for instruction in many situations. However, you may need an aid when:

1. The real object is either too big, too small, or too spread out to be seen effectively.

2. An object or process is not available to the students by any means except through an aid of some type. Newly developed and unavailable items, or those too distant to be visited, may be brought to the class or laboratory through instructional aids.

3. The real object or process is too expensive, dangerous, or delicate for the students to use.

4. The process is too slow-moving, as in the case of plant growth and other phenomena. Motion pictures employing animation or time-lapse photography are useful here.

5. Rapidity of human or mechanical movement prohibits perception of detail. Slow motion photography is an excellent aid in such cases.

6. The process or phenomenon is invisible. The flow of electricity, chemical processes, and the action of many gases are naturally invisible.

The alert instructor will endeavor to find those places in the instructional program that need illustration. He will examine all content to be presented to determine if it can be made more understandable with some type of aid.

No instructional aid takes the place of an instructor, nor does it necessarily make the instructor's job easier. An aid may assist an instructor to teach more effectively, save time, and thus facilitate the instructional program.

Some instructors tend to use films and other aids which are easily available, even though they have little value in terms of the content to be taught. This question should always be asked: "Will this instructional aid help my students learn more effectively that which they are supposed to learn?" If the answer is "Yes," the aid should be used. If an aid is found necessary, the next problem is to develop or select one that meets certain criteria.

What is a Good Instructional Aid?

The greatest value of instructional aids lies in (1) their appeal to the senses, (2) their ability to attract and hold attention and (3) their ability to focus the attention on essential elements to be learned at the proper time. For instructional purposes, a reproduction of a device or process is often vastly superior to a simple description. As one instructor said, "It saves a lot of hand waving."

Every progressive instructor will design, or at least select, instructional aids. In doing this the aid must be judged carefully against certain criteria. Assuming that the workmanship is of good quality (that the work is clean, clear, etc.), the value of the aid will be in direct proportion to the following factors.

Simplicity and unity. The student cannot assimilate a large number of facts presented at one time. A variety of ideas presented simultaneously tends to confuse the student. Many instructional films are prepared with no particular course in mind and with only a broad general objective. Short films on specific phases of a subject contribute to flexibility since they can readily be used as a part of the lesson or course of study. The relationship of the analysis, the course of study, and the content of the film should be clear and consistent.

Colorfulness. This quality may be achieved through the use of an attractive design, color, movement, or form. Care must be exercised to ensure emphasis on important ideas. For instance, the use of bright color on an unimportant detail will draw attention away from the more significant idea.

Flexibility. The competent instructor seldom teaches the same lesson twice in exactly the same way. No two groups of students have exactly the same needs; and technical practices, tools, and materials are constantly changing. In the light of these facts, the instructor should, whenever possible, select or construct aids and devices so that they may be modified if necessary. If the aid becomes obsolete, it should be redesigned or discarded. In this respect, materials for use with overhead and opaque projectors will be found the most flexible, and sound motion pictures the least flexible.

Practically speaking, motion pictures are not flexible. They are comparatively expensive, the order of presentation is fixed, and it is difficult to insert new material. This drawback should be carefully weighed against the tremendous appeal they have through movement. It should be noted that the use of instructor-recorded sound tracks on standard film adds flexibility. By this method the sound can even be translated into another language.

Timeliness. Any aid that is used "out of step" with the presentation of the content tends to lose its effectiveness. Films shown "when the film or auditorium is available" are often almost useless in terms of the educational objectives.

Visibility. Any instructional aid should be of such size that the smallest significant detail is large enough for the most distant student to see. There are other factors affecting visibility. The instructor, students in front seats, or classroom equipment may obstruct a clear view of the aid; glare on glossy surfaces, and so forth, may render an aid useless.

Let us consider the specific characteristics of each type of aid and the procedures for their proper utilization.

Motion Pictures

Motion pictures in the form of 16mm films are available on many subjects and from many sources. Some films are designed to help teach facts and exact steps of procedure. Others are suitable for general orientation to a subject. Still others are effective in developing understanding of complex social-historical problems and for influencing attitudes.

While these films should not be designed primarily for entertainment, they are often of great interest and provide an excellent variation in the teaching process. In order to focus attention on learning, the instructor should refer to the motion picture as a *film* rather than *movie,* which has an entertainment implication.

A typical motion picture projector suitable for classroom use. (Bell and Howell)

Because of the cost of producing motion picture films (about $1000 or more per minute of running time) the producers are often required to design the film for as large an audience as possible. As a result films on certain topics are more available than others. For the same reason they tend to be quite general in nature and more useful for general orientation than for instruction in specific procedures.

Great care should be taken in the selection of motion picture films if they are to be effective and fit in appropriately with the lesson and course. As there are many sources of films, obtaining exact information on all potentially useful films for your course is an important but time-consuming task. You may save time by asking for help from your local audio-visual suppliers. Universities and other educational institutions will also have catalogs available for your use. Film libraries are available in many locations through commercial loan and rental agencies, the military and other government services. Also available is the annual edition of the *Educator's Guide to Free Films* published by Educator's Progress Service, Randolph, Wisconsin, which has over 4,000 annotated listings of free films.

The Educational Media Branch of the U.S. Office of Education, Department of Health, Education, and Welfare, Washington, D.C., can provide valuable assistance and service on all aspects of film procurement and utilization.

There is also available the *single concept loop film.* These are super-8 millimeter motion pictures illustrating one particular operation or step in a technical process. An example would be the use of a torque wrench in assembling an automobile engine. They are mounted in small

Super 8 millimeter film cartridge and projector. (Technicolor Corp.)

cartridges similar to tape cassettes and shown with special miniature projectors. The film is a continuous loop so that it plays continuously until the projector is turned off. Loop films are intended for use by from one to three students at a time outside the regular classroom time. Thus, they are used in much the same way as outside reading.

Suggested procedure for using educational films. If detailed information or steps of procedure are to be learned, the following steps are effective. They are not entirely applicable where the objective is to develop attitudes and general impressions.

1. Preview the film by showing it and making notes on its contents with the following questions in mind: Does the picture's content meet the objective of the lesson in whole or in part? Which points in the picture need re-emphasis or clarification?

   Students will learn considerably more if the instructor leads a good discussion on the main points in the film after its showing. In order to do this most effectively, the instructor must prepare his discussion questions in advance.

2. Consider listing on the chalkboard the title of the film and the points for which the student is to watch. A brief overview and introduction by the instructor sets the tone for better student learning.

3. Prepare the room for showing the film by placing the projector and seats so that everyone can see without straining. In hot weather, it may be advisable to sacrifice a little

darkness for better ventilation. Move the projector closer to the screen if a brighter picture is desired, but further away if a larger image is needed. The width of the image on the screen should be not less than one-tenth nor greater than one-sixth of the distance to the farthest student.

4. Introduce the film. Tell the group what the film is about and the major items to look for. If the film has been designed for general use, it is necessary to emphasize those things on which you want your group to concentrate. Inform students of the ways they will be tested on the content of the film.

5. Show the film. If you have seen the film a number of times, you can make further notes to help lead the discussion that is to follow. The students will be more interested in the film if you stay in the room during the showing.

6. Discuss the pertinent material shown in the film. Main or key points of the film should be discussed. This may be done by asking leading questions. Specific and important steps of procedure may be listed on the chalkboard and reviewed a number of times.

7. Re-screen the film. This may be done at once or several days later, depending on the complexity of the process shown and on how soon the students have an opportunity to use what they have learned. Most films contain more information and concepts than the student can grasp in one showing. Research has shown that students may learn as much from the second showing as from

the first. The discussion following the first showing should stimulate interest in the specific points to be looked for during the second showing.

8. Test. Evaluate the extent to which students have learned by oral questions and, if desired, by written tests or performance tests.

Moving pictures can be very valuable in the instructional program, especially where motion (such as that found in any operation or process) is to be shown. When properly used, they can increase learning, save time, and provide desirable variety to the course.

The Overhead Projector

The opaque projector and the slide and strip film projectors which are discussed later have all been in use for many years. A fourth and very practical projector has come into wide use in more recent years. This is the overhead projector which is known by various trade names. It has a number of advantages under certain conditions and is perhaps the most versatile of projection devices for general classroom use. The major advantages of an overhead projector are:

1. The room need not be darkened.
2. It can be operated from the front of the room so that the instructor can operate the projector and look at his students at the same time.
3. A variety of methods are available for making the transparencies and several sizes can be used. As these transparencies are flat and about the same size as standard file folders they can be filed easily and lend themselves to easy handling along

The overhead projector is a versatile instructional aid. (Bell and Howell)

with other materials used in instruction.

4. It is possible to use transparent overlays or successive layers of transparencies with or without color to show steps of procedure, various stages of construction, or the internal assembly of equipment. It is also feasible to use flat working models to show moving parts of equipment. It is even possible to give the effect of movement such as a heart beat or the flow of liquids through the use of special attachments on the machine.

Some projectors are equipped with a roll of cellophane which can be wound across the stage of the machine, thus making it possible to project a considerable amount of material which has been

Overhead projector in use. Note that the room is not darkened, all students can see the screen and the instructor maintains eye contact. (Delta Airlines)

prepared in advance or material which is developed through discussion in the class.

Many instructors prefer to use the overhead projector much as they would use the chalkboard by writing directly on the cellophane at the same time that it is being projected on the screen. This, of course, saves chalkboard space, retains the flexibility characteristics of good chalkboard use, saves class time and allows the instructor to retain eye contact with students.

In some courses where students are doing individual work on paper, such as in writing improvement, problem solving, engineering and design courses, it is an interesting and useful approach to make Ozalid or other transparencies of student work and project it for analysis. The work need not be identified with any individual student. As each student is on the giving as well as the receiving end of constructive criticism the technique helps to maintain an objective and constructive atmosphere in the classroom.

Transparencies can be used in conjunction with the chalkboard. Diagrams and equations may be projected on the board and altered or developed with white or colored chalks. Green background transparencies projected on a green chalkboard give the best line contrast.

A disadvantage to some instructors who do not have photographic services available is the difficulty and cost of converting opaque illustrations into transparencies. There are, however, several methods available and these should be investigated through your dealer as part of your plan for using this important aid. By means of the Ozalid process transparencies can be made by the instructor or others in a few minutes at reasonable cost.

The thermo-fax process of making transparencies, which has been developed by the Minnesota Mining and Manufacturing Company, has several advantages over older methods. With this equipment, transparencies can be made in a few seconds under normal room lighting conditions. The process is completely electric and requires no chemicals. Editing of material can be accomplished by blanking out unwanted material with a sheet of plain paper as the transparency is being made. Transparency stock is available in several colors.

The overhead projector is so practical that some of the largest users of instructional aids have for several years developed most of their projected materials (other than motion pictures) for use with

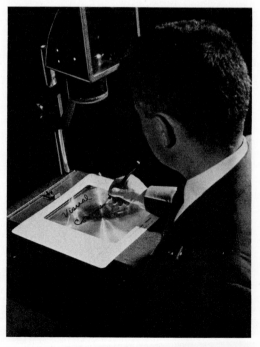

A grease pencil is used to add information to the transparency.

this machine. Suggested procedure for using the overhead projector:

1. Arrange transparencies in proper order for showing.
2. Plan an outline of your commentary while each illustration is to be projected.
3. As the lesson develops plan additional words, symbols, etc. that are to be added to the transparency with grease pencil.
4. Mark the lesson plan to indicate when each illustration is to be used.
5. Set up the projector and try out for focus and screen size. Because of the height of the projector head on some types of equipment it may be necessary to set the machine on a low table and raise and tilt the screen.
6. If possible, set screen across front corner of room and set projector in front of you, but pointed directly at screen. This arrangement keeps you from being between the audience and the screen.
7. As the lesson progresses, show each transparency at the proper time with appropriate comment.
8. Consider re-showing an illustration for review and emphasis.

The Use of Overlays

A distinct advantage of the overhead projector comes through the use of a static transparency with one or more overlays. The static illustration sets the stage. Successive overlays present additional information one step at a time.

This approach may be used wherever the instructor wishes to develop a concept or present the steps in a process. The following copies of transparencies with brief description illustrate a procedure

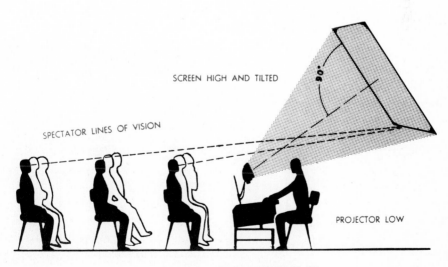

SCREEN HIGH AND TILTED

SPECTATOR LINES OF VISION

PROJECTOR LOW

COMMUNICATOR SEATED

Center line of projection should be at right angles to the screen.

for finding directions when lost in the woods. This method was discovered by Boy Scout Robert Owendoff of Falls Church, Virginia.

1. In an open area (static frame) a straight stake is driven in the ground with at least three feet of

its length above the ground (overlay 1).

2. The tip of the shadow cast by the stake is marked with a small stake (overlay 2).

3. After a wait of not less than ten minutes the "new" spot which the tip of the shadow has reached is

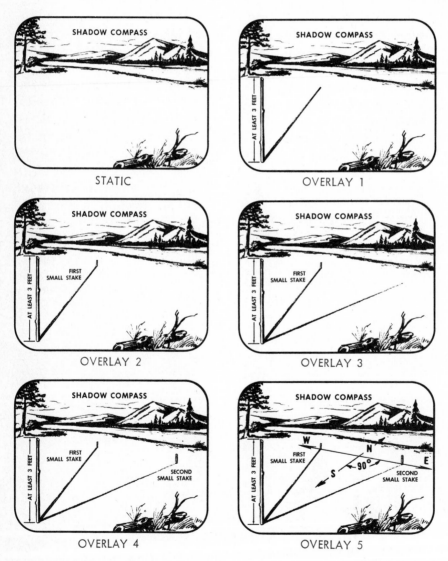

A static transparency with succeeding overlays presents a step-by-step procedure.

marked with another stake (over-lays 3 and 4).

4. A line is drawn to join the two marker stakes (overlay 5).

This line always points east and west regardless of the time of day or year. A line drawn at 90° to the first line will point north and south. Under some conditions, this method of finding directions is more accurate than a compass. The error is seldom more than 20 degrees and it averages only 8 degrees.

The following illustration shows one of a series of transparencies developed by Stanley M. Johnson, Department Head, Machine Drafting, Eli Whitney Technical School, Hamden, Connecticut. He found that the projections overcome the crudeness of hurried chalkboard drawings and saved classroom time.

The overhead projector's step-by-step overlay method of visual buildup makes the component ideas easier to grasp. Retracing steps or reviewing is a simple matter of lifting off the overlays.

The Film Strip Projector

Film strips are very much like a roll of film from a 35mm still camera. In other words, a film strip is merely a strip of film with many pictures. It may contain a few printed instructions as well. These strips are comparable with other projected still pictures for illustrating those things that do not require motion on the screen. The

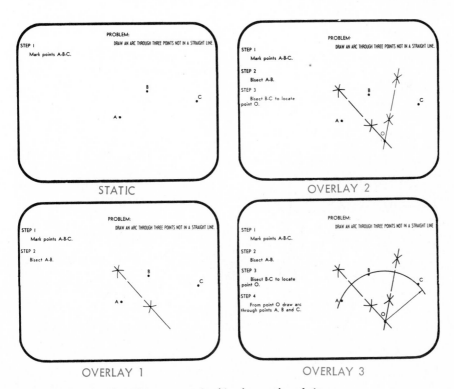

Overlays may visually build up a complex idea in a series of steps.

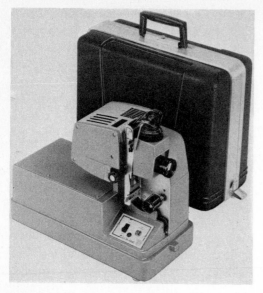

A compact portable filmstrip projector. (DuKane Corporation)

film strip projector is designed to hold and project these strips of film.

Some projectors are used with a record

or tape so that standard instructions can be heard by the student as the film is viewed. Although this type is less adaptable to all situations than the silent type it is usable where the instruction can be made specific and where little class discussion is required. Because of its rather inflexible nature its use is somewhat limited in many types of instruction. Suggested procedure for using a silent film strip projector:

1. Preview the strip and determine the comments that need to be made during the showing.
2. List the title of the strip and the key points on the chalk board.
3. Prepare the room and equipment. Place the projector so that the proper size image on the screen is obtained. Arrange seats so that everyone can see without straining.
4. Introduce the film by previewing

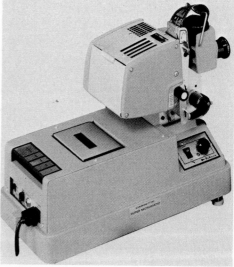

Filmstrip projectors with synchronized sound. (DuKane Corporation)

the content and indicating the key ideas you expect them to get from the showing. Explain the procedures to be used in assessing student understanding of the content presented.

5. Show the film strip. Allow time for students to read the printed explanations on each picture, then make comments and answer questions as needed. The instructor may stand near the screen and use a pointer to help direct attention to specific details. Any student can operate the projector for the instructor. Some projectors have remote controls for the instructor's use.

6. Consider re-showing the strip. This is done to emphasize main points and to clear up any misconceptions.

As with motion pictures, the re-showing may follow at once or may be delayed for some time in order to work it in with other class activity.

7. Evaluate student learning by oral questions, written or performance tests.

The sound film strip may be shown in the same way, except that the instructor cannot make comments during the showing. Some sound strips may be shown profitably a second time without sound. This gives the instructor an opportunity to make comments and to emphasize the key points.

The Slide Projector

Slide projectors have been in use for many years. The popularity of the small 35mm camera and the development of 2″

A typical slide projector. The sequence of the slides may be changed to coincide with changes in the lesson plan. (Eastman Kodak Co.)

× 2″ color film transparencies have made this type of projected aid a common device in the home as well as in the classroom. The amateur photographer with a low cost camera can make excellent slides for instructional purposes.

Slides have an advantage over strips in that the order in which the pictures are used can readily be changed and slides can be eliminated or added.

The procedure for using the slide projector is much the same as that for the overhead projector when it is used for showing transparencies only, the essential difference being that the slide projector does not permit adding ideas to a picture by overlays or by marks made with a grease pencil on the transparency.

Film Slides

During the past several years the flexibility of film-slides has been exploited in an attempt to provide relatively low-cost individualized instruction. Frequently, a set of 2 × 2 (35mm) film slides are prepared with an accompanying audio tape which can be utilized by a single student as a self-instructional "package". This means of packaging instruction has become increasingly popular and a substantial number of mechanical devices are being marketed which bring together both a visual and audio stimulus.

The technology involved in bringing the learner in contact with the *message* through a variety of media materials is quite broad; ranging from the most simple device involving a standard slide projector and an audio recording in disc or tape form to a much more elaborate device having the capability of controlling the visual and audio message electronically as the learner pushes the appropriate button. Through these means,

the time and pace of the learning experience can be selected and controlled.

The Opaque Projector

This machine is capable of projecting a printed picture, photograph, or any flat illustration within the size limitation of the projector. You may clip from a magazine pictures which illustrate a point or process in a lesson, mount them on standard sizes of heavy paper, and project them. Little difficulty is experienced in obtaining pictures to illustrate many processes. The room must be quite dark when the opaque projector is used, since the projected image on the screen is not as brilliant as that from other types of projectors.

Modern projectors of this type have improved lighting and lens systems which permit projecting materials in a partially lighted room. The machine tends to be large and bulky but the newer machines are made of lightweight materials and hence weigh less than older models.

Some projectors come equipped with electric pointers useful in placing a spot or arrow of light at any point on the projected image. This, when carefully used, has many advantages over the traditional pointer.

With modern equipment it is no longer necessary to mount thin materials although this is still recommended for ease of handling and filing. Small illustrations should be mounted on uniform sized heavy paper or cardboard. The size should be determined by the platen or stage of the machine. Colored mounting papers may add interest. Don't use black. Suggested procedure for using the opaque projector:

1. Arrange the illustrations in the proper order for showing during the lesson.
2. Plan the comment that should be made as each illustration is projected.
3. Set up equipment and arrange seating as for other types of projection. Pictures can be kept bright by using the projector near the screen. If pictures vary greatly in size you may wish to move the projector to or from the screen to change the size of the projected image. Since the projector must be re-focused after each move this can be distracting.
4. Use the projected illustrations during the class in the same manner as when using posters or the chalkboard. Use a pointer and stand to one side of the screen. Consider the electric pointer with a beam of light if one is available. If the pictures are arranged in order and numbered a student may assist you by operating the machine.

Wall Charts and Other Non-projected Visual Aids

Graphic aids in the form of large pictures, diagrams, posters, and charts are widely used, and are a most practical form of instructional aid. Their chief advantage lies in their adaptability to almost any classroom, shop or laboratory teaching situation. Many visual aids can be drawn or constructed by the instructor to fit a specific teaching situation. Their chief disadvantage is that they are hard to handle and store properly. The characteristics of a good visual aid are:

1. All unnecessary details are omitted.
2. Lettering is simple and easy to read from any seat in the room.
3. Color is used to identify related parts and to direct attention toward main ideas.
4. Technical details and symbols are correct, although nonessential details may be omitted.
5. The aid is mounted in a way that will provide support yet not limit its usefulness.

A 24 × 30 inch illustration board is excellent for a series of illustrations. An easel should be used to support the charts. Some instructors have used light-colored window shades on which to draw the illustrations of frequently needed material. A series of sketches on wrapping paper may be mounted on a horizontal bar which acts as a binding, and each chart may be thrown over to expose the next. Some visual aids may be placed on the bulletin board or wall for further examination by the students during free time. They must be changed frequently. Pictorial aids should not be left up after they have served their purpose. Here is a suggested procedure for using posters and charts:

1. Select and prepare aids that will help to emphasize or illustrate points in the lesson. Many ideas can be illustrated by sketches drawn on wrapping paper or pads sold for the purpose, using grease pencil, colored chalk or crayon.
2. Mount the posters where they will be usable when needed. If charts are left exposed, they may distract.

3. Plan how and when the aids will be used in the lesson.

4. During the lesson, display the aid at the right time and use a pointer to indicate location of parts or movement of current, gases, and so forth. Always stand to one side of the chart so you can face and speak directly to the class.

5. You may wish to call upon a student to take your position and go through the explanation as you have done. This will help to clear up any misconceptions and will hold students to account for the information.

The Chalkboard

Here is a stone age teaching aid that is one of the most flexible and one of the most practical of all. With imagination and a little drawing ability any instructor can improve a presentation with a chalkboard. The chalkboard can be used to list important points in the lesson, to solve problems, to illustrate ideas. It should never be used as a means of conveying a great amount of written information that can be provided on paper to each student by means of a duplicating machine. The practice of having students copy long outlines or lists from the board is a waste of time. Suggested procedure for using the chalkboard:

1. Plan all chalkboard illustrations before class, giving thought to making parts stand out through the use of colored chalk.

2. Complicated drawings should be

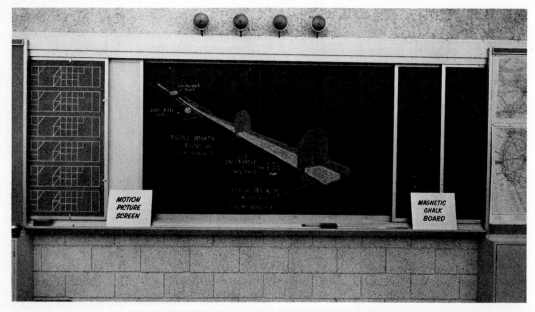

A combination instructional aid with sliding panels. The chalkboard is seen at center. Magnetic chalkboards may be moved in when needed. Note the wall charts at left and right. The entire assembly may be moved aside to use the motion picture screen.

prepared on the chalkboard before class. If the drawing is detailed and complicated, yet for instructional purposes it is desirable to develop it step by step, any one of several techniques may be used. Before class, the drawing may be placed on the chalkboard with very light lines clearly visible to the instructor but not to the class. By merely tracing over these lines with chalk, a neat and accurate drawing may be made quickly while the class observes. Chalk that has been shaped flat on two sides will aid the instructor to make lines that are neat and even.

3. When the same basic outline of a drawing is needed several times, it may be transferred to the board by means of a stencil. This is done by making the drawing on ordinary tracing or wrapping paper. The main line intersections and reference points are then punched or perforated with a pin or nail to make a stencil. By hanging the stencil on the board with scotch tape and patting over the pin points with a dusty eraser the design will be transferred. Chalk lines can then be added.

4. When a semipermanent drawing is desired, showcard color may be used. The chalkboard eraser will not remove the showcard color, and when it is no longer needed it can be washed off with water.

5. When the same outline of an object such as a tool, chemistry flask, map outline, or machine is needed repeatedly it is desirable to make the outline out of cardboard, plastic or plywood and trace this shape as needed. This will save time and

improve the appearance of the drawing.

6. Illustrations may be placed on the board by projecting an image with the opaque or other projector, and tracing the important parts of the image. This is also an excellent way to increase the size of an illustration. A large sheet of paper may be taped to the wall or chalkboard if a more permanent large size illustration is desired.

Models, Cutaways, and Actual Equipment

For some types of instruction, models have several advantages over other instructional aids. They may be examined and handled by students and they show relationships and shapes better than any other aid. Cutaway models and "exploded" models are used chiefly to show location and movement of internal parts of the equipment. Actual equipment, mounted or displayed, is valuable for close examination and adjustment. Working models, either large or small scale, are valuable in demonstrating the operation of tools or machines. Suggested procedure for using models:

1. Select or make the models needed. Many of the best models are made from common shop or construction materials.

2. Mount these so that they can be seen and used conveniently.

3. Plan their introduction into the lesson and the comment you will make about each. Do not plan to pass the model around the class as you talk about it or some other part of the

"Exploded" models of machinery aid in detailed study of components.

A partially dismantled model of an induction motor aids in explaining its operation.

lesson—it only becomes a distraction.

4. During the lesson, and when the model is being used, make sure that it can be seen. An assistant may be used to help handle or hold the model. Do not allow students to crowd up so that some cannot see.

5. Provide for the model to be examined by students in an orderly fashion after the proper instruction has been given.

The Flannel Board

This type of instructional aid has become increasingly popular. It has several distinct advantages for the presentation of material where one idea must be added at a time.

The principle behind the flannel board is that paper or cardboard illustrations, on the back of which sandpaper, felt or flock has been glued, will stick to felt or flannel cloth stretched over a panel. This permits the adding of especially prepared graphics including words, pictures and symbols as the lesson is presented. The technique is useful in explaining organizational structures, parts of equipment and their relationship, and even for emphasizing abstract ideas. It is frequently used for showing such things as the movement of ships and planes. Orientation programs commonly make use of the flannel board in explaining organizations as each element can be added as it is needed.

The major advantage of the flannel board over flip charts or projected pictures is that elements can be added as the

The flannel board is a useful aid in explaining different parts of a training program.

explanation is made and at the exact time they are needed. Of course this can be done to a degree with overlay transparencies used with the overhead projector, but the flannel board is maybe more effective in many situations.

Another advantage of the flannel board is that after graphic materials in the form of pictorial illustrations, symbols, and words are prepared and available they help the instructor to stay on the subject and to keep class discussion on the main points of the lesson. Suggested procedure:

1. Lay out the total illustration as it will be when the lesson is complete. Be sure important parts are emphasized by size and color. Colored construction paper is quite effective for this use.
2. Have each element or part prepared as a separate piece mounted on illustration board and attached to coarse sandpaper, felt or covered with flock. Sandpaper need not cover the entire back of the illustration.
3. Try out the illustrations by running through the lesson and adding each cutout as it is needed. Mark the lesson plan.
4. Stack the cutouts in the order needed for logical development.
5. As the lesson progresses place each cutout on the flannel board firmly. As a summary of the lesson it may be helpful to remove the cutouts, starting with the first one used, and then review the lesson by placing the cutouts on the flannel board as done previously. This is a very effective means of summarizing the lesson. The same procedure may be

employed as a review the next time the group meets.

Recording Equipment

The record player has been used in schools for a long time particularly in music, language and speech training. Other types of recording and playback equipment are available in increasing numbers. Sound can be recorded on disks or magnetically on plastic tapes.

Magnetic recorders are simple to operate and the recording may be retained or it may be erased so that the tape can be reused. Some machines may be operated at different speeds. Slower speeds are used for recording speeches and conferences. Higher speeds, from $7^1/2$ to 15 inches of tape per second, are used for quality recordings of music and other sounds. Tape may be purchased in various size reels ranging from 3 to 14 inches. The 3 inch reel contains 150 feet of tape; the 14 inch reel 4800 feet.

Tapes can be edited by cutting out

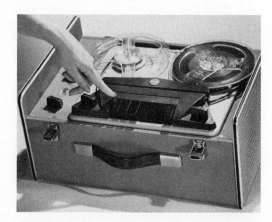

A magnetic tape recorder used in music, language and speech training. (RCA Victor)

sections and splicing the tape or by erasing a section and re-recording that section.

Both disks and magnetic recordings have some advantages and disadvantages. For example, a disk recording may be more useful than a magnetic tape for a short permanent record of a student's performance in the beginning of a speech or language class. Such a record may be filed with other materials in the student's folder. A long playing, magnetic tape would be less suitable since only a section of the tape would be used for each student and the individual record could not be filed in corresponding student folders.

In recent years, the electronics industry has succeeded in making recording equipment much more compact, lighter in weight, less complex to operate with increased sound reproduction quality. The audio cassette provides the user with a self contained magnetic tape cartridge that is easy to load or remove from the cassette recorder. The audio casettes are relatively inexpensive and can be erased and reused indefinitely.

Recording equipment can be most useful for individual, self-instruction or practice in speech, language, or music training. Recordings can be used to aid students in the recognition of sounds like the chatter of an improperly operating cutting tool, a bad bearing, or an overloaded motor. Suggestions for magnetic recording and use:

1. Set up machine following manufacturer's instructions.
2. Record a period of live sound.
3. Rewind and play back for quality.
4. Try again with different microphone placements.
5. If the recording is to be used as a part of a lesson, the lesson plan should, as with motion picture film, include notations on introducing the recording, the recording length and questions and discussion.

Television

As our most powerful means of mass communication, television has demonstrated its effectiveness in influencing the opinion and the buying habits of large groups of people. In educational programs, television has not had that kind of success. It is, however, obvious that we can learn from the television screen just as we learn from the motion picture screen. In fact TV is often a means of showing a film simultaneously in one or more places from a central source.

Educational TV stations put out hundreds of cultural and educational programs. Vocational and technical programs are being added on several stations. Business courses including typing

Audio cassette player-recorder designed especially for instructional purposes. (Bell and Howell)

Educational television provides instruction in many fields. (RCA Victor)

and shorthand have, with the aid of special TV instructional kits, including home study guides, proven to be successful.

Some TV courses are aimed at workers who wish to upgrade themselves, housewives who are considering part-time employment in labor shortage fields, and even retired employees who are willing to consider employment. Almost any subject can be presented via TV. As a special educational aid, TV has demonstrated its usefulness for mass orientation and for reaching those at home.

A major disadvantage of television is that the instructor can't see or hear his students. Although the question and answer relationship can be preserved by "talk back" arrangements the instructor has no simple way of observing and knowing the reaction of individuals in the classes to the instruction. Therefore, it is more difficult to modify a presentation in response to the progress of the individual and groups receiving instruction. If television is used for a part of the lesson and course, then supplemented by discussion and practical work under the supervision of the individual class instructor, some of the required flexibility can be retained.

Closed circuit TV. This method of transmission is being used in a number of situations, including medical schools and military service schools. The picture is sent by wire instead of over the air to the receiving sets in one or more classrooms. Advantages of closed circuit TV are:

1. One demonstration can be "piped" to several classrooms at the same time.
2. Magnification of small and hard-to-see demonstrations is possible.
3. Dangerous, distant, or current phenomena can be picked up by the TV camera and sent back to the viewers.
4. A highly significant procedure which may not be performed again in the same way may be shown to many students through TV. For example, more medical students can now see an operation by a skilled surgeon than was possible formerly by direct observation.

Some programs where several classes are taught simultaneously are making good use of closed circuit TV. It has been demonstrated, however, that the motion picture film made simultaneously by the TV camera (Kinescope) is just as effective for most instruction as live television. For instruction, Kinescope recordings are the equivalent of motion picture film made by more traditional methods.

Television playback. Instant television playback, which has made sports events more interesting, can be used for instruction. For example, the University of Missouri-Columbia has used the technique with closed circuit TV to show counselors in training how an experienced counselor works with a group of young people.

The instant replay makes it possible to go back over important phases of the counseling process immediately after it has been observed for the first time. Video tapes of such sessions can also be used later for more intensive study of counseling behavior. The teacher education program at the University of Missouri-Columbia, as well as elsewhere, is using portable television equipment to "capture" the teaching act and resultant student behavior for analysis and improvement. Microteaching which involves the video taping of a small group instructional setting has become increasingly popular as a means of providing the prospective teacher with immediate feedback.

Closed circuit television allows several classes to be taught simultaneously.

COMPARISONS BETWEEN ◊ ◊ ◊ ◊

	Classroom Films	Closed Circuit TV	Regular TV
1. Good for showing mechanical motion, for describing situations in general, and human relations case studies.	XX	XX	XX
2. Less tendency to show it to everyone regardless of need.		X	
3. Effective use of master teachers.	X	X	X
4. Least subject to loss of time due to mechanical and electrical failure because of availability of technicians.		X	XX
5. Most easily obtained and shown when needed.	XX	X	
6. Can be previewed by instructor and worked into the course of study and specific lessons when needed.	XX	X	
7. Can be re-run for emphasis at the right time.	XX	X	
8. Length more easily determined by content to be covered rather than TV channel time.	XX	X	
9. Less tendency to entertain the public rather than teach and re-teach the student what he needs to know.	X	X	
10. Effective and economical use of color.	XX		X
11. Content easily evaluated at several stages of preparation. Can be edited and changed during production by qualified personnel regardless of geographic location.	XX		
12. Less cost per student showing.		X	
13. Large screen size at low cost.		X	
14. Use is less dependent on conditions beyond the instructors control.	X		
15. Less tendency to interrupt planned schedule.	X		
16. Can make best use of national current events as they occur.			X
17. Can present locally prepared "live" demonstrations in several classrooms at the same time.		X	
18. Best for reaching large audiences at one time.			X
19. Best for reaching those at home.			X
20. Not dependent on availability of TV channels.	X	X	
21. Most easily controlled when using confidential or restricted materials.	XX	X	
22. Capable of magnification & reduction on the screen.	X	X	X
23. Less tendency to use obsolete material.		X	XX

Within the individual classroom, shop or laboratory, television can be used to magnify whatever the instructor wishes to present. For example, the TV camera can be focused on small equipment in motion and, by means of magnification on the screen, make it possible for students as a group to see the action. A camera unit can be mounted on a microscope, thereby making it possible for a large group to see individual slides.

TV makes contributions to training and education in many ways. Like all other aids, however, its advantages must be weighed against its inherent dis-

advantages for each specific situation in which its use is contemplated.

An analysis of three types of projected instructional aids is shown on page 192. It should be kept in mind that the specific situation may tip the scales in favor of one technique over the others.

Portable television. One of the most recent developments in the instructional television field has resulted from the technological advancements which have made possible the production of portable television cameras, recorders and play-back equipment with a relatively high degree of reliability. These technological

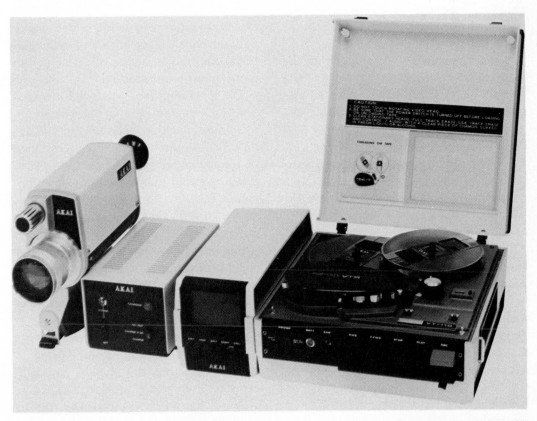

A complete portable television production unit. Contains camera, microphone, audio and video recorders with live monitor and playback capability. (Akai America, Ltd.)

advancements have made it possible for television to be used directly by instructors and students in the regular classroom setting. Greater availability, flexibility, and reliability have brought about increased use of television for instructional purposes. Through these technological advancements, we have definitely moved out of the era which required specialized studios, large capital investments, and technical specialists.

In aggressive steps of technological development, the industry has made available equipment with color capability which in some instructional settings is much more desirable than the more traditional black and white video images. Following the lead of the audio recording industry, the video recording industry is exploiting the convenience and reliability of the video cassette.

Again, the reader is reminded that the *message* to be communicated to the learner is of utmost importance. The media to be used in communicating the message is of secondary concern. The mechanical and electronic devices that are utilized to deliver a message have certain advantages and disadvantages which must be considered by the instructor, and decisions must be made based on a variety of factors.

TV, like chalkboards, motion pictures, or working models, is not in itself good or bad. Each instructional aid has its uses and its limitations, its strengths and its weaknesses. You as an instructor must decide which materials, methods, and aids contribute most to the teaching/learning process.

To ask, "can TV teach better than the individual instructor?", is not pointing up the real issue. The real issue is asked by the question, "How can each type of aid be

made to serve the instructor by making teaching more effective?"

Simulators

A simulator is a device which is similar to but not identical with the real equipment in operation. The degree of similarity required depends on the way the device is to be used in an instructional program.

Simulators are usually designed to provide instruction on selected and critical skills which are required on the actual equipment. Although the actual equipment is generally required for the final phases of instruction, simulators are often superior in several respects for the initial phases of instruction. They are often used for instruction which comes between visual aids, such as motion pictures, and the operation of actual equipment under real conditions.

The need for simulators in educational programs increases as we move into complex man-machine relationships. Thus, high fidelity simulation is most common in military training and on the critical skills required to operate complex equipment. Simple simulators are, however, useful in less complex instructional programs.

One advantage of a simulator is that a portion of the total system can be simulated and thus provide for systematic practice on critical skills not possible or feasible when the total equipment is in operation. For example, a portion of a complex machine can be simulated in such a way that the student can gain experience under the most favorable conditions. This is important with such skills as engine trouble shooting, production line work (the speed of some simulators

An airline hostess trainee being instructed in a simulated aircraft cabin. (Delta Airlines)

can be adjusted), and work to be done under hazardous conditions including extremes of temperature. The simulator need not duplicate the whole task, but it must truly simulate whatever the student must transfer to the operating stiuation.

Of critical importance in the selection or design of simulators is the degree of positive transfer that must take place. Simulator training that results in habits which are not quite the same as those required in the operating situation, may result in negative transfer and can be dangerous. For example, a target simulator used to train military men to fire on a moving target must truly represent the real situation. Otherwise, it would train the men to miss the target!

The last phase of preparation is usually completed on the actual equipment because it provides high motivation and bridges the gap between the simulator and the real equipment under actual operating conditions. Generally such live operation is provided on-the-job by the supervisor responsible for the work or by

Simulators such as these are used extensively in driver education. (AEtna Life and Casualty Co.)

a highly skilled employee reporting to the supervisor. This same principle is followed in the student teaching component of a teacher preparation program. Simulators have their greatest value when:

1. The real equipment is so complex that the trainee cannot be given adequate experience and practice on specific procedures before total integrated performance is required.
2. The real equipment is dangerous in the hands of the trainee until the ability to adjust quickly to emergency conditions has been developed.
3. The unusual or emergency situation does not occur often enough on operating equipment to maintain the degree of skill required for such situations.
4. The real equipment is too expensive to be used exclusively for instructional purposes.

In making decisions regarding the selection and use of simulators, it is important to:

The simulator is an exact duplicate of actual automobile controls. (AEtna Life and Casualty Co.)

1. Determine the critical skills for which instruction is required.
2. Compare costs of simulator vs. real equipment.
3. Plan for simulation as a part of the total program.
4. Analyze the degree of positive transfer required (see Chapter Two).
5. Consider the possibility and danger of negative transfer.

The demonstrator. One of the most common and effective simulators is that used for driver training.

A complete installation consists of several stationary "mock-up" autos equipped with all normal controls. Students operate these cars in response to a motion picture projected on a screen at the front of a special room. Although the cars are stationary, the effect of movement provided by the motion picture is quite realistic.

The action taken by each student driver in response to the simulated driving conditions is recorded by machine at the rear of the classroom. The instructor can thus evaluate each student's progress.

The simulator in this case provides standard instruction on the basic driving skills, thus shortening the time required for practice on actual driving with a dual-control car. It has been estimated twelve hours of simulator instruction when combined with three hours of actual driving are about the equivalent of six hours of actual driving.

Other factors, including safety, instructor time, standardization of instruction and cost of dual-control cars, make this simulator a most desirable instructional device.

Instructional Aids and the Learning Situation

In considering TV, films, synthetic trainers, or any other instructional aid, we should keep in mind the major elements found in effective learning-teaching situations. The importance of each element depends on the subject being learned, the level of the students, the skill or performance required, and other factors. The following paragraphs point up essential elements in most effective learning situations.

Good instruction is organized whenever possible from simple to complex throughout the schedule. Each lesson must be in phase with the one preceding and the one following. The instructor must have control of the aids used and be able to re-show the aid as needed.

The instructor must be willing and able to modify the instruction to fit the level and ability of the students. Learning fails to occur, regardless of how clever the instructor is, if the material is beyond the level of the students. The instructor must be prepared to change the plan of instruction at a moment's notice in order to capitalize on the interest and ideas of the individuals in the group as they develop. This does not mean that the subject matter in the course of study is not covered. It does mean that methods are modified to challenge and capture the interest of the

students. The instructor must know how the instruction is being received and understood.

Classes must be of sufficient size to allow individuals to ask questions frequently and for the instructor to observe the progress of each individual in the class. Students should have an accurate idea of their progress and what is expected of them throughout the course. Mass media such as TV have serious limitations in this respect.

There must be provision for students to practice or apply the content they are learning. This may involve practice work with tools and equipment, or problem solving, or the mental application of information and concepts to practical problems. The instructor is essential for individual coaching of each student.

The class must be reasonably free of interruptions and distractions, and the physical comfort of the students must be considered. Small screen size and poor light control should be avoided.

Provision must be made for the utilization of instructional aids to help teach that which students have difficulty in understanding. Things too small to be seen, too large to bring into the classroom, too expensive or dangerous; things invisible or extremely complicated, may require a special instructional aid of some kind.

Judgment rather than rules should guide the use of instructional aids. In general, however, the following criteria apply:

1. Is the aid consistent with the objectives of the lesson and the course, and is it used at the right time?
2. Are the instructor's comments planned to draw out the important

features of the aid as related to the objectives?

3. Is provision for student "learning

by doing" properly integrated with the use of the aid?

QUESTIONS AND ASSIGNMENTS

1. When is an aid needed?
2. What are some of the characteristics of a good aid?
3. How are aids classified by name?
4. Give an example of a simulation device.
5. What advantages does the overhead projector have over the slide projector? The strip film projector?
6. For what type of instruction should you use the chalkboard?
7. What are the steps that must be taken when using any aid in a lesson?
8. Use the opaque projector to draw a picture on a large piece of paper or the chalkboard by projecting an illustration and tracing the projected lines.
9. List the procedure you would follow in using the 2 × 2 slide projector in a lesson.
10. Make a series of 2 × 2 slides for a lesson by planning the pictures to take and using the 35mm camera.
11. Design a good pictorial aid for use in a specific lesson.
12. What potential uses do you have for on-the-air television? For closed circuit television?
13. What sources of film are available to you?
14. Prepare a series of overlays to present a process of about 4 steps.
15. If more than 4 overlays are required with a single static picture, how could they be hinged to the frame?
16. How can overlays be used to expose one part at a time of a complete illustration, such as an organization chart?
17. List several instructional situations where a simulator could be used.
18. Why are the concepts of positive and negative transfer as presented in Chapter 2 so important in selecting a simulator?
19. Although simulation is generally associated with complex equipment such as an aircraft or automobile, it is very useful with less complex equipment. For example, a student may learn to grind machine tool bits with 1/4" square mild steel. There is no need to grind away expensive high speed steel while learning the fundamentals of tool sharpening. Once the fundamentals have been learned on a "simulated" tool bit, the final degree of skill can be learned with very little practice on the more expensive stock. In what ways is this example similar to learning through simulation?

Individualized Instruction: Programmed Instruction and Teaching Machines

Individualized instruction is not a new concept in education. However, it is a concept that has been receiving increased attention during the past decade. The basic idea of individualized instruction involves a focus on the individual learner rather than upon learners as a group. Instructors of applied subjects have been involved in the individualization of instruction for a long time. This emphasis upon the individual learner has been, in part, due to the nature of the competencies to be developed through applied subjects. There has always been a great deal of attention given to learner performance which is an individual matter and not something that can be readily taught and evaluated by large group techniques.

During the past few years professional educators have been talking a great deal about *competency* or *performance* based instruction. Obviously this relates directly to the identification and specification of behaviors as discussed in Chapter 4. The primary step in instructional design, whether it be for groups or for individuals, involves the identification and specification of behaviors in measurable terms.

The primary advantage of individualized instruction is simply the fact that the teaching-learning process focuses more directly upon the individual which takes into account the individual's unique background, learning rate, and personal need for instruction. In a group instructional setting, all of the individuals in the group are exposed to the same content irrespective of their backgrounds; they receive the instruction at the same pace, in the same sequence, and at the same time even though they may not need the instruction at the same time or be in the same state of readiness for it.

The key to individualized instruction is being able to provide the learner with a learning experience at a time when he or she is *ready* for the experience and at a pace which is appropriate for the individual's learning style.

Instructional materials designed for use by individual learners are packaged in a variety of ways. One of the most frequent terms used to describe an in-

dividualized learning package is the term *module.* These learning packages or modules may be in printed form as a series of individual booklets covering relatively small instructional units, or they may be grouped together in such a way that the individual instructional units comprise a complete course of instruction.

An increasingly popular way of linking the learner with instructional packages is through the use of technology as described in Chapter 10. Instructional technology provides a means for translating

A well designed and programmed audio/visual device for individualized instruction. (Realist, Inc.)

the instructional materials into visual and/or audio formats which can be presented to the learner on an individualized basis through the use of a variety of commercial devices. At this point in time no one device has proven to be most effective for individualized instruction. The effectiveness of the instructional equipment is closely linked with the quality of instructional materials being presented to the learner as well as the nature of the content being presented.

One of the most systematic approaches to individualized instruction is referred to as *programmed instruction.* While many instructional materials and instructional methods can be individualized, programmed instruction is designed specifically for use with the individual learner and for this reason provides the focal point for this chapter.

Although programmed instruction has often been treated as a discovery or break-through in education, its basic elements are as old as Socrates who taught by questioning, so that the student was led by small steps from one concept or idea to the next. Good instructors have always used questions to lead and stimulate students. Instruction sheets as described in Chapter 6 are designed to provide step-by-step guidance toward a given objective. One step at a time is the way we have learned to swim, to read, to drive a car, to solve specific mathematic problems. In learning these things, we have proceeded from simple acts to more complex acts—and gained confidence and increased judgment on the way.

Such an approach does not conflict with the presentation, before detailed instruction begins, of an overall picture or pattern of what is to be mastered. Broad concepts of the total task are often neces-

sary if the smaller steps to be taken from the beginning are to have meaning. The student musician will gain by seeing and hearing the performance of the master musician. This can provide motivation and orientation for the student's step-by-step practice.

Before further consideration of modern programmed instruction, we need a clear understanding of the process. Generally, instruction that will be classified as programmed must have the following characteristics:

1. Material to be learned is presented in relatively small amounts or steps which are referred to as *frames* which consist of information plus questions. (Very small steps, however, are no longer considered essential in programming.)

2. The material is carefully sequenced so that the student is led from one frame to the next by questions, illustrations, or clues.

3. The student responds in some way to the information contained in each frame such as writing a word, manipulating equipment, making a computation, or merely thinking of an answer.

4. As soon as the student has responded to a frame, feedback is provided to indicate whether or not the response was satisfactory. Some programs are designed to practically eliminate incorrect responses. In programs that permit a degree of trial and error learning, it is desirable that the student be shown some reasons for the incorrect responses.

5. The rate of progress through the

course is determined by the individual's ability to master the materials. The learner sets the pace of learning.

6. Each unit of material is prepared so that the student may proceed with little or no help from an instructor.

The recent history of programmed instruction and teaching machines goes back to the 1920's and the work of Dr. Sidney Pressey at The Ohio State University. Dr. Pressey invented several devices that were intended to provide a mechanical grading method for testing students on their knowledge. It became obvious that much was being learned through this machine testing process.

New interest in what is now called programmed instruction came with the work of Dr. B. Frederick Skinner of Harvard University Psychological Laboratories. His article entitled "Teaching Machines" (which was published in *Science* in October, 1958) is generally given as the point of renewed interest in programmed instruction and related machines.

Although there are many variations and combinations of programming, two distinct types used with written materials stand out. These are often referred to as linear and branching.

Linear Program

In the linear program the material or content of the program is arranged, where possible, from simple to complex. The information is presented by brief statements in which a single idea is emphasized. In preparing the program this may be done by first stating the idea in a direct and complete written statement. The statement is then rewritten and a key word or other information is left out and indicated by a blank space. The student fills in the blank. The correctness of the response is checked by uncovering the correct answer as supplied in the program. After observing the correct response and comparing it with his own, the learner proceeds to the next step.

A brief example of a linear program is shown on pages 204 and 205.[1]

Linear programs present information and require responses which provide meaningful practice. They may also use illustrations and diagrams to convey concepts. Page 206 shows a program prepared by Federal Aviation Academy instructors Dicky D. Davis and Maynard D. Hatcher which is an example of this type and quality of programming.

Branching Program

This type of program is characterized by presenting information in larger steps, often several paragraphs at a time. Each unit is followed by a multiple choice question. The student must select an answer. This is done in machine programs by pressing a button. In a programmed text the student's selected answer then refers to another page in the text. Such pages tell the student whether or not the answer is correct. If correct, the student is referred to the next unit in the program. If not, additional information is given including the reasons that the selection is incorrect. The learner is then referred to

[1]Terence J. Trudeau, *Work and Energy, Industrial Arts and Vocational Education*, LIV, April, 1965, pp. 48–49.

the next appropriate unit in the program. The diagram on page 207 illustrates the procedure.

Adjunct Programmed Material

A practical approach to programming, especially for the individual instructor, is to use available material such as a well written text. This is then supplemented with a programmed question and answer sheet and with other materials as needed. This approach has several advantages:

The material following is the first part of a linear program intended to lead the student gradually to an understanding of the operation of the internal-combustion engine and its underlying scientific principles. The photograph illustrates how the program is set up for use with a sliding panel to reveal the correct answer after the student has read the statement or frame on the left.

To use the material as presented here, place a sheet of heavy paper over the answer column at the right. Read the first frame or statement carefully and write the answer in the blank space provided. Now slide the piece of paper down exposing the correct answer for the first frame. The dot below the answer shows you how far down to slide the paper without exposing the response to the next frame.

Proceed in a similar manner through all 57 frames of the set.

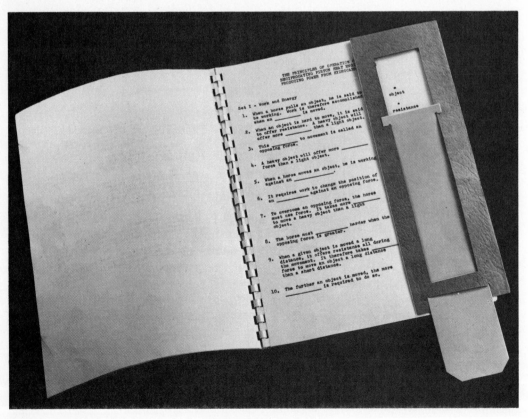

A simple linear program.

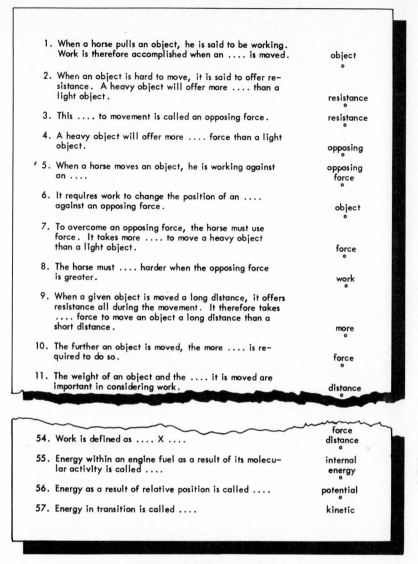

1. When a horse pulls an object, he is said to be working. Work is therefore accomplished when an .... is moved. — object

2. When an object is hard to move, it is said to offer resistance. A heavy object will offer more .... than a light object. — resistance

3. This .... to movement is called an opposing force. — resistance

4. A heavy object will offer more .... force than a light object. — opposing

5. When a horse moves an object, he is working against an .... — opposing force

6. It requires work to change the position of an .... against an opposing force. — object

7. To overcome an opposing force, the horse must use force. It takes more .... to move a heavy object than a light object. — force

8. The horse must .... harder when the opposing force is greater. — work

9. When a given object is moved a long distance, it offers resistance all during the movement. It therefore takes .... force to move an object a long distance than a short distance. — more

10. The further an object is moved, the more .... is required to do so. — force

11. The weight of an object and the .... it is moved are important in considering work. — distance

54. Work is defined as .... X .... — force distance

55. Energy within an engine fuel as a result of its molecular activity is called .... — internal energy

56. Energy as a result of relative position is called .... — potential

57. Energy in transition is called .... — kinetic

Simple linear program (Cont.)

1. The text material may be used for programmed learning and also for review and reference. Adjunct programs have a distinct advantage over programmed materials which are self contained. Self contained programmed materials are generally unsatisfactory for obtaining an overall view of the content. Adjunct programmed materials, however, do allow an overall view of the content for review and serve as a ready source of specific information.

LINEAR PROGRAMING

C SECTION - SERIES AND PARALLEL AC CIRCUITS   Page 129

5

Phasors always rotate in a counter-clockwise direction with passing time.

Assume the three drawings represent the phasor E_1 at three instants of time during the same $\frac{1}{2}$ cycle.

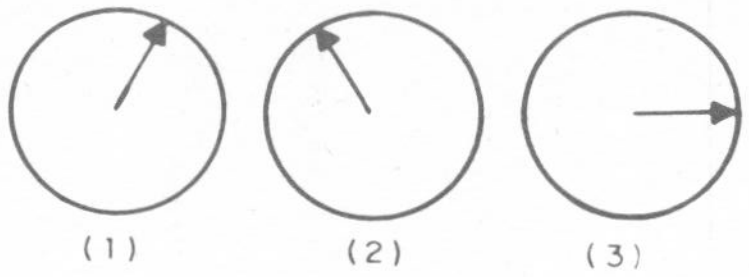

(a) Which drawing represents the first instant of time? _____

(b) Which drawing represents the last instant of time? _____

(1)   (2)   (3)

5 CORRECT ANSWER

(a)   3

(b)   2

6

Two automobiles are racing around a circular track in a CCW direction. One is less than $\frac{1}{2}$ lap behind the other.

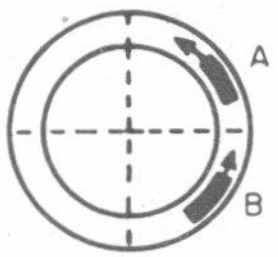

(a) Which one is leading? _____

6 CORRECT ANSWER

(a)   A leads B

7

Phasors also rotate in a CCW direction.

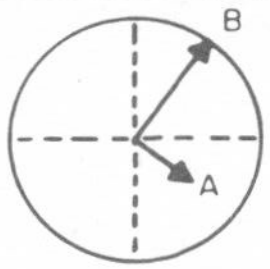

(a) Which of the two phasors to the right is leading by 90°? _____

7 CORRECT ANSWER

(a)   B is leading A

8

Identify the phasor which is leading by 90° in each of the drawings below.

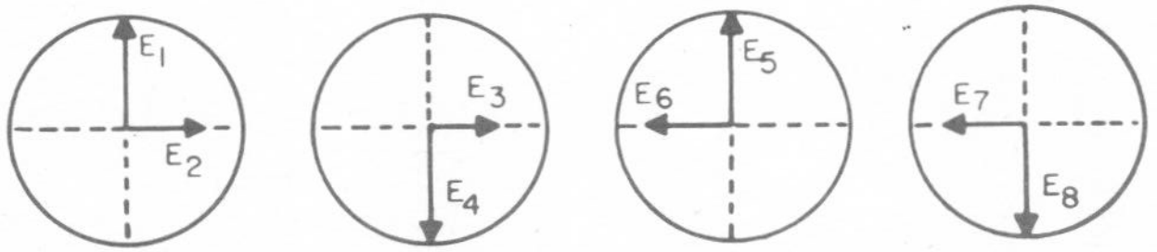

8 CORRECT ANSWER

(a) E_1 is leading E_2

(b) E_3 is leading E_4

(c) E_6 is leading E_5

(d) E_8 is leading E_7

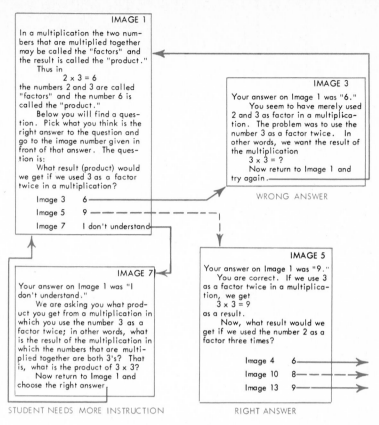

A typical branching program.

2. An adjunct program is relatively easy to prepare and to modify.
3. The student has all the advantages of the textbook, including the table of contents and an index which provide for quick review and the location of specific information at any time.
4. The rapid and experienced learner is not held back by having to read and respond to a large number of small and relatively simple steps as found in linear programs.

An example of a program using adjunct material is shown on page 208.

Some Dividends from Programmed Instructions

The basic concepts of the well publicized programmed instruction movement are having an effect on all instruction. Programmed instruction has helped to improve instructional objectives by insisting that objectives state outcomes in terms of behavior, not merely "appreciation," "familiarization," or "awareness."

Programmed instruction emphasizes the need for an analysis of what the student must know and be able to do. With a thorough and accurate occupational analysis, as described in Chapter 4,

TEXT

Topic — INTRODUCTION TO JOB/TASK ANALYSIS

1. The skills and knowledge required to accomplish assigned work must be determined before we can effectively design a program of training for the work. Therefore, the first step toward a sound training course or program is to analyze the job or task for which training is to be provided.

2. An adequate analysis forms a basis for determining training needs and specific guidance as to the content of proposed training. The analyses also provides standards for evaluating the results of training.

3. Job/task analysis, as required for determining training needs and for planning and evaluating training, is not complicated. It does, however, require careful and accurate work by a team of individuals who are thoroughly familiar with the job/task being analyzed. The analysis process must result in an accurate and detailed listing of all procedures and skills required by the job. In addition, the analysis must contain an accurate outline of the knowledge required to perform the work with judgment under varying conditions.

PROGRAM

Read paragraph #1 before completing the following statements:

The first step toward a sound training program is to analyse _____ · job
or task for which the training will be offered.

The two elements that make up an analysis are __s__ · skills
and __k__ . · knowledge

These are the same elements required to accomplish assigned
__w__ . · work

Read paragraph #2 before completing the following statements:

An analysis is necessary for determining training __n__ . · needs

The analysis also provides guidance as to the __c__ _____ · content
of training programs.

In addition the analysis provides standards for __e__ _____ · evaluating
the results of training.

The analysis then is a basic document for:
1. determining training _____ · needs
2. guiding the selection of _____ · (requirements)
   · content
3. _____ results

Read paragraph #3 before completing the following statements:

An analysis requires the work of a _____ . · team

Members of the team must be familiar with the _____ or · job or task
being analyzed.

Team members must also know the _____ for an analysis to · standards
be used in training.

An analysis includes an accurate outline of the knowledge required to
perform tasks with _____ · judgment
under varying conditions.

An example of adjunct programming.

the job of programming a course of instruction is half complete.

Programmed instruction concepts have helped to develop new interest in constant evaluation of the student's progress. This has often been neglected by the proponents of instruction through mass media, including radio and television.

Good programs emphasize and are built on sound principles of learning, such as:

1. Students work and learn at their own rate. Individual students need not conform to the learning speed of a group.
2. Good programs simulate to a degree the tutorial system—the one student to one instructor approach—which is often too expensive to impliment with a live instructor.
3. The student gains in confidence when informed almost constantly of his progress.
4. Programs may speed up the progress of a group by providing for additional study as needed by individuals. In some situations programmed texts can be used advantageously for out-of-class study so that class time can be used for creative thinking and the use of tools and equipment.

An appropriate and skillfully designed unit of programmed instruction may provide for individual student practice and drill and thus save the instructor's time for more creative work.

Programmed instruction is often highly effective in those segments of instructional programs which have precise standards of performance specified as an objective. Instruction of this type has been used successfully for training air line employees who serve the public when making reservations, and for other training in exact and standardized procedures.

The favorable characteristics of programmed instruction are well understood by educational specialists who have been analytical in their approach. They have always:

1. Required specific objectives for each course and lesson.
2. Analyzed jobs or tasks as a basis for designing instructional programs.
3. Taught through a series of properly sequenced steps.
4. Provided for practice and drill on key elements of the program.
5. Evaluated instruction in terms of the student's performance as defined by the objectives.

Some Factors to Consider

Good programs are expensive. Programs developed under contract with reputable companies cost around $1,000 per hour of material. That is, a program which would take the average student 10 hours to complete will cost about $10,000. It follows that the cost of preparing programmed materials can seldom be justified unless:

1. The subject matter of the course is relatively stable.
2. A large number of students are to be prepared.
3. The content of the programmed unit is essential to meeting the objectives of the total instructional program.
4. A competent staff is available to prepare the program.

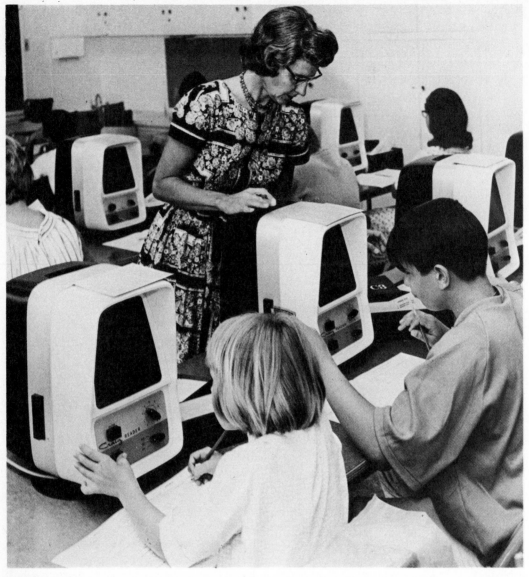

Individualized instruction may be given in groups while allowing each student to proceed at his or her own pace. (Realist, Inc.)

Good programmers must understand educational psychology, the subject matter to be taught, the art of teaching creatively, and the exact situation in which the material is to be used.

Programmed Instruction can be Misused

Programmed instruction like any other approach to instruction, can be misused. Bad programs have been prepared and sold. Good programs have been used in situations which were not consistent with the content of the program. Exaggerated claims have been made for machines and programs. Here we quote Rushton:[2]

> I cannot emphasize too much or too often that qualifying proviso, "when properly used." The wild claims that some have made for programmed learning—that it dispenses with all need for a teacher, that it can, without qualification or preparation, substitute for conventional teaching methods and still produce the same result, that anything can be programmed and that if it cannot be programmed it is not worth teaching, that it can solve the teacher shortage and overnight bring about a new era in education—are without foundation and can only damage the cause of programmed learning. Programmed learning is an educational tool—no more, no less.

The tendency to measure the effectiveness of instruction solely by written achievement tests is responsible for some confusion. The fact that one approach as compared with another produces higher or lower scores on examinations does not provide proof that one method is superior to another.

Written achievement tests at best are rarely capable of measuring all of the desired outcomes from instruction. As Sanford[3] has indicated:

> The advent of the teaching machine, which could be a great boon to education, seems so far to have played into the hands of those educators who believe that the learning of factual content is education, that this learning is neatly separated from everything else that might be going on in the student, and that these other things do not matter much anyway.

The real educational problem is not "how may students most efficiently learn material well enough so that they can pass examinations at a high level," the real problem is "how to make academic material meaningful to them, so that it will play some part in the building up in them of the qualities of an educated person."

How does the learning of factual material contribute to the development of such qualities as the ability to think well, self-understanding, sensitivity to ethical issues, intellectual integrity? This is the key question for educational psychology.

When to use Programmed Materials

Programmed instruction materials like other written instruction materials may be used in different ways. In general, programmed instruction may be used as:

1. A short but complete package intended to provide all of the instruction required to reach a given objective.
2. A means of remedial preparation for those who are to be prepared for classroom or group instruction.
3. An integrated element or part of a total program in which a variety of techniques are used where each is most effective.

---

[2]E. W. Rushton, *The Roanoke Experiment* (Chicago: Encyclopaedia Britannica Press, 1965), p. 62.

[3]Nevitt Sanford, *Will Psychologists Study Human Problems, American Psychologist*, XX, March 1965, p. 195.

A programmed audio cassette reading lesson. This method may be used for a variety of instructional material. (Craig Corporation)

4. Materials for extra study and remedial work by those who need it.
5. A means of post-training and for review of essential content.

Preparing Programmed Materials

The design of programmed materials should be a reflection of realistic and specific instructional objectives. A simple approach may be entirely satisfactory in some situations. A more complex approach may be required in others. It follows that the first step in preparing a unit of programmed instruction (or for that matter any other unit of instruction) is to decide on and state precise objectives. These, it is generally agreed, should establish standards of performance for the student on each task to be learned.

The occupational analysis process as described in Chapter 4 provides a list of doing and knowing elements of an occupation. Each of these may be potentially suitable for programming. It is necessary, however, to establish end-of-course standards of performance as objectives before attempting to prepare programmed material on any unit of the analysis. In defining objectives, we must decide:

1. The precise content to be taught.
2. The most effective way of providing the required instruction.
3. Whether or not the content which we set out to teach has in fact been learned by students.

Broad generalities as objectives are not adequate for the design of programmed instruction where mastery of specific skills is required. Skills may be said to be "the application of knowledge," but our objectives must be stated in terms of demonstrable performance.

The objectives to be attained may be illustrated by referring to this analysis of a plywood cabinet as a student learning activity.

What is to be learned: To estimate the size, shape, and cost of a piece of plywood required to build a cabinet.

Material, methods, and approach: Blueprint, chalkboard, demonstration, text or instruction sheet, and an adjunct program.

Results: Students will demonstrate their ability to accurately estimate the minimum size, shape, and cost of a sheet of plywood required to build a specific plywood cabinet.

Once the objective, conditions of learning and standards of measurement have been stated, the next process is to list the exact steps required to perform the job or task. This process as part of occupational analysis is described in Chapter 4 and is further illustrated in the instruction sheets in Chapter 6.

At this point, it is feasible to consider the programming method or combination of methods to be used. To meet the above objectives, for example, an instruction sheet may be prepared and supplemented with adjunct programmed materials as illustrated on page 208.

Generally, a programmed unit of instruction should be tested with typical students and revised as necessary before it is duplicated and used for regular instruction.

Specific and detailed instruction on the preparation of programmed materials is available in several modern texts. The following texts should be of significant help:

Preparing Instructional Objectives by Robert F. Mager (Fearon Publishers, 1962).

Good Frames and Bad by Susan Meyer Markle (John Wiley and Sons Inc., 1969).

Establishing Instructional Goals by W. James Popham and Eva L. Baker (Prentice-Hall Inc., 1970).

Teaching Machines

All teaching machines use programmed materials. The machine does not teach. It merely holds and controls the use of the program by one or more mechanical methods. Machines range from complex to simple. Some are merely the equivalent of mechanical page turners.

A teaching machine using printed materials and audio tape. (Bell and Howell)

A thorough analysis of the learning-teaching situation and the content to be learned in a total program should precede the selection of a teaching machine. For example, a cheat proof mechanism is important for research and with certain age groups of students. However, the same mechanism may represent an unnecessary expense with other groups. A specific machine may include features which:

1. Hold and present instructional materials in a planned sequence of one frame at a time.
2. Provide for some type of response by the student on each step or frame of the program.
3. Provide immediate feedback on each response by the student.
4. Advance steps or frames as required by the student's response.
5. Keep a record of errors and correct responses made by the student.

This last characteristic is of greatest value in the try-out and development of programs and for research.

As most machine programs are designed for use with a specific type of equipment, the initial purchase of machines must be consistent with the availability of proper programs or with the type of programs to be developed.

For example, one teaching machine uses a combination of microfilm and a projector to show numbered images on a small screen in the order selected by the student. In operating the machine the student (1) reads the material on the screen, (2) makes a choice from a multiple-choice item and (3) indicates the choice on the keyboard of the device. The device then selects and projects another image appropriate in terms of the student's response. For example, if the student has given the correct answer, the teaching device presents further information or perhaps additional problems. If the student has given an incorrect answer, the device presents further material to assist the student in responding

A teaching machine using text, illustrations and multiple choice questions. (TutorSystems)

correctly, etc. The program will continue to provide answers faithfully as long as the student is willing to work.

Self-teaching Texts

Self-teaching books are somewhat similar to teaching machines. Within these books, the page the student is told to read next is determined by the answer given to questions or problems. After providing correct responses, the learner is referred to another page which contains advanced material on the subject. If the response is incorrect or inadequate, the learner is referred to a page which explains the material in one of several different ways depending on the nature of the response made by the student. Thus,

the student is provided with feedback as each small step is taken in much the same manner as would be provided by a teaching machine or tutor.

Instructional Aids and Program Instruction

Each aid and related instructional materials have characteristics which should be considered in planning instructional activities. All aids present information—but some types of information are presented more effectively by one type of aid than others. In general, we can say that most common instructional aids, by themselves, are limited to presenting material. They may, however, do this most effectively.

An instructional aid which presents written material and provides for written student response. (Realist, Inc.)

Programmed materials, including those used in machines, present material and in addition provide for immediate student response and feedback. Programmed materials are generally characterized by written presentation and written response, but this is not an inherent limitation. Still pictures and illustrations in the form of film slides and strips are being used to a limited extent. Motion pictures are feasible, but are more difficult to incorporate as programmed material in a machine.

Some instructional aids and machines provide for feedback—but the type and quality of feedback varies greatly from one approach to another. For example, the feedback on a simple linear program is vastly different from the feedback on an advanced simulator. Simulators provide instruction and require performance involving knowledge, physical skill, and judgment. Feedback is built into the simulator and is inherent in its design. The cost of complex simulators, however, suggests their use in only the most critical (often life or death) situations, such as driver training.

The difference between a simple instructional aid and an advanced teaching machine may be illustrated by the concept of *open loop* vs. *closed loop* instruction. Simple instructional aids by themselves can present information and suggest a response by the student. This is open loop instruction.

By comparison, the advanced teaching machines, including simulators, (1) present information, (2) require the student to respond, (3) provide feedback and (4) lead student into next step. This is closed loop instruction.

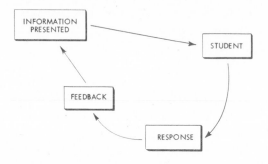

CLOSED LOOP INSTRUCTION

Research on Programmed Instruction

Between 1955 and 1970, there were more than 300 reports on research with various elements of programmed instruction. Probably no other approach to instruction has been subjected to as much research. In addition, a large part of the research conducted in the general field of learning over the years is related to the basic concepts employed in programmed instruction.

Much of this research has been conducted with college students, with the next largest groups comprised of employed adults and secondary level students. Much research has emphasized the learning of facts with the success of the program measured in terms of student performance on written tests.

OPEN LOOP INSTRUCTION

A great many research reports indicate that no significant differences in the quality of learning were found in the comparison of programmed instruction methods with other methods. Also, no significant differences were found in comparisons between various approaches to programming.

Programmed instruction has often demonstrated a saving of student and instructor time. There is some evidence that a linear program using very small steps and fixed at the slow student's level annoys and eventually bores the bright student because of the large number of small items which require a response. It is clear, however, that students learn from programmed materials of all types. It is also clear that all levels and categories of students can learn from programmed materials.

QUESTIONS AND ASSIGNMENTS

1. List in your own words the characteristics of good programmed instruction.
2. What is the major difference between the "linear" and "branching" forms of programming?
3. Prepare a one page program of the linear type.
4. State objectives and describe a teaching situation that would be suitable for programmed instruction (a) on a machine; (b) in book form.
5. Prepare a short unit of adjunct programmed material.
6. Discuss the possible advantages and disadvantages of motion pictures to provide training.
7. Select one related information topic with which you are thoroughly familiar. Discuss the relative advantages of an instruction sheet vs. teaching machine with a class of 20 students.
8. List 10 operations involving tools, instruments or equipment. Which of these can best be taught by demonstration? By teaching machines? By programmed book? By combination? Justify your selections in writing.
9. Describe how overlays could be used in presenting the characteristics of programmed instruction.

Measuring and Evaluating Student Achievement

12

Written achievement tests and other measures of achievement are used to help determine the extent to which the student has learned at any point in the instructional process. They also are valuable in determining the learner's level of knowledge acquired over a longer period of time and may be used prior to the course to determine the level at which instruction should be initiated. Tests can be effective either as daily quizzes or at certain other points in the course for purposes of review and emphasis. After the course is completed, tests may help to measure the amount of information that has been retained and can be applied.

Written tests are valuable tools in the learning process, and few programs are complete without them. However, even the best tests can measure only part of an individual's achievement level. They can provide valuable information, but they never tell the whole story of an individual's development. No written test is capable of measuring all of the developmental changes in the student which occur as a result of an educational experience.

As instructors, our objectives should be to use achievement tests properly, weigh test results carefully, and combine the test results with other evidence of progress and achievement for the best possible evaluation of student all-around development.

When we *measure,* we assess the magnitude of a trait or characteristic, and we secure a score or numerical value. For example, we can report that a student answered 8 of 10 questions or received a rating of 16 on a scale used to assess performance when 20 represented a perfect performance. *Evaluation,* on the other hand, is a broader concept through which an instructor may take measurement results that vary in precision along with more subjective assessments and arrive at as fair and accurate appraisal as his professional judgment permits.

Purpose of Achievement Tests

Achievement tests are different from aptitude tests, mentioned in Chapter 2, that attempt to measure the student's capacity to learn. Achievement tests are specifically designed to find out the extent to which learning has taken place. Both types of tests are important. Each should be used in the right way and at the right time.

Aptitude tests are rarely constructed by individual instructors. Most instructors are concerned primarily with achievement tests—with measuring what their students have learned during a lesson, a phase of the course, or the entire course. Achievement tests can serve a number of purposes. Some of the more important of these are to:

1. Emphasize important points. A test and the discussion that should follow may be used to review, summarize, and emphasize facts, principles, and steps of procedure.
2. Reveal the student's areas of weakness. A test may identify those things on which the student should study or practice. Knowing how well we are doing is essential to continued learning.
3. Locate weaknesses in instruction. A test may reveal to the instructor certain areas that were not well taught, where more thoroughness or another approach is needed.
4. Hold students to account. Tests often make students feel more responsible for learning. They may

challenge the student to learn more. As a general rule students will make greater progress in the course if they know that they will be tested fairly.
5. Provide a basis for grades and advancement. Tests are used to measure how much the student has learned in comparison with known standards and the performance of others in the group. From these comparisons, combined with other assessments of the student's work and progress, a fair and significant evaluation can be obtained from which a grade can be derived.

What is a Good Test or Measuring Instrument?

Good tests are valuable and necessary measuring instruments, but poor tests may be worse than none at all. Tests that measure the wrong things or measure the right things inaccurately and inconsistently may actually detract from the instructional program and discourage the students. The characteristics of a good test are few in number, fairly complex, and often misunderstood. They can be grouped as follows.

Validity. Does the test measure what it purports to measure?

Reliability. How accurately does the test measure what it purports to measure, and how consistently can the measure be made?

Practicality. Is the test easy to give, take and to score properly?

Objectivity. Do test items require interpretation or can responses be judged right or wrong? If two or more people cannot grade the test and arrive at the same score, it is not objective. In other words, our subjective judgment had to be used which reduced the *objectivity* of the test.

Comprehensiveness. This test characteristic refers to the manner in which the test samples all parts of the lesson, unit or course.

These characteristics are not separate and distinct. Each has a bearing on the other. However we may consider them one at a time.

Validity

The most important characteristic of a good test is its validity. This means that the test actually measures what you want it to measure as determined by the objectives of the course. If it measures elements to some degree other than those consistent with the objectives, you can never be sure what you have measured. A test that does not measure what you think it measures gives false information. It can do great harm. For example, the truly creative student who can visualize the unusual application of theory or who may read between the lines may respond in a way that can be misunderstood by the instructor. It is a fact that some questions are answered correctly, according to the instructor's scoring key, by the least capable students. The more intelligent students may read more into the question than is intended and hence a most appropriate response will be judged according to the instructor's concept of the right answer. If the objective of a test is to measure what the student has learned in a lesson or phase of the course, we should be sure that:

1. The questions are on the more important theories, facts, and procedures in the subject. Keep your course objectives in mind.

2. The questions are not so general in nature that the intelligent student can figure out the answer even though he knows little about the specific subject. Of course, we are interested in measuring intelligence, but intelligence should be measured by tests designed for this alone. Don't use trick questions!

3. The reading difficulty of the items is consistent with the reading ability of students. If the student knows the answer, but fails to respond properly because of an inability to read and understand the question, the validity of the test question is weakened. Test items that use illustrations and pictures may be more valid for certain technical content, depending on the subject and the reading level of the student. If we want to measure reading ability or vocabulary, we need another type of test—one that is valid for this purpose and measures this and nothing else.

4. The test is free of insignificant, detailed, or easily measured information of relatively little importance.

5. The test does not overemphasize a learner's ability to memorize facts. This is a common weakness in many tests. The ability to use and apply facts and principles gives a more valid measure of achievement.

How the validity of a test can be determined. The most practical approach is to analyze and judge carefully each test item or question to make sure that it will tell you what you want to know about the student's actual achievement in the course.

Another very practical technique is to have other instructors or individuals who are competent in the subject and know the objectives and level of your course to read or take the test before it is given to the students. This should be very helpful in eliminating or suggesting modification of items.

After the test has been used, validity can be judged by comparing the results of the test with other indications of the student's progress. If the student is outstanding in his class, laboratory, or shop work, but does poorly on the written test, the reason for this should be investigated. Perhaps the test contains many items of questionable validity or, on the other hand, errors may have been made in judging the student's performance in the classroom, laboratory, or shop.

There is no substitute for careful judgment in the application of all measures of achievement.

Reliability

Here we are concerned with the accuracy and consistency of the test as a measuring instrument. Many tests fail to measure consistently. A reliable test measures in exactly the same way each time it is used. In building a test, we can often increase reliability by:

1. Giving clear and understandable directions for taking the test and for answering each type of item in the test.
2. Reducing or eliminating complicated, ambiguous, vague, and confusing questions which encourage guessing.
3. Increasing the length of the test,

thus reducing the chance of the student guessing correct answers. With five questions the student has a chance of guessing most or even all of them right or wrong. With fifty questions the chance of guessing a high percentage of answers either correctly or incorrectly is very unlikely.

Practicality

A test is usable if it is easy to give or administer, easy to read and understand, and easy to score objectively. There are several elements to consider in making a test more usable.

A test is easy to administer if the instructions to the student are clear, concise and easy to read. Type size and legibility, quality of paper, arrangement of the items and use of illustrations are all contributing factors. In addition, the instrument must be designed so that it can be administered in the time period available so that students can give adequate consideration to each item.

Objectivity

Many tests cannot be graded or scored by different instructors with equal results. A good test should be so designed that the scores are about the same no matter who scores the paper. Such a test is said to have objectivity. That is why the modern short-answer test is often called an *objective test.*

Where creative achievement is to be measured (often, for example, in writing and design courses), objective tests must be supplemented by other more subjective assessment procedures. Here the instructor must use judgment and great care in grading so that an appropriate evaluation results.

Tests should be neither too easy nor too difficult. Normally some students should get a high score, but the test should not be so easy that everyone gets a high grade. The mastery test is one exception to this general guide. If you were to test on a dangerous and critical operation on which no mistakes can be allowed, you are justified in drilling on this operation until everyone can pass the test with a perfect score. When teaching or testing for mastery, time must be a variable. The only appropriate grade would be *pass* or *not yet.* Because of individual differences, some learners would take much longer to reach the specified level of mastery than others.

Comprehensiveness

The good test samples all parts of the lesson, unit or course for which the test instrument is designed. A test is not comprehensive if a disproportionate number of items are taken from the several areas of study being assessed. The number of test items should be proportionate to the emphasis given the area during the lesson, unit or course. The more comprehensive the test, the greater will be its content validity and reliability.

Kinds of Tests and Measures

Hundreds of types of tests and other measuring instruments have been designed. These, however, can be grouped as follows.

Oral questions. Used primarily as a spot check of the students' understanding of concepts at the time they are taught.

Written tests. Most useful for measuring the students' information about and understanding of facts, principles, and procedures. Written tests can be based on both knowing, doing, and attitudinal content from the analysis. (Cognitive, psychomotor or affective, if you prefer).

Performance tests. Here the student is required to demonstrate all or part of a procedure. Performance tests are based primarily on the doing of performance elements of the analysis.

Observation of students at work. This is vital part of the educational program wherever practical application of learning is an objective. Rating scales can be prepared that list the essential criteria to be used in making the judgments in a more objective way.

Some General Guides for Preparing Tests

Good judgment rather than rules should be the guide in developing tests. The instructor should ask this question: "What skill and knowledge is essential for the student to meet the objectives of the lesson or course for which the examination is designed?" Each test item should be evaluated to make sure it measures essential knowledge and skill. There is always a tendency to measure those elements that are easy to measure.

Having decided that students should be tested on certain parts of the course, the next question is "What type of item is best suited to measure achievement in each part of the course?" Another problem to consider is, "How can we give the right balance to the total test?" The greatest number of items should be directed to the most important elements of the course.

Types of Written Test Items

These types of items have been selected as being the most common and useful in typical instructional programs:

1. True-false
2. Completion
3. Multiple choice
4. Identification
5. Matching
6. Short answer essay

The following examples and instructions are for preparing each type of item. It should be observed that the term *question* is not to be indiscriminately used for the more appropriate term *test item*. The term question is appropriate only when it is actually a question followed by a question mark (?).

True-false. This is one of the most common types of test items. They are useful for testing on a large amount of information in a short period of time. This type of item is less reliable than the other types because there is more chance for the student to guess the correct answer, and it tends to measure memory rather than understanding or application. A test made up of true-false items should normally contain at least 50 items. The more items in the instrument the less chance the student has of guessing a high percentage of the answers correctly or incorrectly.

The item consists of a single statement which is either true or false. Example: *Spirit stains protect wood from moisture.* T_____ F_____
Here are some suggestions for writing true-false items:

1. Be sure statement are either completely true or false. If the correct answer is "perhaps" or "yes, except when . . ." the item should probably be discarded or rewritten. Don't have one part of the question contain a true statement and another a false one unless the directions specify that the item must be entirely true in order to be correctly marked true.

2. Make about half of the questions to be used in a test true and the other half false. Randomly mix the true and false items so that no pattern of response exists to give unnecessary clues to the correct responses. Avoid double negatives. Example:

One should not work on electrical equipment if he is not sure that no circuits are energized. T_____ F_____

An improved statement might read:

Before working on electrical equipment, one should make sure all circuits are dead. T_____ F_____

3. Keep the language simple.
4. Make the statements as short as possible.
5. Make questions out on important points only, not on unimportant details.
6. Avoid trick questions.
7. Avoid words or construction that may help the student to guess the right answer. Such words as "always," "usually," "none," and "only" may help the student to guess the right answer. Example: All propellers are made of aluminum.
8. Do not make true statements consistently longer or shorter than false statements.
9. Avoid copying sentences from the text. Write the item in your own words. Some students tend to remember exact textual wording better than others yet they may not know any more of the subject than those who do not have this ability.

Directions: Some of the following statements are true, some are false. If a statement is true circle the "T" at the left. If the statement is false, circle the "F" at the left and explain why it is false. The first statement is answered as an example.

(x) T Ⓕ   The WLA model motorcycle has a horizontal engine with opposed cylinders.

Explanation: *The WLA model is equipped with a V-Type engine*

(1) T F   The purposes of the oil bath air cleaner is to clean the oil.

Explanation:

A modified true-false exam in which all false answers require an explanation.

Completion. This type of item will measure the student's memory and ability to recall exact words or facts such as technical terms, tolerances, or exact specifications. Completion items should be used when the course objectives require the student to remember such information.

The item consists of a true statement, one or two important words of which have been omitted and blank spaces left to indicate where the omitted words belong. The student must think of the proper word and write it in the blank or on a separate answer sheet.

Here are some suggestions for writing completion-type questions:

1. Write out a number of short statements covering the most important information you have taught.
2. Go through these statements and omit one or perhaps two important words. Make sure the meaning of the sentence is clear after the words are omitted.
3. Omit only words that call for specific information. Be sure there is only one word that fits or, if more than one word is correct, provide credit for all correct answers.
4. Make all blanks the same length so as not to give a clue to the right word.
5. Omit only those words that will test the student's knowledge of specific content learned during your instruction, not items of general knowledge. Don't omit the verb in the statement and do not use the article *a* or *an* to provide a clue. To place the article as *a(an)* before a blank indicates a further option.
6. Number each blank space. It is often desirable to have the answers written on a separate answer sheet which has corresponding numbers, or in a column along the margin of

Directions: Complete the following statements by writing the correct word or words in the blank space or spaces. The first question is answered as an example. The length of the blanks' is not an indication of the word or phrase to be used in properly completing the statement.

(x)   An important consideration in tool design is the *capacity* and *range* of machine tools.

(1)   Although each improvement in tool material has been accompanied by an increase in hardness, brittleness, and cost, higher _____ _____ have resulted in cutting tools.

(2)   Where shock is an influencing factor in cutting tool applications, it is normally better to use a tool made of _____ _____ steel than a carbide-tipped tool.

(3)   A plant which assigns its designers a specific class of tools, like jigs or bits, is using the _____ _____ system of organization.

(4)   A basic step the tool design follows is to develop tools so they are _____ to make and also give _____ performances.

Examples of completion type items.

the test sheet. An example is shown above.

Test items in the form of a straightforward question rather than an incomplete statement are often possible and desirable. Example:

1.   *What is the name of the machine that changes mechanical energy into electrical energy?* _____

Multiple choice.   These items will successfully measure the student's knowledge of facts. They may also, if skillfully designed, be used to measure understanding and ability to discriminate among several possible alternatives. For this reason such items have greater potential value for use in measurement than others. The item usually consists of a statement followed by a series of alternatives, all of which are plausible but only one of which is best. Example:

_B_   1. Auger bits vary in diameter by:

     A. 1/8 inch
     B. 1/16 inch
     C. 1/32 inch
     D. 1/64 inch

This item is designed to test for facts that the student should remember.

Here are some suggestions for writing multiple choice items.

1.   Include at least four and not more than six responses for each item.
2.   Include no alternative responses that are obviously wrong.
3.   If the responses are to be written on the test paper itself instead of on a separate answer sheet, provide a space for the answers as shown in the preceding example. If the answers are all in a column along the right side of the paper, scoring of the test can be done more easily.

2. Individual instruction sheets should be used primarily to:

A. Eliminate the use of oral instruction
B. Teach information and skills
C. Aid in meeting individual differences
D. Teach the student to dig out information for himself

This item measures the student's judgment and understanding of facts.

4. Include as much of the item as possible in the stem or first part of the question. Make the answers as short as possible.

5. Avoid items on trivial or unimportant facts.

6. Avoid items that can be answered from general knowledge. Measure only content that has been taught.

7. Diagrams, drawings, and pictures add interest and tend to make the questions more practical.

8. Avoid the use of *a* or *an* as the final word in the introductory statement. If the word must be used, insert the other in parentheses beside it. For example:

3. The meter used for measuring resistance in a circuit is a (an):

A. Voltmeter
B. Pitometer
C. Ohmmeter
D. Potentiometer

Other words that should be qualified: *is* (*are*), *this* (*these*), and other verbs that take the singular, such as *show* (*s*) and *use* (*s*).

Matching. This type of item consists of two lists or columns of related information. One column may be made up of names and the other of names or symbols or, as shown below, one column may have names, the other illustrations. The student is asked to match the name with the appropriate illustration. This type of item is highly discriminating where exact information is required.

Here are some suggestions for writing matching questions:

1. Use at least four but no more than twelve items in each matching item.

2. Include more items in the column of alternatives than in the other. The column of answers should contain two or more items more than the other column.

3. Include only materials or information that is related in each matching item. Don't mix numbers, names, and dates in the list of pos-

Directions: Complete each of the following statements by placing the letter representing the best respone in the space provided to the left of the item number. The first statement is answered as an example.

B (x)   The primary purpose for maintenance programs of machine equipment is to:

        A. extend the critical life
        B. prolong the physical life
        C. retard the serviceable life
        D. increase the use-time factor

___ (1)   The acceptable variation from an ideal size is called:

        A. allowance
        B. dimensional control
        C. precision control
        D. tolerance

___ (2)   That tolerance exists in machining

Part of a multiple choice examination.

sible answers. Put numbers and dates in ascending or descending order, and put names in alphabetical order since part of the task is not to find the location of the material but to know the answer.

4. As a general rule, each item should be used only once.
5. The entire matching item should be on the same page. See below.

Identification. This type of test item is useful in measuring the student's knowledge of the names of tools, supplies, utensils, or the parts of a piece of equipment, for example. The student looks at a drawing or picture and writes the proper name in a blank space. See page 228. As another example, you could hang tools or parts on a panel in front of the group with large numbers below each part. The student merely writes the name of the part after the proper number on the answer sheet.

Directions: At the left of the name place the letter identifying each type of fastening device. An item is answered as an example.

(1) ___ Cone head
   B   Button head
   ___ Pan head
   ___ Flat head
   ___ Flat top countersunk head
   ___ Truss head

(2) At the right are shown four types of bolt heads.

Exam item for matching related items.

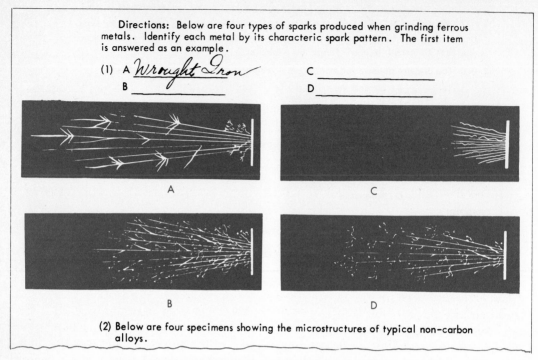

Directions: Below are four types of sparks produced when grinding ferrous metals. Identify each metal by its characteric spark pattern. The first item is answered as an example.

(1) A *Wrought Iron*

B _____

C _____

D _____

A

C

B

D

(2) Below are four specimens showing the microstructures of typical non-carbon alloys.

Exam item requiring identification of pictured objects.

The opaque projector may be used to project pictures on a screen in front of the class. A number from a calendar may be pasted on the picture so that the student knows which blank to fill in on the answer sheet.

Short answer essay. In essay items students respond in their own words in sentence and paragraph form. Essay-type examinations are more time consuming for both student and instructor and are more difficult to grade. They are best when we want to measure the student's ability to organize material and present it in a logical way in writing. They have value in measuring the student's generalized understanding of a subject.

The main disadvantages of this type of examination are that it is difficult to grade objectively, it is time consuming, and it may encourage excessive verbalizing on the part of the student. The following is an example of an essay item:

Compare the characteristics of multiple choice items with those of true-false items with regard to measuring recall of facts, application of theory, measurement of judgement.

In preparing and scoring the essay examination:

1. Ask for specific information that can be given in a short paragraph. Decide on the ideas that must be provided for a complete and correct

response and decide on the point value to be assigned for part or full response.

2. State the basis of the answer, particularly in items where the learner is asked to "discuss".
3. Make sure the item is clear and that the student knows exactly what is expected.
4. Require the student to explain why, describe, and give reasons for the response.
5. Indicate point value of each item in parentheses near lower right of answer space.

The first step in scoring the essay-type examination item is to cover the student's name on each test paper so that you do not know whose paper you are marking.

Read over a group of responses given by the students to each item. This will give you an idea of the average quality of responses and help you decide on the scores to assign. Score one item on all test papers before proceeding to the next item.

Some instructors write out the expected response for each item prior to scoring it. Assign a proper weight to each response by giving one point on the score for each significant element of subject matter to be described properly by the student. One essay item may contain four significant points while another has only two.

Summary of Types of Test Items and their Characteristics

Multiple choice.
  Advantages:
  1. Little chance to guess correct answer.
  2. Objective scoring is facilitated.
  3. May be designed to measure judgment as well as memory.

Directions: Responding to the following items as briefly as possible. Use complete sentences and make your replies clear and direct. Supply specific information as required. The first item is answered as an example.

(x) Describe the procedure you would follow in constructing a partition wall for a typical one-story house.

After framing out, I would nail all headers and cripple studs for the frame openings while the wall is still on the floor, spacing all studs for the partition 16 inches on center. Only after the framework was complete would I set the partition into place.

(1) Describe the master pattern you would make for the joists and studs in the house shown below.

A short essay exam item.

4. Can be varied to suit many types of subject matter.

Disadvantages:
1. Very hard to construct when judgment is to be measured, although it is feasible.
2. May tend to measure student's reading ability to an unfair degree.
3. May be used for specific but trivial information.

Completion.

Advantages:
1. Little chance to guess correct answer.
2. Good when student must be able to remember specific facts, words, or symbols.

Disadvantages:
1. Measures memory rather than judgment.
2. Difficult to make items that call for only one correct answer.

Identification.

Advantage:
1. Good for measuring knowledge of such factors as names of tools and materials, or locations of certain features of a machine or piece of equipment.

Disadvantage:
1. Since pictures or drawings are necessary in written identification tests, pictorial or other graphic representation may pose a problem for some instructors.

True-false.

Advantages:
1. Can be used to cover wide range of content quickly.

2. Easy to score.
3. Easy to make.

Disadvantages:
1. Student has 50-50 chance of guessing correct answer on each item.
2. May measure student's reading ability rather than knowledge of subject matter.
3. May be low in reliability because of the guessing factor.

Matching.

Advantages:
1. Large number of responses can be obtained with one test item.
2. Quite objective and discriminating.

Disadvantages:
1. Not the best method for measuring complete understanding of information and judgment.
2. Difficult to write properly.

Short answer essay.

Advantages:
1. Relatively easy to construct.
2. Gives student chance to organize and express ideas.
3. May give best indication of student's overall knowledge of certain subjects.
4. Essential when measuring written communication skills.

Disadvantages:
1. May measure student's communication skill rather than knowledge.
2. Difficult to score and grade objectively.
3. Will not measure as many objectives in a given time period.
4. May encourage excessive verbalizing.

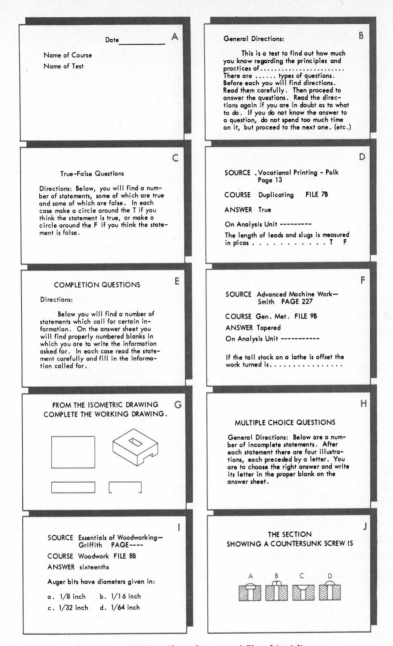

A

Date _____

Name of Course

Name of Test

B

General Directions:

This is a test to find out how much you know regarding the principles and practices of ....
There are ...... types of questions. Before each you will find directions. Read them carefully. Then proceed to answer the questions. Read the directions again if you are in doubt as to what to do. If you do not know the answer to a question, do not spend too much time on it, but proceed to the next one. (etc.)

C

True-False Questions

Directions: Below, you will find a number of statements, some of which are true and some of which are false. In each case make a circle around the T if you think the statement is true, or make a circle around the F if you think the statement is false.

D

SOURCE . Vocational Printing – Polk
        Page 13

COURSE Duplicating   FILE 7B

ANSWER True

On Analysis Unit ---------

The length of leads and slugs is measured in picas . . . . T F

E

COMPLETION QUESTIONS

Directions:

Below you will find a number of statements which call for certain information. On the answer sheet you will find properly numbered blanks in which you are to write the information asked for. In each case read the statement carefully and fill in the information called for.

F

SOURCE Advanced Machine Work—
        Smith PAGE 227

COURSE Gen. Met. FILE 9B

ANSWER Tapered

On Analysis Unit -----------

If the tail stock on a lathe is offset the work turned is . . . .

G

FROM THE ISOMETRIC DRAWING
COMPLETE THE WORKING DRAWING.

H

MULTIPLE CHOICE QUESTIONS

General Directions: Below are a number of incomplete statements. After each statement there are four illustrations, each preceded by a letter. You are to choose the right answer and write its letter in the proper blank on the answer sheet.

I

SOURCE Essentials of Woodworking—
        Griffith PAGE----

COURSE Woodwork FILE 8B
ANSWER sixteenths

Auger bits have diameters given in:

a. 1/8 inch   b. 1/16 inch
c. 1/32 inch   d. 1/64 inch

J

THE SECTION
SHOWING A COUNTERSUNK SCREW IS

A   B   C   D

Some standard headings for a card file of test items.

Card File Test Building

Instructors as a rule agree that a comprehensive program of testing should be carried on in every subject. Yet one is likely to speculate on the questions, "How much use is being made of available test material?" and "How many instructors find time to carry on a good testing and test-building program conscientiously?" Perhaps all too frequently no test is available that meets the needs exactly and a poor test is used or the testing is delayed.

Card files of test items make it possible for the instructor to construct a good test with a minimum of time and effort whenever he needs one. Briefly, this system consists of typing all available and usable items on cards. When a test is needed on a specific unit of work appropriate cards are selected and arranged in desired order. After other cards, which give instructions to the students, are added, the questions are prepared for duplication. Good tests can be organized in a short time by means of the card file system. The tests can be changed and improved easily. The method is usable, flexible, and meets the requirements for keeping the testing program up to date.

Building the Item File

Obtain cards of different colors for the various types of items; for example, salmon for true-false, yellow for completion, blue for multiple choice, and so on. Use $3'' \times 5''$ cards for those items which do not require large drawings, etc., and $5'' \times 8''$ cards for those items which require more space. Or, if you prefer, use $5'' \times 8''$ cards for all questions.

Make standard headings for the cards. Use a standard heading for each card so that the card may be properly replaced when removed from the file. The heading makes it possible for others to use the file intelligently and keep it in order.

The sources and page number make a record of instructional materials being covered. Always include the number of the analysis element on which the ques-

tion is based. These are valuable as a reference when the test item is being discussed by students.

Prepare test items. Write out items of each type on cards of the color selected. For items that make use of drawings, use the $5'' \times 8''$ cards, allowing a margin of one-half inch on each side of the drawing as a seven-inch space is the effective width of stencils or masters used for reproduction on $8^{1}/_{2}'' \times 11''$ paper. As new test items become available or are written for a course, add them to the file.

File the item cards. Several methods of filing the cards have been found practical. That shown above is perhaps best for the individual teacher, since all of the types of questions for one course are located in one box or drawer. The $5'' \times 8''$ cards should be filed separately. Standard sets of general directions to the student on each type of item should be typed on colored cards that distinguish them from the cards on which individual items have been typed. A card for directions should be prepared for each type of item. Other cards carrying standard information can be added.

Preparing a Table of Specifications

A Table of Specifications is nothing more than a systematic way for an instructor to structure the decision-making that is involved in creating an appropriate examination for the lesson, unit or course after test items covering the content have been prepared. Two basic decisions are made by instructors either intentionally or by default. *First,* as a result of the test items chosen, certain objectives or content areas of the lesson, unit or course are tested to some degree (proportionately or disproportionately).

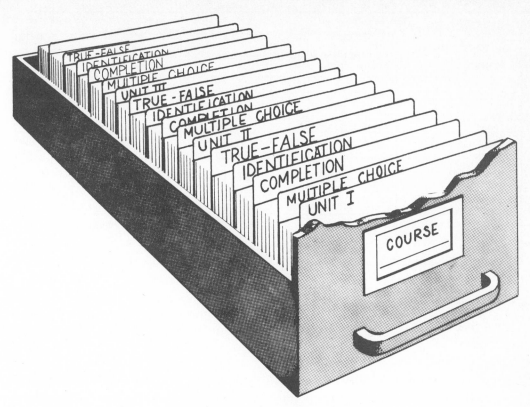

A file drawer of test item cards.

Second, as a result of the type of items selected, the instructor emphasizes recall of facts, recognition, or application.

Since these decisions are going to be made, it seems appropriate for the instructor to make the decision on purpose in a systematic and rational way. The Table of Specifications is a means of accomplishing this end. In the Table you will note that the objectives or content areas are written on the left hand side of the Table. The first column marked (1) provides an opportunity for the instructor to decide the percent of emphasis or amount of weight to be given each of the objectives or content areas. The second column marked (2) can be used to specify the number of items needed to provide the percent of emphasis desired. For example, if an 80 point examination is planned and 10 percent emphasis is desired for a given objective or area of content, the number of items entered in column (2) would be 8. The next three or more columns will be used to specify the extent to which the items chosen should measure the student's ability to recall facts, recognize, identify, apply, etc.

The last two columns are not completed until all selections have been made. In

ABBREVIATED OBJECTIVES OR CONTENT AREA TO BE TESTED	(1) Emphasis in Percent	(2) Number of Points	Recall of Facts 10%	Recognition 30%	Application 40%	Knowledge of Concepts 20%	Actual Number of Points	Actual Percent
1. Principles of learning	10%	8	1	3	3	2	9	11.25
2. Selecting and organizing content	30%	24	3	8	9	5	25	31.25
3. Instructional aids and devices	15%	12	1	3	4	2	10	12.50
4. Developing and using instructional material	20%	16	2	4	6	3	15	18.75
5. Measuring and evaluating achievement	25%	20	2	6	9	4	21	26.25
TOTALS	100%	80	9	24	21	16	80	100.00
PERCENT	--	--	11.25	30.0	38.75	20.0	--	100.00

A typical Table of Specifications.

essence they are the "reality" columns and reveal the decisions you made on the basis of the guidelines provided by the other columns in the table. Due to multiple point items, percents that yield fractional points and other factors, the examination will not always yield the exact percent and number of items as initially planned in the Table of Specifications, therefore, the need for the last two columns.

Constructing a Test from the Table of Specifications

These steps are suggested in constructing a written achievement test after you have a Table of Specifications as a guide.

1. Take all multiple choice item cards that relate to a given objective, content area or unit from the file and select those that are appropriate for your test.

2. Run through the selected stack of cards and eliminate the least desirable questions in order to get the proper or desired number of questions.

3. Repeat this process for the other types of items you plan to use.

4. Arrange the cards at random, in the order of difficulty or in any way desired.

5. Add a heading card for the test and a direction card for each type of item.

6. Have the test typed, if possible; make out the answer sheet; and refile the cards. The fact that the items are already typed and in good order will aid in the final preparation of the test.

The method of selecting and filing questions facilitates keeping tests up to date. As they can be changed easily, there is less tendency to use tests which do not exactly fit the lesson, unit or course. Due to the relatively large number of items on file, the cards may be used for review purposes and special on-the-spot examinations without repeating the use of an item in later tests. As new test material becomes available, the file can easily be improved by the addition of new items. Here are some further suggestions in constructing the written achievement test:

1. Use no more than four or five different types of items.
2. Include some reasonably easy items and some more difficult ones.
3. Arrange the items of each type together in the order of difficulty, starting with the easier items.
4. Organize the questions so that scoring is simple, rapid, and accurate.
5. Consider using answer sheets.
6. Prepare clear and precise directions for the student.
7. If at all possible, try out the test on other instructors before giving it in its final form to the group for whom the test was constructed.
8. Check with other instructors and specialists on every phase of test construction.

Scoring and Evaluating a Test

If the test has been prepared so that the students' answers are placed along one margin of the test paper or if an answer sheet with columns is used, scoring of the test can be done quickly with an examination key as shown in Figure 12-13.

Such a key on heavy paper can be made up for each page of the test or for each column on the answer sheet. Correct answers to each item are written on the key.

When the key is placed next to the answers on the test or answer sheet it is possible at a glance to note answers that do not match the key.

An important addition to the examination key is the record of times each item is missed. This provides information necessary for decisions regarding the validity, reliability, and usability of each item. It can also be used to highlight information that should be re-taught or perhaps taught by a different method.

If an item is missed a great many times, the following type of analysis should be made:

Is the item missed by good and poor students alike? We may have a poor item, perhaps so ambiguous or poorly written that everyone is guessing the answer. Such items should be re-written or discarded.

Is the item missed by the least capable students but generally answered correctly by the most capable in the class as shown by total scores on the test? This would tend to indicate that the item is valid, reliable, and discriminating.

If an item is generally marked correctly by both strong and weak students, it may mean that the item is too easy, that the answer has been given to the students through other items in the test or that by the use of such words as "always" or "never" we have helped the students to guess the right answer. On the other hand, it may only mean that this material has been taught very thoroughly. A careful reading of the item in the light of the way the material was taught will usually indicate its strengths and weaknesses.

If we are to use tests for teaching as well as evaluating, the results of each test should be carefully analyzed. Both the instructor and the student can learn much from a study of the results of a good test.

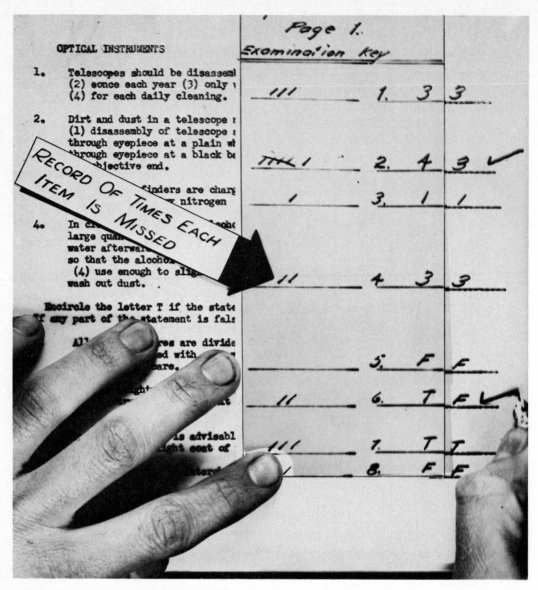

Scoring a test with an examination key.

Time should be provided in the schedule for a thorough discussion of the test. This will help to clear up any misunderstandings and will provide information of value in improving the course and the test itself.

An interesting practice found in one industrial training program is described below.

The trainers of one course followed an interesting policy regarding grading. All students were encouraged to make scores above the class average on each test. All students whose scores were below the class average for that test were called in for a conference with instructors; thus, exactly half the class received such a call after every examination. But the student was neither berated for making a score below the class average nor exhorted to do better. The conference was for the sole purpose of determining whether there were any company-controlled factors responsible for the student's low score. If such factors did exist, immediate steps were taken to correct the situation.

This policy is one of several used by this company to protect the substantial investment it has in training programs and in students. Seeing to it that the student has every assistance and opportunity for learning the subject matter of the course is said to be one of the soundest ways of getting the most from the training dollar.

Translating Test Scores into Grades

Whenever possible, it is best to report only scores to students for the various measures taken during a course. In this way, only one translation to a letter grade is made. Do not get trapped into trying to average a dozen or so A's, B's, C's, D's and F's for a course and arrive at a defensible course grade. Many schemes are available to assist in the translation of numerical scores into letter grades, but there is no substitute for the instructor's judgment based on experience. The following illustration of a translation graph may prove helpful. For simplicity of explanation, a single test score is used; however, as indicated, in actual practice the translation of a composite or cumulative score for the course is a better practice. The graph is a convenient means of translating a raw score into the commonly used

marking or grading systems. Here is a typical procedure.

1. Select a piece of graph paper which is divided into inches and tenths of inches.

2. Along the lower line place grades starting with 100 at the right of the sheet and moving toward the left as shown in the example of the graph on page 238. Usually the lowest grade will not be below 40.

3. On the vertical line projecting upward from the left end of the lower line, place marks which cover the range of raw scores from highest to lowest made on the test. Since the lowest mark on this test was 51, we could have started with 50 as the lowest point on the vertical scale. Extra high or low marks on this scale do not effect its use.

4. Draw a vertical line through the lowest passing mark on the base line as set by you or the administration. This will usually be 60 on a percentage system and *D* on the five letter *(A, B, C, D, F)* system.

5. Determine the value of the highest score on the test. In terms of your past experiences with the course and your experiences with other groups of students, you are best able to say how much the highest score on the test is worth. Place a mark at this value on the base line. In our example, we have decided that a score of 78 on the test is equal to a grade of 99. (There were only 80 questions in the test.)

6. Project a line upward from 99 and another to the right from 78 until they meet at point *A*.

7. Determine the lowest passing score

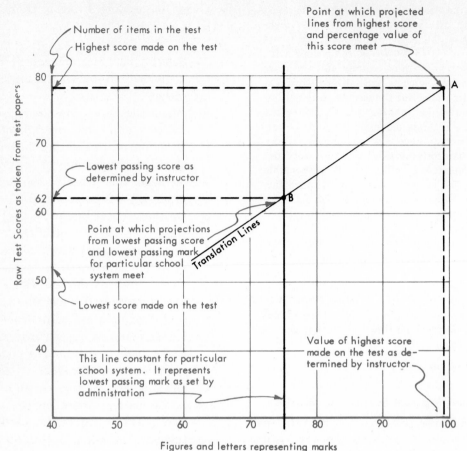

Number of items in the test

Highest score made on the test

Point at which projected lines from highest score and percentage value of this score meet

Raw Test Scores as taken from test papers

Lowest passing score as determined by instructor

Point at which projections from lowest passing score and lowest passing mark for particular school system meet

Translation Lines

Lowest score made on the test

Value of highest score made on the test as determined by instructor

This line constant for particular school system. It represents lowest passing mark as set by administration

Figures and letters representing marks

A translation graph.

on the test. This choice is a matter of good judgment based on your knowledge of the amount the student should know and the difficulty of the particular test. Statistical methods may be used to determine the lowest passing score; however, they are fairly complicated and will not work very well for small classes. Your judgment will be aided if you first make a distribution of the scores from the test as shown in the example below. Study the test papers with scores near

failing to determine the lowest passing score. In our example we shall select the raw score of 62 as being the lowest score that a student should receive and yet pass the test.

8. From this point (score 62) on the vertical line of scores, project a line to the line drawn in step 4. This gives us point B.

9. Through points A and B draw a line and allow it to extend down below the level of the lowest score on the left hand scale. This line is called the translation line.

Using the translation graph. To use the graph, take any raw score from a test paper and find a corresponding point on the left hand scale. Follow along a horizontal line from this point to the translation line and then drop down to the scale of marks on the base line. Example: Score of 71 is worth a mark of 89 or a *B*. The mark at this point on the base line represents the equivalent of the raw score on the test and is the mark given the student in his record.

Steps	Tally scores made by one class.	Total tally of scores after test has been used with several classes.
80–84		I
75–79	II	IHT I
70–74	III	IHT IHT
65–69	IHT I	IHT IHT IHT III
60–64	I	IHT I
55–59	II	IIII
50–54		II
45–49		

Distributing raw test scores to determine the lowest passing score. The highest passing score is 80.

Both the raw scores and their equivalent marks should be placed on the test paper and students should be informed about the method used in marking the papers.

How to use Performance Tests

Performance tests can be designed to measure a student's competence on some phase or operation of the work for which instruction has been provided. The performance test is the best type of test to use where you wish to measure the student's skill on a practical job. It is not the best type of test for quickly measuring

knowledge, basic concepts, or information. For this you would use written tests. The performance test rates high in validity and reliability if it is carefully constructed and properly given. Performance tests can be designed to measure the student's skill on such operations as:

1. Dividing on C and D scales of the slide rule.
2. Changing feed on metal lathe.
3. Preparing a salad
4. Sharpening a hand saw
5. Typing a letter
6. Locating cause of wiring failure on an automobile engine

Constructing a performance test. Select an important operation on which the students have received instruction. This operation should require a reasonable length of time to perform and should generally include from 10 to 25 steps.

Perform the operation yourself in the same manner that the students have been taught—just as they would do it on the job. As you work, list the steps that you take and note any key points where the students must be particularly careful. Use the proper doing or performance element from the analysis as a guide.

If possible, have another instructor or skilled operator check the steps of procedure on your list.

Determine the standards or criteria against which the student's performance will be judged. There are a number of factors that must be considered and you should decide beforehand which are the most important and, therefore, those you will attempt to measure. Some of these factors are:

1. Accuracy in following the proper

steps of procedure. This includes work habits.

2. Speed at which a person can complete the task properly.
3. Quality of the completed task. This would apply to operations or tasks requiring skill and judgment, such as those required in assembling two parts with screws.
4. Safety precautions. Insure that all reasonable safety precautions are taken where applicable.
5. Write instructions for the students so that they will know exactly what they are to do and why. If there is a time limit on the test they should know about it.

Giving a performance test. Make sure all necessary tools and materials are available and in good condition.

Instruct the students on the nature of the test, the time limits, what they are expected to do and on the criteria or standards to be used in assessing their performance.

Allow the student to perform the operation or task without obtrusive supervision. Observe those points that you have listed on the test and mark the degree of satisfactory performance. Do not interrupt except where the violation of a safety practice might be detrimental to the student, others or the equipment.

Measuring Achievement by Observation

Direct observation of students at work can provide a measure of achievement not available in any other way. It is rarely possible to evaluate student achievement on the basis of written and performance tests alone. This type of measurement can

at best represent only samples of achievement. Certain attitudes, work habits, and creative ability can be measured best by observing the student at work in typical situations. Such observation should not be done in a careless fashion. Both the instructor and the student should know the characteristics being observed and by the standards. In observing, you should look for certain things at each stage of achievement.

The figure on page 241 shows both sides of a 5″×8‴ card, designed to assist in evaluating the performance of students in a specific course. Observation check tests are used to establish standards and as an aid to fair and consistent evaluation of student progress and achievement. Evaluate performance as carefully as possible and at predetermined points in the course. Keep a written record. Don't rely on your memory.

Remember always that results of learning are difficult to evaluate. For example: A mother punished her four-year-old child for pulling the cat's tail. Some time later she found the child in his room, with the door closed, and pulling the cat's tail very hard. The child had learned not to pull the cat's tail *while being watched.*

Student Evaluation of Instruction

So far we have discussed the measurement of the student's progress in a course of instruction. This is our primary concern in measurement. Student opinion of the course itself is, however, another type of evaluation.

We gain valuable information for the improvement of our instruction through the students' evaluation of the course. In doing this it is well to keep in mind that the patient doesn't always know what

	PARTICIPATION	CARE & USE OF TOOLS	WORK PROCEDURE

ABOVE AVERAGE 3	Makes a real effort to learn
	Always industous
	Logical and thoughtful
	Always prompt in starting to work
	Does more than his share of work
	Solves all problems
	Shows initiative—Has helpful ideas
		Repairs, replaces tools and
		  cleans equipment and shop
		Proud of tools and equipment
		Conserves materials and supplies
		Excellent selection and use of
		  tools and equipment for
		  specific job
			Always follows standard procedure
			Always takes safety precautions
			Looks out for the safety of others
			Always has organized plan for the
			  work
			Always more than meets require-
			  ments

AVERAGE 2	Shows average effort to learn
	Works well with little special
	  attention
	Usually prompt in starting to work
	Usually cooperates with others
	Has some good ideas
	Does his share of work
	Solves some problems
		Generally careful with tools
		Interested in tools and equipment
		Generally careful with supplies
		Selects tools & equipment fairly
		  well
			Usually follows standard prc
			  cedure
			Usually works safely on the job
			Usually looks out for safety of
			  others
			Shows some plan and organization
			  for working
			Usually meets requirements

BELOW AVERAGE 1	Puts forth very little effort to
	  learn
	Wastes time and bothers others
	Usually slow in starting to work
	Seldom cooperates with class-
	  mates
	Shows little imagination—has
	  few ideas
		Continually misplaces and breaks
		  or dulls tools
		Indifferent about tools and
		  equipment or shop
		Wasteful of materials and sup-
		  plies
		Incorrect selections of tools and
		  equipment
			Seldom follows standard procedure
			A dangerous worker
			Does not look out for safety of
			  others
			Disorganized and slip-shod habits
			Always behind time
			Low quality of work
			Not very dependable

Division
Group No
Instructor

Participation
Work Procedure
Care and Use of
Tools & Equipment

Scale of Points
Above Average-----3
Average----------2
Below Average-----1

Place check
below if
student is
instructor
material

COMMENTS

Front and back of a student evaluation card.

medicine is best for him. Easy and entertaining courses are often rated too high by the less serious students. Nevertheless any instructor can be helped by systematically gathering students' opinions on a number of factors important to the success of the course. The presentation below shows an opinion gathering form used in the Executive School of the Federal Aviation Agency. Self-evaluation by the instructor is a constant element in good instruction.

THE EXECUTIVE SCHOOL

Evaluation of Presentation

Instructor: Date: Time: to

Subject:

Directions: For each of the first six questions, circle the expression which most nearly expresses your feeling. For each of the last three questions, please indicate briefly your feelings.

1. In general, how do you feel about the level of interest of class members in the subject?

| At a very low level throughout | Somewhat below average | About average | Well above average | At a very high level throughout |

2. How do you feel about the organization of the material?

| Not organized at all | Poorly organized | Fairly well organized | Well organized | Extremely well organized |

3. How do you feel about the quality of instruction?

| Very poor | Poor | Average | Above average | Very superior |

4. How useful do you feel that the subject will be to you in your work?

| Not useful at all | Of little use | Probably of some use | Generally quite useful | Extremely useful |

5. How much benefit did you personally derive from the presentation?

| No benefit at all | Very little benefit | Some benefit | Considerable benefit | A g... |

6. Consider your estimate of the v...
   ...omparis...

A questionnaire for the student's evaluation of a course.

QUESTIONS AND ASSIGNMENTS

1. What is an achievement test?
2. How does an achievement test differ from an aptitude test?
3. What are some of the purposes, other than grading, for giving tests?
4. What is validity? Reliability? Can a test be reliable without being valid?
5. What is meant by "level of difficulty" of a test item?
6. Name the four techniques for measuring student achievement.
7. What type of information can be obtained by direct observation of students at work?
8. When would you use a performance test?
9. For what types of information would you use true-false items?
10. When would you use short answer essay items?
11. From the content of one lesson in your course, prepare a multiple choice, a completion and a matching item.
12. Which type of item measures best the student achievement in terms of the objective for the lesson?
13. From available tests in your subject start a card file of test items.
14. Prepare a Table of Specifications for a unit examination in a course you are taking or teaching.
15. Make a performance test based on one of the doing units.

Improving the Learning Environment

13

The nature of good management in teaching can be illustrated by a description of two contrasting classes. Upon entering the first laboratory we find groups of students pushing their way around a few congested areas, including that in front of a tool storage area. There is the sound of voices raised above the noise of someone striking an anvil and the starting and stopping of machines.

The instructor, in dingy apron, moves from one student to another, from one machine to the next, takes the tools out of the student's hands, makes a few adjustments and gives hurried instructions or warnings. Wherever he stops, a group of students crowds around to ask him what to do next. In the pockets of the apron are carried special instruments and supplies which are reserved for students that can be trusted.

No one seems to have the material needed for efficient or effective work or knows exactly what is expected. There is little evidence that the students have seen a demonstration recently. There are no instruction sheets, only a few ragged old blueprints. In the corner is a cluttered desk piled with more old blueprints, broken tools, and a dog-eared classbook. As the bell rings, the instructor shouts a few orders about cleaning up the shop as the

A good instructional situation. The work stations are clean and orderly. The tools are neatly arranged and accessible. The instructor is well prepared and able to give individual as well as group instruction.

students push out through the doorway past another group filing in for more of the same kind of instruction.

Our instructor stops to comment to us about people these days not wanting to learn anything. As we leave, the instructor is hunting for the six-inch scale and a micrometer that disappeared during the period.

We decided to go to a different school. Here are brightly lighted well-adjusted machines, racks of tools arranged in an orderly fashion, benches with clean smooth tops, and an area set aside for organized demonstrations and planning.

A group of young people enter and go to individual lockers where they get into clean work aprons. By the time all have taken their positions on chairs provided for them, the instructor, a well groomed person wearing a clean shop coat is standing before the group and ready for a few minutes of discussion and a short, well-planned demonstration. It is evident from the students' habits on entering the room that these short group meetings are an important part of the class period and that they know the instructor has something of value for them.

Following the meeting, during which the instructor asks several questions to test the students' understanding of the demonstration, each student goes to a designated work station and proceeds with an appropriate learning activity. Written instruction sheets are in evidence and provision has been made for their proper storage. There is no waiting in line for tools or equipment because commonly needed items have been mounted on panels or in cabinets near the work stations. Good instruction, plus a

A well organized tool cabinet facilitates speedy issue and return of tools.

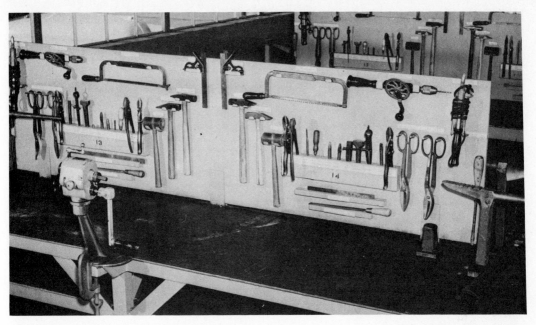

Tool panels at individual work stations result in better tool usage and save time and confusion. (U.S. Navy)

glance at the panels at the beginning and end of the period, eliminates the need for tool checks and toolroom. The habit of replacing tools on the racks was easily developed because proper instructions were given and enforced from the start.

As the students work, the instructor moves from one station to the next giving words of encouragement or caution, or asking questions. At one point, three students are called together for a short demonstration on a procedure which all three needed to perform. Shortly before the end of the period the order to clean up is given, each student puts his or her station or machine in order, returns tools to the racks, washes hands, returns work clothes to the locker, and takes an assigned seat. A few words of instruction or information about the next day's lesson are given and the group is dismissed.

What makes the difference? At first thought, it may seem that we have merely compared a scatter-brained individual with a born teacher. A look at the techniques of management may give us a better indication of the basic causes of each situation. Instruction in any of the practical fields related to Business, Agriculture, Home Economics, Industrial, Distributive, as well as other technical and applied fields must follow certain basic management techniques to facilitate effective teaching and learning. These include:

1. Laboratory and classroom planning for good instruction.
2. A practical analysis of the content to be taught and a systematic procedure for teaching.

A well prepared demonstration laboratory. (Federal Aviation Administration)

3. The use of organized demonstrations and formal instruction, coordinated with individual on-the-spot instruction.
4. The appropriate use of instructional aids and individual instruction sheets.
5. Sound application of good human relations so that each student knows the instructor's expectations.
6. Evaluation of individual progress by first-hand, day by day observation of each student at work, supplemented by other measures.

In this chapter we will deal with some of the techniques that help maximize learning from every minute of instructional time.

The Classroom, Shop, and Laboratory

Time will be lost if the room is too hot, too cold, or too stuffy when the students report for class. Because it takes a little time to change the temperature of a room and to let in some fresh air, it may be desirable to open doors and windows for a few minutes before the class arrives. Instructors exchanging rooms should work out a cooperative system for leaving the room in the best possible condition for the next class.

Prearranging chairs in accordance with the type of instruction planned for a given period may be an instructional time saver. If a film is to be shown, a different arrangement of chairs will be required from that used for a demonstration. Arranging chairs and other equipment should, of course, be done before the students sit down and preferably before they arrive. Early arrivals can help arrange the room.

Chairs and desks should be clean. Instructional time can be lost by students cleaning up chairs and equipment before they settle down for instruction. Unused equipment, publications, and materials of all kinds should be arranged as neatly as possible or removed from the room when they have served their purpose.

Roll Call

Many teachers waste time by calling the name of each student and meticulously recording the information in the class record. There are several ways to save this time. First, if a seating chart is made out and students sit in an assigned seat each day, the checking of the roll can be done by the instructor almost at a glance. In some situations it may be preferable to pass around a sheet on which each individual either signs his name or puts his initials after his name on a typed sheet. While some distraction may occur from passing a sheet around during instruction this should not be very significant once the routine is established. The presence of individuals can be verified by calling on them by name as instruction proceeds. Probably the one excuse for calling the name of each student as a part of taking the roll is to learn the names during the first few class periods. However, this is something the alert instructor can do in other ways, and it should not be necessary to waste the time of a class by calling the name of each student every period.

Tools, Equipment, Supplies and Materials

Some instructors are more interested in "things" than in people. This doesn't mean that one should be careless about machines, equipment, etc. but it does mean that in the learning situation the instructional items must be available to the students when they are needed. The students are the focal point of all instruction and their needs must be met by the most efficient and effective means at our disposal. To have a class of twenty persons stand in line while tools and other

Checking out equipment from a tool room wastes time.

249

instructional items are distributed or collected for ten minutes of the hour cannot possibly be justified on a dollars and cents basis. Common items used frequently by the students should be available at work stations, in convenient cabinets or on open panels. A few tools may be kept in locked cabinets or under more careful security arrangements. However, this practice should be kept to a minimum. The toolroom has little place in an instructional program. As a matter of fact, more tools may be lost through storage in a special tool or equipment room than having them on panels or in open cabinets where they can be checked at a glance whenever necessary. It only takes one careless student in the toolroom to foul it up to the point where a complete inventory must be made.

It should never be necessary to send for a tool or a piece of equipment during the demonstration, yet this happens frequently. The way to avoid this delay and waste of time is to plan the demonstration ahead of time, using the aids and tools in the proper order. This is part of lesson planning. Delay which results from having to send for materials and tools during a demonstration is inexcusable.

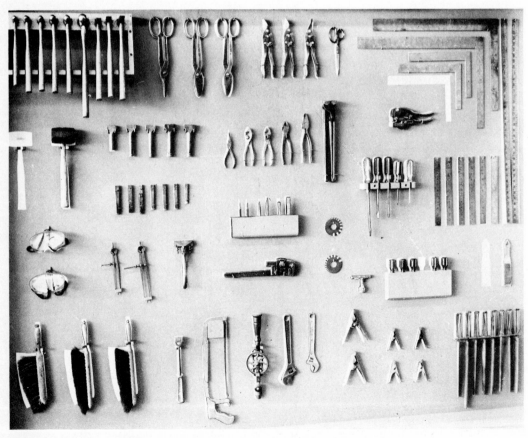

A display panel of tools prepared in advance of the demonstration.

The U.S. Naval School, Norfolk, Virginia, is using individually fitted tool drawers with excellent results. In each drawer the student has all the tools for the equipment to be worked on. This enables the learner to concentrate on the task to be accomplished because all the tools are available. By merely glancing at the open drawers at the end of each day, the instructor can readily see whether or not any tools are missing. If a tool has been broken or misplaced, responsibility can be readily determined and it can be replaced or recovered promptly. In addition to preventing the loss of tools, this system eliminates the confusion and time lost by students and instructor. This type of tool drawer has saved time for both the students and instructors. After this system was put in effect at the Naval School in Norfolk, not a single tool was lost for several years. The combination of time and tools saved has greatly reduced the operating cost of this program.

Distribution of Material

If students are to be given a number of instruction sheets, publications, charts, etc., during the period, these may be placed on desks before the students arrive or they may be arranged in such a way that they can be passed out quickly as students come into the room.

Occasionally the break between classes may be used by the instructor and one or two individuals from the class to distribute instructional materials to the students' desks or benches. Obviously, time spent by students going to and from a library or a central storage space for instructional materials is time wasted. If this must be done, a note to the librarian in advance indicating the exact material desired and the exact amount required will assist in the efficient distribution of materials. If a good deal of mimeographed material is to be used during the course, consideration should be given to placing all material in notebooks or folders before it is given to students. Students may be issued loose leaf notebooks and the handout materials can be punched to fit as a means of promoting the learner's organization of instructional materials.

Printed material may be distributed as the students arrive.

Instructional Aids and Demonstration Equipment

Much has been written about the proper use of instructional equipment and particularly teaching or learning aids, but many instructors still take class time to set up a projector, to thread the film, place the screen, and adjust the machine. If it is not possible to do all this before class, it may be possible to plan the instruction period so that the instructor can set up equipment when students are otherwise occupied in some form of individual work, such as working a problem, preparing an assignment, or making a plan for a learning activity or project. Visuals to be used with the overhead, opaque, and slide projectors should be arranged right side up, and in proper order. It is distracting to have the instructor fumble with instructional aids, project them upside down or in the wrong order.

Some time savers can be worked out in connection with the chalk board. If the demonstration or lecture involved the development of an idea by sketches on the chalkboard, it may be desirable to put part of the sketch on the board before class. Rough sketches on a piece of paper may help to plan where these will be located on the available chalkboard space during the instruction. The alert instructor estimates the amount of space available for chalkboard illustrations and plans the instruction to make the best use of the available space.

A motion picture presentation should be set up and ready before class time.

Lesson Plans

The lesson plan, of course, reflects the planning for the instructional period and should be a major help in saving time. A technique that many have found helpful is to put a time schedule on the side of the lesson plan. This tends to remind the instructor of the time that can be used for the various parts of the lesson. This is particularly helpful with instructors who tend to hold a class overtime because they cannot quite get the last idea across or have not quite made the assignment clear. Notes made on the lesson plan after class can save time the next time the plan is used.

Distractions

The administration should be careful about the use of loud speakers and intercom devices that interrupt classes. Instructors should be called from their classes only in the case of an emergency and never for the convenience of the administrative office. The practice of sending messengers into a classroom to deliver notes and information is also distracting. This information can almost always wait until the end of the class period. In one school, it became the practice to shove notes under the door during the class in order to avoid interrupting the instructor. This proved to be more distracting than having the messenger walk into the room. The instructor should try to have an alternate plan of instruction in mind to be used when unavoidable distractions occur, such as a loud machine in the next room. Moving the class to another location or switching to some kind of individual application work, such as problem solving, writing reports, or sketching

design ideas, may be advisable under these conditions.

Written Instructions

Too much time is wasted in some classes by having the students copy information from the chalkboard. If the material is worth giving to the students it should be duplicated and handed to them. Little is learned by copying. An equal amount of time spent studying the material and thinking about it will result in more learning.

A number of schools have made up notebooks containing outlines of the instruction with space available for student notes. This is an excellent practice and a great aid to the student in keeping notes in usable form.

The Habit of Talking Too Much

The instructor who talks too much is wasting time. Too frequently, the authors have observed that some instructors spend twenty minutes explaining something that could be covered adequately, although not exhaustively, in one sentence. As an experiment, you may want to make a recording of one of your lessons and then analyze this carefully to see if the material could have been presented more clearly with fewer words in less time. There is the old quip about the teenager who when asked why he didn't ask his teacher about a particular point, replied, "I didn't want to know *that* much about it."

When you think you have put the subject across, ask some questions of individuals in the class to test their understanding of your meaning and proceed on to the next part of the lesson as quickly as possible. The habit of looking for signs of restlessness and boredom on the part of students and of changing the approach to the lesson when this happens may make the difference between a dull lesson and an interesting one.

Planning and Scheduling

Scheduling is the process of making the best use of all the different phases that comprise an instructional program. It deals with instructors and students, work loads, equipment, supplies and space. Good scheduling leads to economical use of these factors to facilitate maximum instruction. Anticipating the sequence and timing of planned activities is essential to program effectiveness. Anticipatory thinking is an excellent habit for instructors to develop.

It is not desirable to lay down or to follow rigid rules of scheduling. Two schools, identical in mission and curricula, should not necessarily have identical schedules. Such things as availability of equipment, classroom facilities, instructor load, and the level of instruction are never the same. However, some fundamentals of scheduling should be useful as guides in establishing a sound school program. These fundamentals should be adhered to as closely as possible whenever a schedule is developed or modified. Let us take up the problem of practical work first.

The term "practical work," as used here, includes all types of application, both mental and physical. The solving of mathematical problems is a form of practical work just as is learning to type a letter, although the two are different in that one is primarily mental in nature and the other is both mental and physical.

Improving the Rate of Learning

Experienced instructors know that the rate of learning decreases rapidly when students are kept in a classroom in a listening situation for periods of time that exceed their attention span. In thinking about instruction we need to apply the same common sense that we would in preparing food. We readily recognize that poorly prepared food is not worth serving. Regardless of how badly we need food, it is useless to serve it unless it is suitable to our needs. Men who have had starvation diets in prison of war camps have to undergo a gradual change of diet before they can consume normal food in normal amounts again. Further, regardless of the excellent quality of well prepared food, no one cares to continue to eat hour after hour. Even the best steak becomes distasteful when we have reached our capacity.

These same principles apply to instruction. In many cases, the point at which the rate of learning decreases rapidly may be after as little as ten or fifteen minutes. If provision is made for strengthening the learning process by practical application, discussion, summary, questions and tests, a much longer period of instruction may be used. These periods of application or practical work should follow as closely as possible the presentation of information, procedure, or concepts to which they are related. Short periods of application in each period of the daily schedule are desirable. In any event, some practical work should be included in every day's plan.

A further illustration of the way in which learning takes place can be shown by two ways of presenting a film. If we take a specific sixty-minute film, show it to a group of students, we may find that they are able to remember only a relatively small part of the film's content. This, of course, will depend somewhat on the type of film and on the background of the students. If, however, we show this same film, stop the film several times where there is a natural division in the subject matter, and discuss portions that have already been seen, we can expect to find that much more has been learned.

The fact to remember is that long periods of concentrated instruction of one type do not pay dividends unless there is considerable variety in the presentation. Short periods of practical instruction followed by discussion questions and some form of practical work will provide for a more stimulating environment, more interested students and greater learning.

Relationship of Theory to Application

There should always be a definite and planned relationship between information content and application. Facts, concepts and principles are necessary in order to provide a thorough understanding of the practical work and in order to provide information necessary for applying judgment as the practical situation changes. In scheduling, the relationship of theory to practice must always be considered. You are usually operating according to sound principles of teaching and learning when certain basic and essential information is presented first, and followed immediately with a practical application of the information. If one were to teach the characteristics of the handsaw (how to identify the cross-cut from the rip, the sizes and types of teeth and the uses of each type of saw), this would be taught prior to actual practice in using the handsaw. While the theory must be taught prior to the practical work, it should be taught in small amounts and as close to application as possible. A questionable practice is to teach a great deal of informational content several weeks in advance of the time when students have an opportunity to apply the theory in practical situations. Dividing instruction

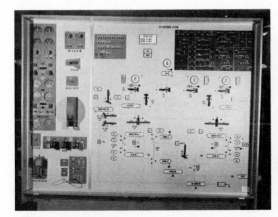

Left: Theory or informational content may be taught in the classroom. Right: Application is taught in the shop or field. (United Airlines)

into small units which may be followed immediately by periods of practical work is recognized as sound educational practice.

For example, it appears that such subjects as mathematics, principles of machine operation, and electrical principles should normally be taught over a considerable expanse of time in the schedule, enabling each part of it to be more closely related to the practical work as it occurs in the course. It is wasteful of time and energy to teach all of the mathematical principles needed at the beginning of the course even if this means only one or two full periods devoted to mathematics. The more essential mathematical principles should, wherever possible, be spread throughout the course so that, as they are learned, they may be applied to practical problems as they occur in the natural instructional process. It is recognized that this increases scheduling difficulties and may affect teacher loads and the use of classroom and laboratory spaces. However, in general it will pay dividends to space the informational content so that it is taught in relatively small amounts throughout the course.

Content Covered and Amount Learned

Another problem always present in scheduling is the decision about the amount of content to be covered in a given period of time. Should the instructor plan to cover a great deal of material or to cover less material and provide for more discussions, questions, tests, and other forms of application? Since the primary mission of any educational program is to facilitate the development of desirable attitudes, to teach information as well as

to assist students in acquiring mental and physical skills, the only accurate measure of the success of a course is its effect on the behavior of students during and following the educational experience. We cannot measure the value of an educational program by the amount of content in the curriculum. We can only measure its effectiveness in terms of lasting changes in the students.

Curriculum builders are frequently under pressure to include the maximum amount of content in each hour of the schedule. The time allowed in the schedule for putting this newly acquired knowledge into practice and thereby strengthening the learning by doing is frequently challenged by those who wish to expose the students to a large amount of content in a short period to time. Perhaps there is no entirely satisfactory solution to this problem. However, we should always give consideration to the fact that *students may actually learn more if they are exposed to less.* Schedules crowded with lectures and demonstrations often result in little learning when insufficient time is allowed to consider and apply the content.

The first practical step to take in trying to solve this difficult problem is to analyze the content very carefully and attempt to eliminate non-essential content and to decrease the time spent on minor points in order to allow more time for summary, review, and drill on the essential points.

We must be careful not to include content in the daily schedule merely because it is *nice to know.* Occasionally we find content included in courses because of custom or just because the instructor knows and likes to teach it.

Each item of subject matter in a schedule should be challenged on the basis of whether or not it is needed for the individual to achieve competence in terms of the objectives of the program.

Breaks and Rest Periods

Occasionally two or more periods are combined into a longer session by eliminating the normal break between periods. This, it is argued, makes it possible to dismiss classes earlier in the day and provided for greater leisure time away from the school. Breaks between periods may have a definite educational significance in that more will be learned and retained if these breaks are worked into the schedule at the end of each normal period of instruction. It may be argued that there is lost time resulting from the more frequent stopping and starting of classes when break periods are scheduled. This may be true if a great deal of equipment has to be put away at the close of each period and re-issued at the beginning of the next period. However, for courses where very little equipment is involved, there should be almost no loss of time in reconvening the class. If there is loss of time, it probably indicates that the instructor is at fault and has not adequately planned and scheduled the lesson.

Excessive Work Schedule

Excessive hours of work are wasteful of human energy and do not increase production. In some industries, for example, workers have produced more in a seven or eight hour day than they did in a nine or ten hour day. It is doubtful whether most students can concentrate effectively on new subject matter for more than five or six hours per day. In addition, longer work days are likely to result in significant morale problems. There are, of course, exceptions to this which occur under unusual circumstances. With an unusual stimulus provided by emergency conditions, it is possible in many instances to increase the school day over short periods of time without noticeably decreasing efficiency. However, the long range programs do not bear this out. Some types of subject matter, particularly those involving a considerable amount of practical application with tools and materials, lend themselves to longer instructional periods.

Time of Day and Learning

Some consideration should be given while scheduling to the fact that learning is accomplished more easily at certain times of the day than at others. This will vary with the individual. Some people work better late at night while others do their best work early in the morning. In general, however, we can assume that the best results will be obtained if we schedule the most complex learning activities during the morning hours. The period just after the noon meal is not very satisfactory for the showing of films, for lecturing, or other relatively passive learning processes. Whenever it is necessary to schedule a lecture or film just following the noon meal, every effort should be made to make the introduction interesting and to provide for some type of student participation such as discussion.

Points to Remember

1. Include some practical application in each day of the schedule. Application is not only working with tools and materials. Problem solving, discussions, and tests will

also help to provide variety and strengthen learning.

2. Teach informational content in small amounts just preceding the practical work to which it is related. Don't teach large blocks of informational content at one time.

3. Keep lectures and talks short. Provide for questions and discussion.

4. Cut down non-essential content in order to allow time for review, discussion, and application of more important content.

5. The value of all content in the curriculum should be easily justified on the basis of its future use in a real situation.

6. Allow breaks between periods for relaxation and time to consider instruction. Well-scheduled breaks will increase the amount learned.

7. Keep the instructional day at a reasonable length. This may be supplemented by additional practical application or by individual study after the more formal instructional period.

8. Schedule the most complex work in the morning. Avoid scheduling lectures and films at periods of the day when students are apt to be sleepy or tired.

9. Provide for maximum variety in teaching through the use of a number of teaching methods, well-planned application, and well selected instructional aids.

Instructional costs are always high. With adult classes and with paid employees each minute of instruction may cost several dollars. No one can afford poor management of an educational program.

QUESTIONS AND ASSIGNMENTS

1. List the things that should be checked in the classroom prior to the arrival of the class.
2. Describe a practical method of saving time during roll call. How would you learn the names of students?
3. Make a list of the advantages and disadvantages of open tool panels in a specific shop.
4. How would you distribute written material to a class?
5. What steps would you take to save student time when using a 16mm projector?
6. List distractions in your classroom. What can be done to minimize them?
7. How can the habit of the instructor talking too much be corrected?
8. Why should some practical work be included in each day of the schedule?

9. Why should informational content be taught throughout the course?
10. Why is the amount of content in a course of study a poor indicator of how much will be learned?
11. Of what importance are rest breaks in the schedule?
12. How long should the instructional day be for your subject?
13. When in the daily schedule should the most difficult subject be taught?
14. Of what importance is variety in teaching methods?
15. List all costs of one period of instruction. These should include cost of materials, the hourly wage of students if they are on the payroll, your pay, a prorated estimate of the cost of the shop or laboratory facilities, and any other obvious costs. What does your instruction cost by the minute? How many minutes of each hour can be saved for good instruction by a specific management procedure you plan to use?

Supervision and On-the-Job Training

14

On-the-job training (OJT) includes many techniques and approaches, and there is no precise definition of OJT that fits all situations. At one extreme, we may consider all instruction, even that done in a classroom, as on-the-job training if the student or trainee is on the payroll while receiving instruction. At the other extreme we can say that OJT means over-the-shoulder coaching by the supervisor as the employee works and produces a useful product or provides a service.

In one sense, the application step in an effective lesson is *simulated* OJT. This step may be of short duration such as that following a typical classroom demonstration or may consist of a longer phase of instruction in the course. For example, in a program of instructor preparation we provide for application when a student gives a five minute talk or gives a practice demonstration to the rest of the class. More application of the basic principles of instruction occurs when the student writes a lesson plan, designs a teaching aid, prepares a test, or demonstrates a full length lesson.

Projects and exercises used in the course of study are often designed to provide for the application of knowledge in the development of skills required on the job. Work on such projects may be quite similar to actual work on the job.

On-the-job experience is more easily simulated in the classroom with some subjects than with others. Job standards and skills in typing and shorthand, for example, can be established in the classroom. It is more difficult to simulate job

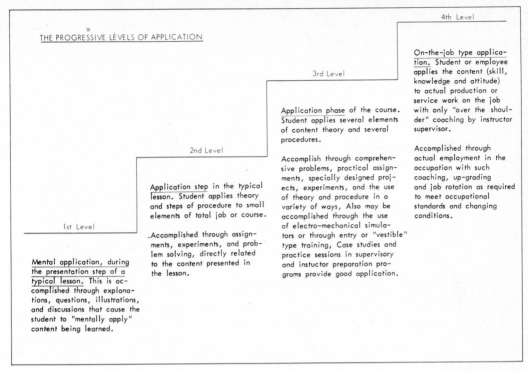

THE PROGRESSIVE LEVELS OF APPLICATION

4th Level

On-the-job type applica-
tion. Student or employee
applies the content (skill,
knowledge and attitude)
to actual production or
service work on the job
with only "over the shoulder" coaching by instructor
supervisor.

Accomplished through
actual employment in the
occupation with such
coaching, up-grading
and job rotation as required
to meet occupational
standards and changing
conditions.

3rd Level

Application phase of the course.
Student applies several elements
of content theory and several
procedures.

Accomplish through comprehensive problems, practical assignments, specially designed projects, experiments, and the use
of theory and procedure in a
variety of ways, Also may be
accomplished through the use
of electro-mechanical simulators or through entry or "vestible"
type training, Case studies and
practice sessions in supervisory
and instuctor preparation programs provide good application.

2nd Level

Application step in the typical
lesson. Student applies theory
and steps of procedure to small
elements of total job or course.

Accomplished through assignments, experiments, and problem solving, directly related
to the content presented in
the lesson.

1st Level

Mental application, during
the presentation step of a
typical lesson. This is accomplished through explanations, questions, illustrations,
and discussions that cause the
student to "mentally apply"
content being learned.

Application of knowledge or skill occurs in all steps or phases in a course of instruction.

working conditions with such subjects as the building trades and production line work involving heavy equipment.

On-the-job training is a constant factor in a great variety of work situations. Such factors as turnover of personnel, changes in the work tasks or product, reorganizations, and expanding work programs make OJT a permanent part of almost any organization's activity. Normally, the supervisor has the major responsibility for OJT although this responsibility may be shared by others. If the individual is to be trained effectively and economically on the job and yet not interfere with the production work schedule, the OJT instructor or supervisor should:

1. Make intelligent use of the required work, whether it be routine or specialized in nature, to provide opportunities for realistic learning experiences. Too often the person who knows how to do the job continues to do it. A better way in the long run is to give less experienced personnel a chance to do the job, perhaps under the supervision of a highly skilled worker. This may take a little longer at first, but it results in a more versatile work force and better team approach to major problems of changeover and production when they occur.

2. Make good use of slack periods for instructional programs. In many

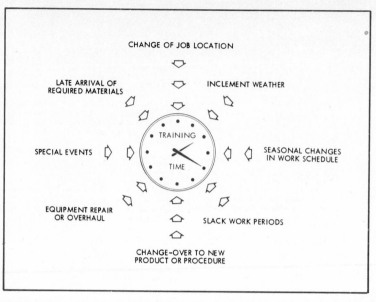

CHANGE OF JOB LOCATION

LATE ARRIVAL OF
REQUIRED MATERIALS

INCLEMENT WEATHER

TRAINING

TIME

SPECIAL EVENTS

SEASONAL CHANGES
IN WORK SCHEDULE

EQUIPMENT REPAIR
OR OVERHAUL

SLACK WORK PERIODS

CHANGE-OVER TO NEW
PRODUCT OR PROCEDURE

Many job-related factors allow time for additional OJT without interfering with the production work schedule.

occupations the work load varies from hour to hour and day to day. Such things as bad weather, product changes, variation in production schedules, and peak work periods in the day affect the work load.

Slack periods provide good opportunities for instruction at lower cost. Care must be taken, however, not to use the available time in such a manner as to give instructional programs a negative image. If the plan for instruction is carefully prepared, is made known to the employees in advance, is provided fairly to all employees who need it, and becomes a regular and effective part of the day's work much can be gained.

3. Have employees see demonstrations of new technical developments.

Whenever a new process, product, tool, or system is under consideration, opportunities may occur for worthwhile learning by selected employees. Knowledge of technological changes being considered broadens the employee's concept of the job, may motivate self preparation for new assignments, and may facilitate early and proper use of the new process. As a by-product, it may help to generate cooperation because the employee sees the job responsibilities as part of the team effort.

4. Keep an open door for employee suggestions. Intelligent employees have many ideas for improving work whether it results in a service or a product. A natural by-product of the discussion, investigation, and development of employees'

suggestions is the further development and encouragement of the employees as they help implement their own ideas. Here is real motivation.

It pays to establish an atmosphere in which the employee is encouraged to think, improvise, and improve work methods. Obviously, these improvements pay off directly, but the motivation, satisfaction, pride, and development of the person may have an intangible but vitalizing effect on the entire operation. Good supervision is the process of getting things accomplished through people. The development of the person on the job is vital to good supervision and management.

On-The-Job Training and Progress Charts

The plan for OJT must always be flexible so that proper use can be made of opportunities when they occur. Basic to the plan is knowledge of the extent to which each person has progressed toward full competency. An on-the-job training chart has value here. In regular classroom or laboratory instruction, this same type of chart is typically referred to as a *progress chart.*

People under instruction in almost every program have different degrees of skill and knowledge. Some may need instruction in basic elements of the occupation while others may need only specialized or upgrading instruction. To ascertain the needs of each individual, we must compare the skills and knowledge possessed with the present and future requirements of the work expected.

Few will disagree with this idea. However, in practice it is frequently ne-glected. Much time and effort can be expended on unnecessary instruction. This often leads to neglecting instruction that is important or vital. A partial answer to the problem is found in the proper use of charts as shown on page 264. Such a chart is merely a device to help spotlight training needs and a means of recording progress of individuals.

Our aim in using the chart is to compare the present abilities of students or employees against present and future requirements of the job to which they are or will be assigned. A training chart may be made for each block of your analysis, or several blocks may be included in each chart.

On the chart shown on page 264, the doing or performance elements are listed across the top and the names of those to receive instruction are listed along the left side. Those with demonstrated proficiency in an operation or task are given an X under the appropriate operation. Other codes may, of course be used to indicate that the operation has only been demonstrated by the instructor or to show degrees of skill developed.

With on-the-job training, such a chart is essential as a means of deciding who shall be assigned specific tasks as they occur on the job, both to get the work done as required and to simultaneously provide appropriate learning and work experience for individuals.

Similar charts are also desirable to use with knowledge elements of content. Records may be kept by indicating results of simple oral and written tests for each individual for each knowledge element of content.

The most important chart for OJT, however, is based on the doing or performance elements. An X on this chart

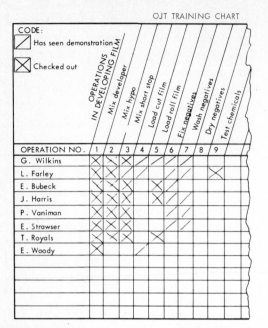

OJT TRAINING CHART

CODE:
⊘ Has seen demonstration
⊠ Checked out

OPERATION NO.	Mix developer	Mix hypo	Mix short stop	Load cut film	Load roll film	Fix negatives	Wash negatives	Dry negatives	Test chemicals
	1	2	3	4	5	6	7	8	9
G. Wilkins	⊠	⊘	⊠	⊘	⊘	⊘	⊘		
L. Farley	⊠	⊠		⊘		⊘	⊘	⊠	
E. Bubeck	⊘	⊠	⊠		⊠				
J. Harris	⊠	⊠	⊠		⊠				
P. Vaniman	⊠	⊠	⊠			⊘	⊘		
E. Strawser	⊠	⊠	⊠						
T. Royals	⊠	⊠	⊠		⊠				
E. Woody	⊠			⊘					

A progress chart for a course in photographic lab skills.

should indicate that an individual has the skill and can properly use, in practice, the information and concepts to which it is related.

The analysis of the occupation, as compared with the demonstrated ability of trainees, provides the basic list of OJT needs. Other needs for on-the-job training are revealed whenever undesirable conditions such as the following occur:

1. Poor cooperation among employees
2. Harmful rumors
3. Excessive complaints
4. Poor housekeeping
5. Unsatisfactory use of safety equipment
6. Excessive waste in materials
7. Abuse of equipment
8. Absenteeism
9. Orders ignored
10. Lack of pride in workmanship
11. Inaccurate records
12. Time killing

Instruction alone may not solve all of these problems, but an effective on-the-job training program is usually an essential part of the solution.

The Job Instruction Method

In other chapters we have explained several techniques that are applicable to both formal instruction and OJT. The main difference in the methods lies in the length of instruction periods and in the fact that OJT is more of a "catch as catch can" approach because it is integrated with productive work. The OJT approach may appear to the casual observer to be quite disorganized. This is not, however, an accurate picture of effective OJT. It, too, is planned and organized, but provision for great flexibility must be built into the plan.

During both major world wars the on-the-job training method was used extensively in rapidly preparing large numbers of people for specialized employment. The method is so simple and logical that, on paper, it seems obvious and perhaps inconsequential. However, a little first hand observation on the job is usually all that is needed to remind anyone that effective work practices need constant attention by capable supervisors and instructors. There are two phases to the OJT method of instruction: (1) preparing to instruct, and (2) instruction on the job.

Phase I: Preparing to instruct. Analyze the job or work task to be learned. This was explained to a large extent as the analysis process in Chapter 4, especially in listing the steps of procedure in the doing or performance elements. Some further analysis may be needed because of the specific conditions or requirements of the job or task to be learned. Then, too, some of the needs for instruction as determined by difficulties on the job may require an additional job or task analysis.

Make a plan for teaching the content involved in the performance of the job or task. In some simple jobs the instruction can be done in minutes. In others, instruction may be spread over a much longer period of time. OJT is seldom a full time activity for more than a portion of each day. Although it may not be feasible

OJT LESSON PLAN OUTLINE

LESSON PLAN FOR_____

CONTENT FROM ANALYSIS _____

INSTRUCTOR_____

TOOLS AND EQUIPMENT NEEDED FOR LESSON

1._____   4._____
2._____   5._____
3._____   6._____

STEP 1. PUT TRAINEE AT EASE. FIND OUT WHAT HE KNOWS. AROUSE HIS INTEREST.

STEP 2. PRESENT THE JOB OR TASK: Show, Tell, Stress and Discuss Key Points.

Steps	Key Points
1.	
2.	
3.	
4.	
5.	
6.	

STEP 3. TRYOUT
Let the Trainee Show and Tell you how to do the job.
Ask questions and correct errors.

STEP 4. ASSIGN JOB: (Date   )_____

STEP 5. Follow up (dates _____ , _____ , _____ , _____ , _____ , _____ ,
DRAWING NEEDED:_____ STANDARDS & PERF._____
MATERIALS:_____

TOOLS:_____   _____
_____   _____

A simple OJT lesson plan.

to develop a full lesson plan as described in Chapter Five, a simple schedule of content items to cover, with appropriate checking points, should be developed and kept in mind.

Have everything ready. This sounds simple, but a lot of time is wasted because a tool, a piece of material, or safety device has been forgotten. Check to see that needed power and extension cords are at hand. Arrange the available facilities and work area to aid learning. Consider the use of written instructional materials.

Phase II: Instruction on the job. Put the new employee at ease. Assuming you are starting a new trainee who has had some basic instruction but not very much experience with a particular type of work assignment, your first step should be to put the individual at ease.

Be at ease yourself. Act natural. Don't continue to do anything that seems forced or unnatural after you have given it a fair trial. Remember, however, that good methods may seem awkward at first. Try to remember how you felt the first day you reported to a new job.

Be friendly. Don't be in too much of a hurry. Explain simple things first— where tools and equipment are located, the schedule, any special rules and regulations. Introduce the trainee to others. Take time to ask questions about the trainee's experience. Find out if there are job related problems such as transportation and parking problems. Is anything needed before going on with the job related instructional program?

Find out the initial level of job competence. What experience has the trainee had that will transfer to this job? Does he have a high degree of skill in some part of the job but no experience in another? Such information should be recorded on

the training chart as an aid in planning OJT for the individual.

Try to interest the trainee in the program of work and study. In Chapters 2 and 3 we discussed the basic needs of most individuals. Try to understand what desires each person is striving to satisfy and the opportunities the job offers in meeting these needs. Is this a job with opportunity to learn and to develop a wide range of skills? Is the job likely to remain when schedules change? Is there a chance for extra pay for extra work? Try to see the job from the employee's point of view.

Present the content. Refer again to the points on giving a demonstration in Chapter 9. Remember: Show one step at a time. Discuss. Illustrate, ask questions. Present steps in proper sequence. Make key points stand out. Don't try to present too much at one time. Remember how long it took you to reach your present level of skill.

Provide opportunity for tryout. In some instruction the tryout is completely interwoven with the other steps. In Chapter 2 we discussed "learning by doing" during the lecture. This is one form of application. In questioning, we attempt to motivate the student to apply the principles to practical problems. The application step is emphasized in the demonstration lesson. This phase of instruction is so vital, and yet so often neglected, that it has been mentioned several times in this book.

In OJT as in other types of instruction, the tryout under supervision is an inherent part of sound instruction. The tryout in OJT has some special problems. The person doing the job for the first time in your presence is likely to be highly motivated but so keyed up or nervous that difficulty is experienced in doing even

A good instructor or supervisor is patient and helpful during initial training. (United Airlines)

simple things. Learning is difficult, if not at times impossible, in this situation. As you have had a part in the instruction, you are also emotionally involved. When both instructor and student are thinking of themselves, are concerned with their own performance, the situation can become tense and unproductive from the learning point of view. In effective learning, we must be able to give our full

attention to the subject. Here are some suggestions for the tryout phase:

1. Step aside and give the individual a chance to give his full attention to the job.
2. At the proper time, depending on the person and the job, observe the method used as well as the job itself. Don't be too quick to suggest

changes on small things—the trainee will feel better if permitted to solve even the smallest problem without the help of an over eager coach or instructor.

3. Prevent job failure by prompt action but in as impersonal a manner as possible. Criticize the act but *never* the person.

4. Watch your blood pressure. When you get that aggressive feeling, take time to cool off. Walk away or do some physical work to relieve the tension. Come back and re-demonstrate in a calm manner. Put yourself in the other person's shoes.

Don't forget to ask questions. There may be a reason why the trainee is performing the job a certain way. It is best to know why before making suggestions for corrections.

Follow up. Our objective in following up after the individual has been working independently for awhile is to provide encouragement, to provide assistance if needed and to assure ourselves that incorrect procedures do not become habits.

Several actions help to make the follow-up phase more valuable. When the individual has developed to the point where more responsibility can be given, and has demonstrated that the task can be performed under close supervision, a degree of confidence has been developed. Good habits are being learned. Our next action then is to permit the trainee to function independently. At this point he should be told where to get help if needed, and encouraged to ask questions.

For a while you should visit the worker quite frequently to provide encouragement, provide the opportunity to ask questions or make suggestions. Then taper off.

In writing about the on-the-job instructional approach, we have illustrated the ideas with simple jobs and tasks involving specific skills and steps of procedure.

After supervised instruction, the trainees are encouraged to work independently and to ask questions when necessary.

All or part of the OJT approach to instruction can be used with any subject, although it takes a little imagination. Take any subject from first aid to general safety, from introducing new procedures to improving the quality of work. In each case we should:

1. Prepare to teach by identifying the instructional content inherent in the job or task, plan for teaching, and having everything ready before we start.
2. Put the learner at ease, find out the initial level of competence and assist the trainee to develop an interest in the competencies to be acquired.
3. Present the procedure concepts one step at a time by showing and telling. Make key points stand out. Ask questions.
4. Give the individual a tryout under supervision. Have trainee explain what has been learned and then perform. Provide suggestions as necessary.
5. Allow independent performance but follow up to give encouragement and help when needed and to prevent the development of improper habits.

Proficiency Development on the Difficult Job

The employee on the job must perform adequately to justify wages paid by the employer. The employer expects an acceptable level of performance from the

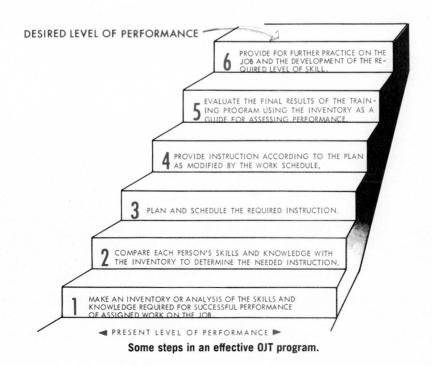

DESIRED LEVEL OF PERFORMANCE

6 PROVIDE FOR FURTHER PRACTICE ON THE JOB AND THE DEVELOPMENT OF THE RE-QUIRED LEVEL OF SKILL.

5 EVALUATE THE FINAL RESULTS OF THE TRAIN-ING PROGRAM USING THE INVENTORY AS A GUIDE FOR ASSESSING PERFORMANCE.

4 PROVIDE INSTRUCTION ACCORDING TO THE PLAN AS MODIFIED BY THE WORK SCHEDULE.

3 PLAN AND SCHEDULE THE REQUIRED INSTRUCTION.

2 COMPARE EACH PERSON'S SKILLS AND KNOWLEDGE WITH THE INVENTORY TO DETERMINE THE NEEDED INSTRUCTION.

1 MAKE AN INVENTORY OR ANALYSIS OF THE SKILLS AND KNOWLEDGE REQUIRED FOR SUCCESSFUL PERFORMANCE OF ASSIGNED WORK ON THE JOB.

◄ PRESENT LEVEL OF PERFORMANCE ►

Some steps in an effective OJT program.

first. This may mean that the new employee should be assigned to relatively simple tasks in the beginning. The plan for OJT should provide, however, for each willing and competent individual to progress as fast and as far as practical. Some individuals of high aptitude have lost interest, become discouraged, or quit because they were assigned to simple tasks for too long.

Good judgment on the part of the supervisor to determine the point at which the employee is ready to be instructed in and assigned to a more advanced task is essential. A good employee likes a challenge but doesn't want to be put in a position where there is a high potential of failure.

Job Rotation

This approach to on-the-job training involves placing an individual temporarily in another job for the purpose of training. The technique tends to slow down production and to create a degree of confusion in a smoothly running organization. These disadvantages are offset by having more than one person capable of doing a specific job and by having, among employees, a better understanding of the jobs of others.

Planned rotation of employees from one specific job to another is often a productive part of the total on-the-job training program. Mr. Bob Arthur, Assistant General Foreman, Tool Department, Timkin Roller Bearing Co., has this to say about job rotation:

> Because of the precision and geometry of our product, our work in the tool rooms at the Canton Bearing Plant of The Timkin Roller Bearing Company demands maximum skills . . . This demand for a high level of skills led to the over-specialization of tool room craftsmen. Over a period of time, unique job assignments were repeatedly given to the same employees. This, of course, saved a lot of the foreman's time by reducing the need for instruction and followup. Consequently, a limited number of employees had all the know-how of these select jobs, and we became more or less dependent upon their skills and integrity. Eventually, this led to several crippling situations. It meant a one-shift operation or overtime. In many cases this not only meant unnecessary production delays and increased costs, but it also had a demoralizing effect on the off-shifts . . . All this has been eliminated by a constant job rotation program. A timetable is kept on the critical machines and assignments. Men are periodically rotated to avoid over-specialization and to maintain versatility.

Job rotation has many advantages; we are continually getting new and different suggestions for method improvement; we are able to give service to the producing departments on a twenty-four hour basis; absenteeism does not impair our production planning in any one spot; and the morale of the department has improved immensely with the passing of the 'one job specialist.'

Over-The-Shoulder Coaching

Effective on-the-job training programs are always a blend or combination of methods each of which is used at the right time. Not the least of these methods is *over-the-shoulder coaching*. Here the trainee is attempting to develop and apply skills in typical work situations under the watchful attention and guidance of a more qualified person. The advantages of this type of training are that:

1. It can often be provided at the moment it is needed.
2. It tends to be practical and realistic.

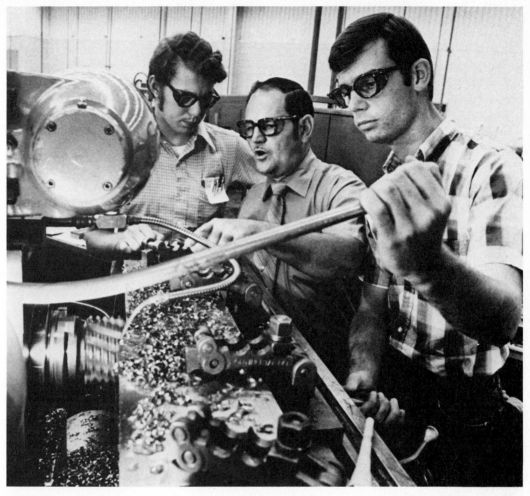

Over-the-shoulder coaching is an excellent instructional technique in aiding trainees or workers in perfecting skills. (Western Electric Company)

3. The worker is motivated to learn because of an immediate need to know.
4. The supervisor can easily identify specific performance deficiencies in the worker and take immediate and proper action.
5. The results of the training are readily apparent because the employee is working with real equipment and the finished work can be judged by known standards.

Good coaching techniques like all other instructional strategies must, however, be mastered if good results are to be expected.

Perhaps the most vital element is timing. Trainees must be allowed to develop their own skills and there is no way to do this except by practice. The clumsy performance of the trainee may, however, tempt the supervisor or instructor to make too many suggestions too soon. At the other extreme the trainee may be allowed to develop incorrect skills if there is inadequate supervision and correction. The skilled supervisor analyzes each worker's performance progress continually so that guidance may be given when it is needed, but over-supervising is to be avoided.

Learning is an emotional as well as an intellectual and physical experience, and all learning is affected by human relations on the job. The supervisor should take time to set the standards carefully for the job and make sure they are understood. An atmosphere of mutual trust, respect and approval must be created. The worker should never feel "on trial" or that the "cards are stacked". We can expect the conscientious employee to be keyed up, but a supervisor can do much to prevent feelings of fear of the job or supervision. Progress should be recognized and a word of encouragement used whenever it is deserved, especially with the new employee.

Good over-the-shoulder coaching instills confidence in the worker and improves performance. (RCA Electronic Components)

Questions are also important. Questions may be used when there is a need to focus the worker's attention on key steps of procedure. A series of questions can lead the employee/trainee through a procedure or thought process and thus develop confidence and ability. Questions are often of value in checking on an individual's readiness for the next element of work. Proper answers to questions let the worker know where he stands and help to develop self confidence.

The skilled supervisor never forgets that the tasks that are so easy for him now were once hard. One must remember one's own thoughts and problems when first learning a new job. By continual study, the supervisor retains a learning point of view and also stays up-to-date in the skills required of personnel being supervised.

Criticizing the Employee

It is never easy to talk to someone about deficiencies. Most of us tend to procrastinate and avoid the unpleasant task of criticizing a student or employee whose performance or attitude needs to be improved. Sometimes this unpleasant task is put off until it becomes so pressing that we tend to act on the spur of the moment and with considerable emotional feeling. This, of course, may do much more harm than good. A session with an employee in which deficiencies will be discussed should not come as a part of an angry response.

Failure to correct errors and coach individuals for the improvement of their performance inevitably results in poor performance, poor attitudes and a lowering of morale. This, in turn, affects the supervisor's own self concept because of guilt feelings about his performance as a supervisor. Correcting deficiencies is an essential part of every supervisor's or instructor's role and should be done with maximum effectiveness and with minimum unpleasantness for both the supervisor and the employee.

All available facts should be gathered and evaluated before criticizing, and some thought should be given to one's actions and the words to be used while talking to the employee. This does not mean that one has to avoid a direct approach to the problem. Sometimes it is necessary to point out deficiencies in a very direct and forceful manner, but to the extent possible, this should be done in an impersonal, fair, and firm manner. *Criticize the act, not the individual.*

When you are about to give a reprimand or criticize and correct major deficiencies:

1. Always get the facts. This may, in itself, eliminate the need for any further steps. Most supervisors have had experience in criticizing with too few or inaccurate facts, and consequently finding themselves in an embarrassing situation because they had to either admit they were wrong, or try to use some "face-saving" technique to get out of the situation. With all the facts, the proper course of action becomes more obvious.

2. Consider the circumstances. By this we mean look behind the facts. Was there an emotional reason (perhaps a personal problem) behind an individual's behavior? The circumstances may do a great deal to bring the facts into proper perspective and to suggest a constructive approach for improvement.

Pick a time for the interview when both you and the employee are most able to view the facts with an open mind and with minimum irritation.

3. Have a flexible plan. Think through the questions you may ask. Be prepared to change your course of action if information brought out in the interview suggests it. Give the individual a full chance to talk at the beginning. Don't act with a closed mind. Your plan should be as flexible as possible so that you can make use of all the information available including the reaction of the employee during the interview.

Remember, the purpose of criticizing and coaching the employee is to bring out the means of correcting deficiencies and leaving the individual with a desire to improve. We fail, if we destroy the person's confidence and willingness to try again.

Key Factors in Effective OJT

Sound supervision and high achievement on the job is made up of several key factors which should be integrated with on-the-job training. A brief discussion of these factors follows.

Using known and understood standards. Blueprints for production work give dimensions in precise terms and include the tolerance that will be allowed. For example, $3.50 \pm .005$ means $3^1/_2$ inches plus or minus 5 thousandths of an inch. This procedure sets standards that must be maintained. It also recognizes that obtaining more accuracy than is required is expensive and generally results in wasted time and materials.

One of the first steps toward effective supervision, including OJT, in any area

of work is to establish the standards against which achievement or work will be measured.

The occupational analysis as described in Chapter 4 provides a method for systematically identifying job related skills. The degree of proficiency expected on the job can be included in the analysis. This is really the essence of "behavioral objectives."

Standards should be explained and well illustrated during an instructional program so that each employee develops confidence and the ability to meet the standards. In day-to-day supervision, each worker should be well informed on the specific standards for each job or task as it is assigned. When this is not done, the employee may either spend too much time in reaching standards higher than are required or may fail to meet desired standards. The net results are either increased costs or unacceptable work. Unreasonable standards discourage the employee and after a while he may quit trying. Sound, well-planned OJT, including good instruction on the standards for each job, is a large part of the solution to this problem.

Two way communication. As supervisors we should do as much or more listening as we do talking. Employees often fail to get through to their supervisors with questions that must have good answers if the employees are to learn the job well and proceed in the work with confidence and enthusiasm.

The supervisor who believes that he must provide and take credit for all the good ideas is limiting the brain power of the unit being supervised to that of one person—himself—and he is not necessarily the most creative person in the unit.

Two way communication is important in OJT.

Research in many organizations clearly shows that employee motivation grows out of a feeling of worth and self-respect. This feeling is increased when the supervisor takes the time to talk with individuals and to listen thoughtfully to their ideas and concerns. This is especially true in all coaching and OJT situations. The supervisor who is too busy to talk to people is perhaps busy because of a lack of communication and as a result is not getting the whole hearted support and best efforts from the group.

OJT is more than communication, but effective communication is an essential part of all OJT.

Full participation in planning and decision making. Competent supervisors take responsibility for the performance of their group. However this never means that the group or its members should not have a part in planning the work. Participation (not manipulation in sheep's clothing) bears a positive relationship to motivation, cooperation, and team spirit—all of which are needed for high productivity.

Since a feeling of worth and self respect is essential to motivation and high productivity, it follows that participation in planning has a positive bearing on effective supervision. When employees have a share in planning their work, they are far more inclined to:

1. Try to do whatever is required.
2. Support the need for changes and innovations in the work.
3. Give the supervisor information needed to take action on problems.
4. Make labor and time saving suggestions.
5. Work with the supervisor as a willing team member.

As supervisors we are responsible for results and at times must make decisions without guidance from the team. However, such decisions will receive more support if employees believe that their ideas have been considered and that the decision is reasonable in the face of facts. Participation in planning and decision making can result in significant new insights and an educational experience for the employee. The job may be viewed in a new light, and the employee may be more inclined to develop the skills to meet a greater challenge.

Team spirit. The importance of good human relationships within a group is often underestimated. When an individual likes people and enjoys associating with others on the job, a more positive attitude toward the job result, and there is more of a desire to contribute as a member of the working team.

Many studies have shown that high morale and productivity result more from good human relationships than from increased pay, improved physical working

APPROPRIATE PERFORMANCE
STANDARDS

TWO-WAY COMMUNICATION
BETWEEN SUPERVISOR
AND EMPLOYEES

EFFECTIVE TRAINING

PARTICIPATION IN
DECISIONS

CLEAR INSTRUCTIONS
AND ASSIGNMENTS

High
Achievement
on the
Job

TEAM SPIRIT

EFFECTIVE
DELEGATION

RECOGNITION
OF
ACHIEVEMENT

COACHING TO
CORRECT DEFECTS

AN ATMOSPHERE
OF APPROVAL

ANALYSIS OF
UNDERLYING CAUSES
OF ERRORS

FREEDOM
FROM FEAR

GOOD WORKING
CONDITIONS

Factors in OJT which contribute to a common goal.

conditions, and other tangible benefits. As supervisors we need to give careful thought to the relationships that develop on the job.

On-the-job training helps to build team spirit as people who receive training together get to know each other better and find a common ground for communication and understanding. Many strong friendships and loyalties to the organization come as a natural by-product of the relationships that occur during well planned and productive educational programs.

On-the-job training helps the supervisor to understand the members of the unit

and helps them to understand him. Success in an on-the-job training situation and the resulting increase in competence on the job leads to greater job satisfaction and a feeling of belonging to a good team.

Recognition of achievement. We have all seen employees who, although well paid, are not highly motivated to do a good job. Sometimes motivation is lacking because an employee receives little recognition for work well done. When efforts appear to go unnoticed, the employee is likely to assume that the supervisor judges the work to be of little worth or of poor quality.

As pay and working conditions become more satisfactory, the employee has an increased need for satisfaction through recognition and praise for good work. Direct and sincere praise through comments, verbal or written should, or course, be given at once for a job well done. There are other ways of giving recognition which may have a more permanent value. One way is to show a continuing interest in the work, in problems, and in the employee's progress in developing desirable skills. A training chart can aid the supervisor in identifying this progress.

It's easy to praise. It takes more effort to develop and show a continuing interest in each person's work. Employees may take praise for granted, especially if it is given frequently and indiscriminately, but they will appreciate and respond to the supervisor who takes time to understand their work and problems as they occur. David Ogilvy's comments in *Confessions of an Advertising Man* illustrate this concept.

> Thirty years ago I was a chef at the Hotel Majestic in Paris . . . I have always believed that if I could understand how Monsieur Pitard, the head chef, inspired such white-hot morale, I could apply the same kind of leadership to the management of my advertising agency. To begin with, he was the best cook in the whole brigade, and we knew it . . . (Following Chef Pitard's example, I still write occasional advertisements myself, to remind my brigade of copywriters that my hand has not lost its cunning.)
>
> M. Pitard praised very seldom, but when he did, we were exalted to the skies . . . (Today I praise my staff as rarely as Pitard praised his chefs, in the hope that they too will appreciate it more than a steady gush of appreciation.)

When the supervisor takes time to discuss the job and to provide whatever coaching and help is needed, the employee is more likely to believe that the work being done is important and that recognition is being provided when deserved. Encouragement and help through coaching as a part of on-the-job training are important in meeting the employee's needs for recognition and self-respect.

Analysis of underlying causes of errors. All significant problems on the job should be analyzed in recognition of the fact that the apparent cause may not be the real cause.

Sometimes the employee knows the cause but is reluctant to reveal it. An acceptable reason may be given but may conceal the basic reason for the problem. For example, if an employee has received conflicting instructions from two or more supervisors, this fact may not be revealed out of loyalty or out of fear.

Only after the real cause of error is identified can we take appropriate action. We must recognize that a problem may be the result of many interrelated causes. In analyzing the cause of errors, we should assess:

1. The quality or thoroughness of instruction provided.
2. The physical working situation.
3. The physical limitations or other handicaps of the employee.
4. The adequacy of job preparation.
5. The relationship between the employee and others in the work situation.
6. The prevailing atmosphere and the morale of the group.
7. The amount of wasted effort caused by changes in organization, rules,

regulations, special studies, and surveys.

Once the underlying cause of errors is determined we can make a sound decision regarding corrective action. In some instances the lack of adequate training is the cause of errors, but it must be recognized that training cannot solve all supervisory problems.

Training may help the employee to adjust to the working situation or to find ways of improving it. The handicapped employee—and remember that all of us have limitations—may need special instruction in order to do the job in a particular way. Morale and working relationships may be improved through appropriate instruction related to the work to be done. Supervisors and managers need substantial management and supervisor training in order to understand fully the various and interrelated effects of management decisions and actions.

Good working conditions. Physical surroundings are important for efficient and orderly work. Such things as color scheme, light, temperature, and noise level have direct effects on productivity.

Working conditions, however, include more than physical conditions that can be seen or felt. The people in an organization, the supervisory relationships, the career plans, and the job opportunities are logically a part of the working conditions.

On-the-job training provides an important element in the improvement of working conditions when it helps to develop people, give them a feeling of pride and success, and leads to a more meaningful life both on and off the job.

An atmosphere of approval. All of us do better on and off the job when we work in an atmosphere of approval—when we feel competent and are rewarded for achievement in various ways by the people we work with and for. This, of course, does not mean that there are no work standards and that poor work goes without notice. It does mean that each individual's work is judged fairly, and that an opportunity is provided to work toward genuine results. Productivity is fostered in an atmosphere where new ideas may be tried without fear or reprimand for an occasional failure. On-the-job training is vital in developing an atmosphere of approval as it:

1. Develops confidence in one's ability to do the job well.
2. Lets a person know of the job expectations and precisely those things that must be done to develop the required skill.
3. Recognizes progress and provides a basis for recognition and self-respect.
4. Helps to establish work standards and to gain acceptance of standards by the employee.
5. Gives the supervisor greater perspective on the problems that are encountered by the new employee on the job.

Points to Remember

Coaching on the job. The word coaching is usually associated with sports and its value there is seldom questioned. Successful athletic coaches and their teams are rewarded in many ways because they are in the public eye.

Good coaching on the job may go unnoticed except by the supervisor and the personnel directly involved. However, coaching is as essential in the development of a winning team in the office, laboratory, or shop as it is in sports.

Coaching on the job may take many forms; it usually involves analyzing employee performance, identifying performance that can be improved and correcting improper or dangerous procedures, discussing the work with the employee to get his point of view, and providing assistance and encouragement as the employee attempts to improve performance.

Over-the-shoulder coaching is perhaps the purest form of OJT because the worker is actually doing work at the same time assistance and guidance is given.

It is important to keep in mind that the relationship between the supervisor and the employee at the time of coaching is likely to be sensitive. The act of coaching suggests a degree of criticism which the employee may tend to resent. It follows that coaching is an important and difficult task—but a major OJT technique that must be mastered. (See page 270 for more information on coaching.)

Clear instructions and assignments. Goals and objectives in the supervisor's mind are of little value to the working team if instructions and assignments are not made perfectly clear to each employee.

Many supervisors and managers at other levels rush through the process of assigning work. They may fail to check for understanding, and they often leave the employee completely confused. The cavalier approach to giving assignments results in confusion and resentment and the employee may well ask, "If the job is important why not take the time to assign it clearly?" The net result is poor work. The more capable employee may seek another job.

Good assignments are required if we expect people to work up to capacity. Such assignments are vital and are included in our list of on-the-job training techniques.

Effective delegation of responsibility. Most supervisors know how to take responsibility. A smaller number know how to share responsibility or how to give responsibility to others without losing control. Delegation is one of the best approaches to high production, as well as to the development of personnel at all levels from beginner to manager.

How else can the supervisor measure or judge the employee's ability in areas beyond the job presently being done? By what other means can the supervisor check on the employee's actual competence and identify specific needs for coaching or other types of training?

Too many supervisors believe that they cannot delegate because the work must be finished and after all they are the best qualified. However, responsibility along with recognition and self-respect brings out the best in people. When the going gets tough, supervisors who have developed their people through delegation and related on-the-job training may well deserve the credit for success.

Delegation as a way of developing people is worthy of top priority in our plan for OJT.

Effective supervision is interwoven with sound on-the-job training. Supervision without training becomes an unproductive "straw boss" operation with little long range benefits to the employee, to the supervisor, or to management.

When a competent supervisor shares work problems and goals with personnel, and encourages them to plan and provides opportunities for their development as a part of normal everyday work, we can expect good results.

Get to know each new person on the job before you try to provide instruction. Show an interest in the employee and encouragement by listening.

Keep in mind that we are all alike in some ways but different in others. As people do not come in standard packages each person must be treated as an individual. Who wants to be treated as just another "warm body" in the ranks?

Remain patient with individuals who are slow to catch on—they may, with time and good preparation become one of the best. If you show irritation you're giving yourself and the trainee more of a handicap. Harold Mayfield in a recent issue of *Harvard Business Review* said:

> In my experience, I have been surprised, not with the reluctance of subordinates to accept constructive advice, but with their readiness to listen. I believe this is explainable in part by their feeling for intent. If the supervisor genuinely means to be helpful, they will make allowances for words which in another context would be unforgivable.

Let an employee know how he is doing. This should be done soon, especially with a new employee. The employee wants to know if the level of performance is satisfactory and will appreciate some suggestions for improvement if they are given in an understanding manner. Like shooting at a target, it's best to know where each shot hits before the next shot is fired.

Give explanations and reasons for each process taught. We learn faster and remember longer when we know the reason behind the method.

When practical, give the individual a broad view of the whole process before providing detailed instruction on the parts. This helps to provide an understanding of the work being done.

Spread out the training schedule. A person learns more for the total time spent in training if the instruction is paced or provided a little each day, in order to permit one to fully understand one step before going on to the next. Several short training periods are usually more effective than one or two long periods.

Pick the best time for training. We learn best when we are feeling well—when we are rested. This suggests some breaks in the schedule for relaxation.

When fatigue and/or boredom become evident, change the method of instruction or, if practicable, stop training until the next day.

Remember that skill does not increase at a steady rate. There are ups and downs. Rapid progress may occur for some time and then slow down to the point where the trainee becomes discouraged. When this occurs, let the person know that this plateau in learning is to be expected, that others have experienced these peaks and valleys on their way to successful performance. Provide reassurance and encouragement to continue efforts. This is also a good time to look for better methods of doing the job.

Instruction is a natural and necessary part of supervision on the job. It helps to reduce labor turnover, conserve materials, reduce training or learning time, prevent or reduce machine breakage, increase the quantity and quality of production, lower production costs, and improve morale.

The well prepared employee requires a minimum of supervision in planning and performing assigned tasks.

Competent people are the most vital asset of an organization. With effective OJT through a variety of approaches a competent workforce can be developed.

QUESTIONS AND ASSIGNMENTS

1. Of the following, which is typical of training provided on the job?
   Demonstration on operating machine
   Job rotation
   Laboratory experiment
   Lecture and film to large group
   Over-the-shoulder coaching
2. What is meant by simulated OJT?
3. Which level of application is typical of the lecture? Which of over-the-shoulder coaching?
4. List several job related situations that result in a need for OJT.
5. Lay out a training or progress chart and include the skills or procedures from at least one block of an occupational analysis.
6. On a training chart, how could you record levels of skill developed by individuals?
7. List several conditions on the job that suggest a need for instruction.
8. List several undesirable conditions that may not be correctable through training.
9. Make up a plan of instruction for a simple job or task.
10. Demonstrate the above plan with individuals who can play the role of trainees on the job.
11. Why should a worker be challenged to do his best work?
12. List several advantages of job rotation in a training program.
13. Why is over-the-shoulder coaching said to be the most direct form of OJT?
14. What are some advantages of over-the-shoulder coaching?
15. Why is it important to get the facts before criticizing an employee?
16. Why are specific work standards important in training?
17. How would you use two-way communication in training on the job?
18. List several actions that may result from including workers in the planning of their work.
19. How can organized OJT contribute to the development of team spirit in a group?
20. Is it possible to give too much praise? Why?
21. List several factors that may lead to work errors on the job.
22. What is meant by an atmosphere of approval?
23. Why is it important to take time for clear instructions and assignments on the job?
24. Why in your opinion do so many supervisors fail to delegate responsibility and authority to their people?
25. What are the characteristics and advantages of job rotation?

26. List the steps in each phase of job instruction.
27. Illustrate each level of application with examples from the subject you teach.
28. Prepare a training or progress chart for use in your course or for OJT. If you have not already done so, list the steps of procedure in one of the doing or performance elements of the analysis, or take a simple task such as starting a power lawn mower and break the task down into steps. Be sure to add after each step or in a separate column the key points of information and the safety precautions. Teach someone how to do the job. For example, you might teach a young man or your wife how to start the mower. Be sure to use all the steps of the job instruction method.

Appendix

Instructional Techniques Check-off List

Instructional techniques, to be effective, must be used at the right time and in the right way. The significance of any instructional technique depends on a number of things, including the subject matter and objectives of the lesson, the background of the students, the personality of the instructor, and the available tools, materials and instructional aids.

It is suggested that you read through the following list after teaching a typical lesson and mark yourself on those techniques you consider significant for that lesson. The check list may also be used after several lessons with the idea of gradually developing the habit of applying the principles involved.

The spaces to the left of the numbers are for your check marks.

A.   THE LESSON PLAN

With regard to your lesson plan:

___ 1   Does the title of the lesson indicate the exact content of the lesson?

___ 2   Do the objectives state the outcome of instruction in terms of students skill

and understanding?

___ 3   Are specific references and instructional aids listed?

___ 4   Does the introduction explain in a general way the content to be covered in the lesson?

___ 5   Does the introduction explain the relation of the lesson to previous lessons?

___ 6   Does the introduction describe the way in which the class will be conducted?

___ 7   Does the introduction indicate potential applications of skills acquired from the lesson?

___ 8   Is there a timetable showing the approximate amount of time to be spent on each part of

the lesson?   Is the amount of time spent on various parts of the lesson consistent with the importance of

those parts?

___ 14   Does the lesson plan provide for maximum student participation and drill without sacrificing

other important phases of the lesson?

___ 15   Is there provision for repetition and emphasis of important points?

B. DURING THE INTRODUCTION TO THE LESSON, DID YOU:

___ 1   Test the group's knowledge with well-planned questions?

___ 2   Indicate the information and what degree of skill to be learned in the lesson?

___ 3   Emphasize the need for knowing the information and skills to be learned?

___ 4   Illustrate (from your own past experience or that of others) how content of lesson will

be used on a practical job.

___ 5   Tell the students how the class was to be conducted?

___ 6   Try to develop student interest in the subject by illustrations, personal stories, and

information on related new developments?

C. IN TEACHING PRINCIPLES DID YOU:

___ 1   Give sufficient information to properly introduce the principle?

___ 2   Build on students previous knowledge?

___ 3   Bring out each idea in logical sequence?

___ 4   Clearly explain relationship of one idea to the next where possible?

D. IN TEACHING AN OPERATION BY DEMONSTRATION, DID YOU:

___ 1   Do and tell?

___ 2   Then do while student told?

___ 3   And then did selected students do and tell?

___ 4   And finally did all students do under your supervision?

E. ON KEY POINTS OF THE LESSON DID YOU:

___ 1   Go over main points more than once for emphasis?

___ 2   Drill on those points that must be known?

___ 3   Ask challenging questions so that students had to think through basic principles?

___ 4   Illustrate or empasize key points with instructional aids?

___ 5   Explain new terms?

___ 6   Use personal experience or stories where appropriate to emphasize points?

___ 7   See that note-taking was significant, was not just "busy work" and did not interfere

with presentation?

___ 8   Show students how to record notes on main points of lesson? (It is often more effective

to give students a mineographed sheet of basic notes to which they can add notes and comments.)

F.   WHEN QUESTIONING, DID YOU:

___ 1   Where appropriate, first direct the question to the class as a whole—pause— and

then call on one student to answer?

___ 2   Provide for individual responses to most questions?

___ 3   Evaluate ansers and emphasize correct responses?

___ 4   Ask clear, brief, and challenging questions?

___ 5   Contact as may students as possible?

___ 6   Encourage accurate, complete answers?

___ 7   Call on students by name "at random" rather than follow an alphabetical list or seating

arrangement?

___ 8   Use questions all through the lesson?

___ 9   Frame questions extemporaneously to clarify dubious points or to follow up when questions

are partially answered?

___ 10   Use the question to correct errors as well as to detect them?

G.   IN PROVIDING FOR LEARNING BY DOING, DID YOU:

___ 1   Ask questions at proper checking or measuring levels?

___ 2   Encourage students to take notes on key points in the lesson?

___ 3   Provide problems to solve and thoroughly check for errors?

___ 4   Introduce problems that made use of facts taught in lesson and which made the students

think in order to apply those facts?

___ 5   Stay with the student after the correction was made to make sure that the right way is put

into practice?

___ 6   Give students a definite level of skill to work toward?

___ 7   Secure maximum student participation and drill without sacrificing other importants phases

of the lesson?

___ 8   Let students practice under your supervision and with suggestions, without "taking over"

yourself when difficulty was encountered?

H.   DURING THE SUMMARY TO THE LESSON, DID YOU:

___ 1   Repeat important points of lesson?

___ 2   Question students about major points seen?

___ 3   Write unfamiliar words on chalkboard if there is doubt about spelling or menning?

___ 4   List important steps of procedure on board or use charts?

___ 5   Make appropriate use of competition between individuals or group as a means of

keeping up student interest during practice or drill?

I.   WITH REGARD TO INSTRUCTIONAL AIDS, DID YOU:

___ 1   Have aids arranged for smooth, easy presentation?

___ 2   Keep extraneous tools, materials and devices out of sight during class?

___ 3   Evaluate the aid to make sure it was worth the time spent using it?

___ 4   Make sure mechanical devices operate properly?

___ 5   Introduce the aid adequately?

___ 6   Employ humor when it would add to the lesson?

___ 7   Change the pace of speaking where it would make the lesson more interesting?

___ 8   Keep interested in the subject and in the job of teaching?

J.   WHILE TEACHING, DID YOU:

___ 1   Use colorful and yet accurate language?

___ 2   Stay on your feet or in a position to demand attention?

___ 3   Use meaningful gestures?

___ 4   Know your subject so that you were sure of yourself?

___ 5   Stimulate discussion but remain in control at all times.

___ 6   Employ humor when it would add to the lesson?

___ 7   Change the pace of speaking where it would make the lesson more interesting?

___ 8   Keep interested in the subject and in the job of teaching?

K.   WITH REGARD TO HUMAN RELATIONS, DID YOU:

___ 1   Try to understand the reason for each student's behavior?

___ 2   Avoid sarcasm and ridicule?

___ 3   Refrain from being "one of the gang" (fraternizing)?

___ 4   Give credit for good work?

___ 5   Attempt to judge students on their present behavior rather than on their past records?

___ 6   Try to be a good sport but maintain sufficient reserve?

___ 7   Avoid unfavorable references to personal beliefs that may be sacred to others?

___ 8   Use informal methods yet hold the respect of the class?

L.   IF DISCIPLINARY ACTION WAS NECESSARY, DID YOU:

___ 1   Reprimand with justice and tact after determining the causes of student's behavior?

___ 2   Adjust any disciplinary action to produce the desired results with individuals?

___ 3   Consider student's mental and physical condition at the time of the reprimand?

___ 4   Stay calm and avoid all arguments?

___ 5   Speak with objectivity?

___ 6   Have and use facts?

M.   WITH REGARD TO PARTICIPATION, DID ALL STUDENTS:

___ 1   Participate in directed discussion?

___ 2   Contribute ideas?

___ 3   Appear interested?

___ 4   Ask questions that indicated thought on the lesson?

___ 5   Answers questions in full and with apparent understanding?

___ 6   Use tools and/or equipment while learning?

___ 7   Voluntarily have their work checked by the instructor?

___ 8   Appear anxious to develop skills?

___ 9   Show appreciation for equipment properly used?

N.   CONSIDERING VOICE AND APPERANCE, DID YOU:

___ 1   Speak loud enough without shouting?

___ 2   Keep tone of voice friendly?

___ 3   Speak with enthusiasm?

___ 4   Speak clearly and with careful selection of words?

___ 5   Use your voice to give emphasis (such as pausing before and after important points)?

___ 6   Use the correct pronunciation of words?

___ 7   Dress properly for the job?

___ 8   Present a neat appearance?

___ 9   Avoid mannerisms, such as playing with belt buckle,--mannerisms that were withoug force and meaning?

___ 10   Control temper at all times?

___ 11   Face and talk to the class?

___ 12   Show enthusiasm?

O.   WITH REGARD TO MANAGEMENT, DID YOU:

___ 1   Do all you could to provide proper temperature and ventilation?

___ 2   Make the best use of available light?

___ 3   Keep instructional area clean and orderly withoug limiting worthwhile activity?

___ 4   Make sure that all students could see and hear?

___ 5   Move students when this would provide a better learning situation?

___ 6   Help students to be as comfortable as facilities permit?

___ 7   Keep standing students from gradually working forward until some could not see or hear?

___ 8   Manage to that front seats were filled first and all seats filled from front to back?

___ 9   Arrange seats properly before the group reported for instruction?

___ 10   Manage charts, models, and other aids, so that they were available when needed and properly stored when not in use?

___ 11   Tactfully discourage interruptions by other instructors or office personnel?

___ 12   Provide for equipment to be ready and placed so that it would be used with minimum disturbance.

Instructional Bibliography

The following texts have been selected to provide supplemental information on various subjects covered in *Instructors and Their Jobs.* The accompanying chart shows which parts of the reference texts are relevant to specific chapters in *Instructors and Their Jobs.* An asterisk indicates that the entire text may be used as a reference.

Instructors and Their Jobs

Topic	1	2	3	4	5	6	7	8	9	10	11	12	13
Supervision and On-The-Job Training													Ch.7
Improving the Learning Enviroment											Ch.18		
Measuring and Evaluating Student Achievement						P.52 to P.63						*	
Programmed Instruction and Teaching Machines													
Instructional Aids and Devices						P.226 to P.232	Ch.4 Ch.5	Ch.10 Ch.11 Ch.12		Ch.6			
Demonstrating								P.143					
Questioning													
The Lecture Discussion, and Group Participation Method	*					P.254 to P.261		Ch.9					
Written Instructional Materials											Ch.12		Ch.17
Preparing Courses of Study and Lesson Plans			Ch.3								P.175 Ch.11		Ch.12 Ch.14
Identifying Content and Specifying Behaviors										Ch.3	*		Ch.8
Influences of Learning		*	Ch.2 Ch.4	*	*	P.64 to P.68		*	Ch.3 Ch.4				
Gaining Insight into The Learning Process				*	*	P.26 to P.39		*	Ch.5		P.157		Ch.4
The Instructor's Role					Ch.11	P.139 to P.162		Ch.4			Ch.10		

INSTRUCTIONAL BIBLIOGRAPHY

These texts give additional information.
An asterisk indicates the entire book can be used as a reference.

1. Baird, A. Craig, and Franklin H. Knower, ESSENTIALS OF GENERAL SPEECH COMMUNICATION. New York: McGraw Hill Book., 1973 4th edition.

2. Beach, Leslie, and Elon L. Clark. PSYCHOLOGY IN BUSINESS. New York: McGraw Hill Book Co., 1959.

3. Banathy, Bela H. INSTRUCTIONAL SYSTEMS. Belmont, California: Fearon Publishers, 1968.

4. Bernard, Harold W. PSYCHOLOGY OF LEARNING AND TEACHING, New York: McGraw Hill Book Co., Inc., 1965.

5. Bigge, Morris L. LEARNING THEORIES FOR TEACHERS, Evanston and London: Harper and Row, 1964, 2nd edition.

6. Cooper, Russell. THE TWO ENDS OF THE LOG: LEARNING AND TEACHING IN TODAY'S COLLEGE.

7. Erickson, Carlton W. ADMINSTERING INSTRUCTIONAL MEDIA PROGRAMS. New York: MacMillan Co., 1968.

8. Fleck, Henrietta, TOWARD BETTER TEACHING OF HOME ECONOMICS, New York: The Macmillian Co., 1974 2nd edition.

9. Foster, Charles R. PSYCHOLOGY FOR LIFE TODAY. Chicago: American Technical Society, 1973, 3rd edition.

10. Fryer, Douglas H., Mortimer R. Feinberg and Sheldon S. Zalkind. DEVELOPING PEOPLE IN INDUSTRY, PRINCIPLE AND METHODS OF TRAINING New York: Harper and Brothers, 1956.

11. Fryhlund, Verne C. OCCUPATIONAL ANALYSIS: TECHNIQUES AND PROCEDURES. Milwaukee: Bruce Publishing Co., 1970.

12. Gerberich, J. Raymond. SPECIMEN OBJECTIVE TEST ITEMS. New York: David McKay Co., 1956.

13. Giachino, J. W. and Ralph O. Gallington, COURSE CONSTRUCTION IN INDUSTRIAL ARTS AND VOCATIONAL EDUCATION. Chicago: American Technical Society, 1967, 3rd edition.

	1	2	3	4	5	6	7	8	9	10	11	12	13
14				*									
15			*						Ch.16				
16				*									
17			P.201	P.179 to P.195									P.147 P.337
18			*										
19			Ch.15 Ch.16 Ch.17 Ch.18			Ch.24	Ch.7 Ch.8	Ch.4	Ch.1 Ch.9				
20						*							
21				*									
22			Ch.9				Ch.3		Ch.5				
23								*					
24							Ch.1 Ch.2 Ch.3	Ch.4					
25										*			
26				*									
27	Ch.7								Ch.5 Ch.6	Ch.5 Ch.6			
28	P.97	Ch.8	P.126										P.79
29			*										

14. Glaser, Robert. TEACHING MACHINES AND PROGRAMMED LEARNING, DATA AND DIRECTIONS, Department of Audio-Visual Instruction, NEA of the United States, Pittsburg, Pennsylvania.

15. Gronlund, Norman E. MEASUREMENT AND EVALUATION IN TEACHING, New York: The MacMillian Co., 1971, 2nd edition

16. Hass, Kenneth B., and Harry Q. Packer. PREPARATION AND USE OF AUDIO-VISUAL AIDS. New York: Prentice Hall, Inc, 1955.

17. Hatcher, Hazel M. and Lila C. Halchin. THE TEACHING OF HOME ECONOMICS, Boston: Houghton Mifflin Co., 1973, 3rd edition.

18. Jordon, Arthur M. MEASUREMENT IN EDUCATION AN INTRODUCTION, New York: McGraw Hill Co., 1953.

19. Larson, Milton E. TEACHING RELATED SUBJECTS IN TRADE AND INDUSTRIAL AND TECHNICAL EDUCATION, Ohio: Charles E. Merrill Publishing Co., 1972.

20. Lee, Irving J. HOW TO TALK WITH PEOPLE. New York: Harper and Row, 1952.

21. Lumsdaine, A.A. and Robert Glaser, Joint Editors. TEACHING MACHINES AND PROGRAMMED LEARNING. Washington, D.C.: National Education Association of the United States, 1960.

22. Mager, Robert F. DEVELOPING ATTITUDE TOWARD LEARNING. Belmont, California: Fearon Publishers, 1968.

23. Mager, Robert F. GOAL ANALYSIS. Belmont, California: Fearon Publishers, 1972.

24. Mager, Robert F. PREPARING INSTRUCTIONAL OBJECTIVES, Belmont, California: Fearon Publishers, 1962.

25. Mager, Robert F. and Peter Pipe. ANALYSING PERFORMANCE PROBLEMS, "YOU REALLY OUGHTA WANNA". Belmont, California: Fearon Publisher 1970.

26. Markle, Susan M. GOOD FRAMES AND BAD: A GRAMMAR OF FRAME WRITING. New York: John Wiley & Sons, Inc., 1969, 2nd edition.

27. McGehee, William, and Paul W. Thayer. TRAINING IN BUSINESS AND INDUSTRY. New York: John Wiley and Sons, Inc., 1961.

28. McMahon, Gordon G. CURRICULUM DEVELOPMENT IN TRADE AND INDUSTRIAL TECHNICAL EDUCATION. Columbus, Ohio: Charles E. Merrill Publishing Co., 1972.

29. Micheels, W. M., and Ray Karnes. MEASURING EDUCATIONAL ACHIEVEMENT. New York: McGraw Hill Book Co., Inc., 1950.

Topic	30	31	32	33	34	35	36	37	38	39	40	41	42
Supervision and On-The-Job Training													
Improving the Learning Environment			*										
Measuring and Evaluating Student Achievement	Ch.8	Ch.14 Ch.15		*	P.137			P.87	Ch.9				
Programmed Instruction and Teaching Machines												*	
Instructional Aids and Devices	Ch.5	Ch.12											Ch.30 Ch.32
Demonstrating									P.100				
Questioning		P.122							P.102				
The Lecture Discussion, and Group Participation Method								P.91	Ch.5				
Written Instructional Materials													Ch.31
Preparing Courses of Study and Lesson Plans	Ch.6	Ch.4,5 Ch.6,7 Ch.10			P.5	*	*						
Identifying Content and Specifying Behaviors						*	*	*		Ch.2	*		
Influences of Learning									P.24	Ch.3			
Gaining Insight into The Learning Process	Ch.2							P.43		Ch.3			
The Instructor's Role		Ch.1									*		

INSTRUCTIONAL BIBLIOGRAPHY (CONT'D)

30. Musselman, Vernon A. METHODS IN TEACHING BASIC BUSINESS SUBJECTS. Danville, Illinois: The Interstate Printers and Publishers, Inc., 1971.

31. Pautler, Albert J. TEACHING SHOP AND LABORATORY SUBJECTS. Columbus, Ohio: Charles E. Merrill Publishing Co., 1971.

32. Perry, William G. Jr. FORMS OF INTELLECTUAL AND ETHICAL DEVELOPMENT IN THE COLLEGE YEARS. New York: Holt, Rinehard and Winston, Inc., 1973.

33. Popham, W. James, EVALUATING INSTRUCTION, Englewood Cliffs, New Jersey: Prentice Hall, 1973.

34. Popham, W. James, and Eva L. Baker. CLASSROOM INSTRUCTIONAL TACTICS, Englewood Cliffs, New Jersey: Prentice Hall, 1973.

35. Popham, W. James, and Eva L. Baker, ESTABLISHING INSTRUCTIONAL GOALS, Englewood Cliffs, New Jersey: Prentice Hall, Inc, 1970.

36. Popham, W. James and Eva L. Baker. EXPANDING DIMENSIONS OF EDUCATIONAL OBJECTIVES. Englewood Cliffs, New Jersey: Prentice Hall Inc., 1973.

37. Popham, W. James, and Eva L. Baker. PLANNING AN INSTRUCTIONAL SEQUENCE. Englewood Cliffs, New Jersey: Prentice Hall., Inc., 1973.

38. Popham, W. James, and Eva L. Baker. SYSTEMATIC INSTRUCTION. Englewood Cliffs, New Jersey: Prentice Hall Inc. 1970.

39. Proctor, John H. and William M. Thornton. TRAINING PROGRAMS. New York: American Management Society, 1964.

40. Rosner, Benjamin. THE POWER OF COMPETENCY--BASED TEACHER EDUCATION A REPORT. Boston: Allyn and Bacon Inc., 1972.

41. Schramm, Wilbur. THE RESEARCH ON PROGRAMMED INSTRUCTION ANNOTATED BIBLIOGRAPHY. Washington, D. C. U. S. Printing Office, 1964.

42. Silvius, G. Harold, and Estell H. Curry. MANAGING MULTIPLE ACTIVITIES IN INDUSTRIAL EDUCATION. Bloomington, Illinois: McKnight and McKnight, 1971.

	Ch.15	Ch.1	Ch.2 Ch.3			Part V	Ch.17 Ch.18		Ch.5 Ch.7		Ch.6	Ch.19		Part VI	Part I
				Ch.2								Ch.10	*	Ch.12	Ch.11
						Ch.25				P.20 P:40			*	Ch.8	
						P.39	P.175					P.117		P.133	

43. Silvius, G. Harold, and Estell H. Curry, TEACHING SUCCESSFULLY IN INDUSTRIAL EDUCATION. Bloomington, Illinois: McKnight and McKnight, 1967.

44. Staton, Thomas F. HOW TO INSTRUCT SUCESSFULLY. New York: McGraw Hill Book Co. Inc., 1960.

45. Stolurow, Lawrence M. TEACHING BY MACHINES. Washington, D. C.: Department of Health, Education and Welfare, U. S. Government Printing Office, 1961.

46. Taber, Julian I. Robert Glaser, and Halmuth H. Schaefer. LEARNING AND PROGRAMMED INSTRUCTION. Massachusetts: Addison-Wesley Publishing Co., 1965.

47. Toone, Herbert, Estelle Popham, M. Herbert Freeman. METHODS OF TEACHING BUSINESS SUBJECTS. New York: McGraw Hill Book Co. 1965.

48. University of Texas. THE PREPARATION OF OCCUPATIONAL INSTRUCTORS. Austin, Texas: Division of Extension, 1965.

Index

Numerals in **bold type** refer to illustrations.